Uncharted Windows™ Programming

Uncharted

Windows™ Programming

PROGRAMMING

William Roetzheim

SAMS
PUBLISHING

A Division of Prentice Hall Computer Publishing
11711 North College, Carmel, Indiana 46032 USA

Copyright © 1993 by Sams Publishing

International Standard Book Number: 0-672-30299-3

Library of Congress Catalog Card Number: 92-82086

96 95 94 93   4 3 2 1

Interpretation of the printing code: the rightmost double-digit number is the year of the book's printing; the rightmost single-digit, the number of the book's printing. For example, a printing code of 93-1 shows that the first printing of the book occurred in 1993.

Trademarks

Composed in Utopia, Bodoni, and MCPdigital by
Prentice Hall Computer Publishing

Printed in the United States of America

To old friends,
Who made me the person I am today,
For better or worse.
To Dick and Al.

To new friends,
Whose love of life and joyful personalities
Are both a pleasure and an inspiration.
To Ray and Cheryl.

To tried-and-true friends,
Those few individuals in life a person can count on
Always, forever, and completely.
To Dan.

To best friends.
It's such a wonderful thing to have a best friend,
And an even more wondrous thing to be married to her.
To Marianne.

And to all friends everywhere,
Those who entertain, sympathize, share,
Laugh, cry, and make life worth living.
I'm thinking about you. I appreciate you.

Publisher
Richard K. Swadley

Acquisitions Manager
Jordan Gold

Acquisitions Editor
Stacy Hiquet

Development Editor
Dean Miller

Senior Editor
Tad Ringo

Production Editor
Gayle L. Johnson

Copy Editor
Greg Horman

Editorial Coordinators
Rebecca S. Freeman
Bill Whitmer

Editorial Assistants
Rosemarie Graham
Sharon Cox

Technical Editors
Bruce Graves
Scott Parker

Cover Designer
Dan Armstrong

**Director of Production
and Manufacturing**
Jeff Valler

Production Manager
Corinne Walls

Imprint Manager
Matthew Morrill

Book Designer
Michele Laseau

Production Analyst
Mary Beth Wakefield

Proofreading/Indexing Coordinator
Joelynn Gifford

Graphics Image Specialists
Tim Montgomery
Dennis Sheehan
Sue VandeWalle

Production
Katy Bodenmiller
Christine Cook
Lisa Daugherty
Carla Hall-Batton
John Kane
Sean Medlock
Michelle M. Self
Susan Shepard
Greg Simsic
Suzanne Tully
Alyssa Yesh

Indexers
Loren Malloy
John Sleeva
Suzanne Snyder

Overview

ix

Contents

Uncharted
WINDOWS PROGRAMMING

Acknowledgments

I would like to thank Steve of Oracle Corporation for his help with Chapter 8, Nan Borreson of Borland International, Inc. for her help with Borland products, and Teresa Polito and Arnold Waldstein of Creative Labs, Inc. for providing me with a Sound Blaster and Video Blaster board. I would also like to thank the following individuals who helped in the production of this book: Stacy Hiquet, Dean Miller, Gayle Johnson, Greg Horman, Bruce Graves, and Scott Parker.

About the Author

William Roetzheim is a Senior Associate with the consulting firm of Booz, Allen & Hamilton and a well-respected writer on both management and technology. The author of six popular books on computer-related topics, he lives and works in the San Diego area.

Introduction

I've become bored with Microsoft Windows programming books. They certainly give you a lot for your money—many are well over 1,000 pages—but they all say pretty much the same thing. I already know what a display context is. I know how to draw lines into the display context. I don't even have a hard time displaying a standard dialog box. I don't need an introduction to Windows programming.

I want something that's more fun to read. I want something that tells me things about Windows I don't already know. I don't necessarily need all the nitty-gritty details; that's what reference books are for. I *do* want enough specific examples to see exactly how things work. In short, I've been looking for a book exactly like *Uncharted Windows Programming*. I think you're going to enjoy this book.

Because this book is a series of essays about topics of interest to Windows programmers, some chapters are short and some are long. I chose to let chapter length vary with the complexity of the topic, instead of forcing the chapters to be of the same length by splitting up long topics and combining short topics. The organization I use simplifies skipping around within the book to topics of immediate interest or utility. I expect and encourage you to do just that.

All code examples in this book use C++, and I assume that you are familiar with this language. If you need some help learning C++, pick up any one of the dozens of excellent introductory books on the topic. I also assume that you are familiar with Windows programming using C++ and with Borland's Object Windows Library (OWL). If either topic is new to you, you might want to read my book *Programming Windows with Borland C++* (2D Press, 1992). Finally, I assume that you are fluent in MS-DOS and Windows. You should be completely comfortable writing, compiling, and debugging a Microsoft Windows program in C++.

Requisite Hardware and Software

A bare-bones configuration for your development environment consists of an 80286-class machine, 4MB of memory, a mouse, an 80MB hard disk, and a Hercules-compatible card and monitor. A better configuration consists of an 80386 computer, 4MB of memory, a mouse, a 120MB hard disk, and a VGA card and monitor. This latter configuration is adequate for both testing and developing even very large applications.

The programs in this book were tested using Borland C++ version 3.1 and its accompanying Application Framework. The Application Framework provides the Resource Workshop—the tools to build and edit program resources. It also provides the OWL to simplify Windows development using C++. If you are using the Turbo C++ for Windows compiler, all the programs should run without problems. Code that is not OWL-specific should work properly with the Microsoft C++ compiler, although I have never tested code using Microsoft C++.

In addition to a version of the Borland compiler, you must have a copy of Microsoft Windows version 3.1 or later. Examples in this book were tested using version 3.1.

What You'll Find in This Book

This book-and-disk package consists of 12 chapters, one appendix, and a disk containing source code for each class presented in the text. The following sections give you a preview of the contents of the book and the disk.

Road Map to the Chapters

Chapters 1 and 2 help you produce reusable C++ code, and they also help you improve your efficiency and consistency while coding C++ classes. If you prefer to hack, you may safely skip these two chapters and jump to the "good stuff" starting in Chapter 3.

Chapter 3 explains the principles behind dynamic link libraries (DLLs) and describes how to create your own DLLs. You need this knowledge for some later chapters, so skip this chapter only if you are already comfortable with creating custom DLLs.

Chapters 4 through 6 deal with topics related to dialog boxes. Chapter 4 describes how to create your own custom controls, add them to dialog boxes, use them within your application, and make them available within Borland's Resource Workshop. Chapter 5 describes how to give your dialog boxes a custom appearance similar to Borland's dialog boxes. Chapter 6 describes how to implement dialog boxes too big to display on a single page.

Chapters 7 and 8 deal with database access. Chapter 7 describes how to use Paradox within your Windows application. Chapter 8 describes how to use embedded SQL within your application.

Chapter 9 demonstrates how to implement a screen saver, using a presentation graphics `SlideShow` class as an example.

Chapters 10 and 11 deal with multimedia topics. Chapter 10 describes how to add sound or voice to your application, and Chapter 11 describes how to incorporate video. Both of these chapters require special hardware to take full advantage of the examples.

Chapter 12 presents some miscellaneous tricks and techniques.

Appendix A contains the code for the `WStr` supporting class used in more than one example in this book.

After reading this book, you may want to correspond with me about the subject matter. I invite you to do so. My address is 13518 Jamul Drive, Jamul, California 91935. I am also available for paid consulting support through Booz, Allen & Hamilton, Inc. (619 223-5681).

What's on the Disk

The accompanying disk contains files you will use as you work with the examples in this book. The disk will save you hours of typing and debugging. In addition, many of the classes described in this book and included

on the disk are designed to be added to your reuse library for use with other projects. Be sure to read the README.TXT file on the disk for any last-minute updates.

The disk also includes U/Win, a set of Windows file management and support functions for software development. The U/Win utilities perform in a manner similar to utilities found in the UNIX operating system. Most of the U/Win utilities use the concept of *standard input* and *standard output* and can be connected with *pipes*. Thus, commands can be chained together to perform more complicated tasks.

U/Win can be run in batch or interactive modes. In batch mode, U/Win is executed with command-line parameters. In interactive mode, you enter commands through the U/Win dialog windows. Those familiar with the use of these utilities in the UNIX environment will find the command line quickest to use, and those unfamiliar with the environment will benefit from using the dialogs to build command strings interactively.

To order this product, or for more information, contact

> The Boolean Group, Inc.
> 20332 SW Rock Court
> Beaverton OR 97006

or direct electronic mail to CompuServe account 72077,506.

Conventions Used in This Book

This book uses the following typographic conventions:

> ➤ Keywords, function names, variable names, class names, code listings, and so on appear in `monospace`.

> ➤ Placeholders appear in `italic monospace`.

> ➤ New terms appear in *italic*.

> ➤ Filenames appear in all uppercase.

> ➤ Directory names appear in all uppercase.

> ➤ Optional parameters are enclosed in flat brackets (`[ ]`).

In addition, Hints, Tricks, Notes, and Warnings appear in gray-screened sidebars.

CHAPTER

1

Designing
Reusable C++
Classes

The big advantage of C++ over C—or most other languages—is the ease with which C++ code can be enhanced and reused. Unfortunately, it is possible to write C++ code that is neither easily enhanced nor reusable. I firmly believe it is worth a few dozen pages of this book, and a small amount of your time, to demystify some of the tricks for producing reusable C++ classes. After reading this chapter, you will have greater knowledge of many issues, including the structure of inheritance hierarchies, persistence, re-use libraries, and STRICT compliance.

Reuse: The Promise Versus the Reality

It is possible to write C code that is easily reused and maintained. The C runtime libraries are a good example. C++ simplifies writing reusable and maintainable code by using object-oriented features such as polymorphism, inheritance, and encapsulation of data and functions. C++, however, does not, and cannot, force you to write reusable and maintainable code. Reusable and maintainable code is the result of careful planning during design and development. C++ merely facilitates this process.

Reusable Components

Coding is typically 15 percent of the effort in development. If you reuse about 50 percent of your code, you save approximately 7.5 percent of the development effort. Most of the remaining effort in development is spent on documentation and testing. The only way to save a significant amount of time is to reuse documentation, code, and testing. C++ greatly simplifies this reuse.

In C++, a reusable component includes a C++ class. The class consists of the class header file and source file. The header file typically has the .H extension, and the source file typically has the .CPP extension. I recommend that you include only one class in each file to simplify reuse.

OTE: I apply my reuse rules to classes in this book that are reusable. I don't apply my rules to code that is only for illustrative purposes or when deviating from those rules improves the simplicity and readability of an example.

I name a file with the class name it contains. To avoid conflicts with the names of someone else's classes, I begin all class names with a one-character identifier. For example, I use W for all my classes. The `Str` class is called `WStr`, and the header file for the class is named WSTR.H.

For each class, you should have a file containing the class documentation and a file containing a test driver. The documentation file should contain class documentation in a format compatible with your word processor, and it should document the class according to the company's internal standards. I use a .DOC extension for the documentation file.

The test file should contain a test driver that tests every function and overloaded operator. Ideally, a test driver should run without human interaction and should print a message that the class is OK or that a problem was discovered. Whenever you make changes to a class, you should recompile and run its test driver to ensure that the class continues to perform as expected. I use a .CPP extension for the test file, but I prepend a T rather than a W to the front of the class name. For example, the test file for the `WStr` class is called TSTR.CPP.

If you follow this approach, you can easily reuse class documentation, class code, and class unit test drivers. When you design a new software application, document the design in terms of classes and their interaction. You then can include detailed documentation for the reused classes simply by inserting the appropriate class documentation files.

Single Versus Parallel Inheritance Hierarchies

There are two schools of thought on developing class hierarchies. Some people argue that all objects should originate from a single point, often an abstract class called `Object` or something similar. I call this the *single-hierarchy* approach. Borland's container class is an example: all objects are

derived from the TObject class. Most Smalltalk-based class libraries, which include Borland's container classes and the NIH (National Institute on Health) class libraries, use this approach, and most C++ programmers with background in Smalltalk prefer a single hierarchy.

Other people prefer an alternative approach that I call *parallel hierarchies.* They say that objects should be related through inheritance only if they share common data or functionality. A library of objects contains multiple independent inheritance hierarchies; each grouping contains objects with common data or functionality. Most programmers learning C++ as their first object-oriented programming language find this approach more logical. In addition, it is simpler to collect objects from a wide variety of sources when there is no need to force them into an artificial, predefined inheritance scheme. I prefer the parallel hierarchy for these reasons.

Setting Up a Reuse Library

Whether you are a member of an organization or a lone software developer, it pays to establish a software reuse library. For each class, this library should contain the previously described class header file, source file, documentation file, and test driver. Object code and library modules may be included, too. If several individuals share the reuse library, files in the library should be placed under configuration control. Typically, this means that the files should be read-only. Changes to the files should be approved by one or more individuals. Class modifications should be analyzed for their impact on existing code before being implemented. People using the object should be notified of modifications and bug fixes so that they can recompile their code with the new version.

I believe that all objects used in an application should be designed with reuse in mind. This includes providing member functions and operators with capabilities that future developers are likely to expect. All objects should be submitted to the reuse library after being completed and tested.

HINT: Unless performance is absolutely critical, you're better off using virtual functions whenever possible. This allows descendant classes to override your function definition when necessary.

Portable Persistence

In Smalltalk, objects you create during program execution are automatically saved when the program terminates and reloaded when the program starts again. In C++, objects that are created during program execution simply disappear when your program terminates and thus must be re-created when you need to access them again. The process of allowing objects to be written to disk and later read from disk is called *object persistence*. I am familiar with three methods of implementing object persistence in C++: object-oriented databases, Borland's TStreamable class, and custom persistence. I address each in turn.

Object-Oriented Databases

Object-oriented databases (OODBs) are commercial products that enable you to write and read objects to the disk, normally using static or dynamic link libraries linked with your code. The physical storage format on the disk is hidden from your application. The format may be flat files, relational files, hierarchical files, or any other organization. The most primitive OODBs use a custom file format and enable you to only store objects on disk. These products offer little advantage over the two approaches discussed next. Likewise, the manufacturers of these products require you to purchase their software and, occasionally, a runtime license for each product distributed.

More-advanced OODBs either store their objects using a format compatible with existing commercial database management systems such as

Oracle, Sybase, dBASE IV, or Paradox, or exist in parallel with a commercial database management system that mirrors the data in the object-oriented database. Both approaches enable the sophisticated user to use query and report-writing database tools. Storing data in a native database format is appealing because data consistency is ensured and all translations are performed internally by the OODB. The disadvantages of this approach are technical difficulties (and the resulting unavailability and immaturity of these products) and the relatively slow performance.

Storing data in parallel relational and object-oriented database formats requires an update scheme to ensure that the data in both databases remains in synch. This technology is becoming more available. Accessing data in an object-oriented database typically is much faster—2 to 10 times faster—than in a relational database. It is on par with flat file implementations for many accesses.

Every approach requires purchasing an OODB, and many products require that you or your users purchase a commercial database product as well. For corporate software developers building large centralized databases, these products are an obvious choice. If you simply need a convenient way to store and retrieve objects to disk, the TStreamable or custom persistence approaches described next might be just what the doctor ordered.

Two examples of OODBs are Poet from BKS Software (800 950-8845) and IDB Object Database from Persistent Data Systems (412 963-1843).

Persistence Using *TStreamable*

Borland includes an easy method of implementing object persistence with its compiler—the TStreamable class. Borland calls classes that offer persistence *streamable*. Making a class streamable simply involves including TStreamable in the class inheritance list, and implementing four persistence-related functions and a new constructor. For example, if you developed a string class called WStr and wanted to make the class streamable, you would add TStreamable to the inheritance list as follows:

```
class WStr : public TStreamable
{
    .
    .
    .
};
```

If WStr had other classes in its inheritance list, you would need to ensure that each of those classes was also streamable.

Using TStreamable to implement persistence is relatively simple and foolproof. Unfortunately, it is not portable to environments that Borland C++ does not support (UNIX, for example). If you are certain that your code will never need to be ported to UNIX, you might want to use Borland's approach to persistence as defined as follows. If your code needs to be ported to UNIX, skip the remainder of this section and jump ahead to the section "Persistence Without TStreamable."

The four functions you must implement for each streamable class are

```
virtual const Pchar streamableName () const;
static PTStreamable build ();
virtual void Write (Ropstream);
virtual void Read (Ripstream);
```

Many types use the P/R convention defined in the Borland-supplied macro _CLASSDEF. This macro is invoked once for each new class to automatically define a reference to the class and a pointer to the class. The reference is defined as the class name preceded by a capital R, and the pointer is defined as the class name preceded by a capital P. For example, _CLASSDEF is invoked for the WStr class as follows:

```
_CLASSDEF (WStr)
```

If you need to implement _CLASSDEF in another environment (UNIX, for example) for portability, the following implementation should work:

```
TBD _CLASSDEF code
```

The function streamableName simply returns the class name. For our sample WStr class, this function looks like the following:

```
const Pchar WStr::streamableName () const
{
    return "Wstr";
}
```

The function `build` simply creates a new instance of the class by using the streamable constructor that must be implemented for each class. For our sample `WStr` class, this function looks like the following (the constant `streamableInit` is defined by Borland C++):

```
PTStreamable WStr::build()
{
    return new WStr (streamableInit);
}
```

The function `Write` outputs a binary copy of the class to the specified output persistence stream (`opstream`), using a reference to the stream as an input parameter. For example, `WStr` stores the string it contains in a private variable called `szBuffer`. `WStr`'s `Write` function looks like the following:

```
void WStr::Write (Ropstream os)
{
    os << strlen (szBuffer) + 1;
    for (int i = 0; i <= strlen (szBuffer); i++)
    {
        os << szBuffer [i];
    }
}
```

To output user-defined data types, such as other classes, in this fashion, the user-defined data types must be streamable. For all the built-in types (`character`, `double`, and so on), Borland overloads the `<<` and `>>` operators to work properly with output persistence streams (`opstreams`) and with input persistence streams (`ipstreams`).

The function `Read` performs the reverse action of the `Write` function. This function reads each variable from the specified input persistence stream. `WStr`'s `Read` function looks like the following:

```
void WStr::Read (Ripstream is)
{
    int    size;
    is >> size;

    char *szTemp = new char [size];
    for (int i = 0; i < size; i++)
    {
        is >> szTemp [i];
    }
    *this = szTemp;  // Overloaded assignment operator
```

```
    delete[] szTemp;
    return this;
}
```

The streamable constructor for a class initializes the class to a default value in preparation for a subsequent call to Read. Both the streamable constructor and the Read call are invoked automatically when you are reading a new instance of a class from an ipstream. For the WStr class, the streamable constructor looks like the following:

```
WStr::WStr (StreamableInit)
{
    delete[] szBuffer;
    szBuffer = new char [1];
    szBuffer [0] = 0;
    nBufSize = 1;
}
```

As a last step in making a class streamable, normally you want to overload the << and >> operators for an ipstream or opstream argument to simplify reading and writing the classes. For the WStr class, this is accomplished as follows:

```
// Input to a WStr reference
inline Ripstream operator >> (Ripstream is, RWStr str)
{
    return is >> (RTStreamable) str;
}

// Input to a WStr reference to a pointer
inline Ripstream operator >> (Ripstream is, RPWStr str)
{
    return is >> (RPvoid) str;
}

// Output from a WStr reference
inline Ropstream operator << (Ropstream os, RWStr str)
{
    return os << (RTStreamable) str;
}

// Output from a WStr pointer
inline Ropstream operator << (Ropstream os, PWStr str)
{
    return os << (PTStreamable) str;
}
```

To use streamable classes in your program, you must register them with the Borland stream manager. Do this by placing the following code for each streamable class in your main source file, normally just before the `WinMain` or `Main` program loop. Substitute your class name for `WStr`.

```
TStreamableClass RegWStr ("WStr", WStr::build, _ _DELTA (WStr));
```

To write a class, open an output persistence stream (`opstream`) or output file persistence stream (`ofpstream`), then call the `Write` function for each class while passing the output stream as a parameter. To read a class, open an input persistence stream (`ipstream`) or input file persistence stream (`ifpstream`), then call the `Read` function for each class while passing the input stream as a parameter.

Persistence Without *TStreamable*

I prefer to implement most features of streamable classes without using Borland's `TStreamable` class. The biggest advantage of this technique is that the resulting code is portable to any environment supporting a C++ compiler, including UNIX. However, you give up the ability to store pointers to shared memory and have them come back still pointers to shared memory, and you must explicitly remember to call the parent function when storing or retrieving an object.

Implementing persistence is actually quite simple. Each persistent object contains a `Read` function and a `Write` function that take a standard C++ input stream or output stream, respectively. Using whatever format is appropriate, the class reads or writes all local data to the stream. If your class contains pointers to data, you must be sure to read or write the actual data rather than the pointer.

This approach has two major disadvantages. The most significant problem—one that I have not attempted to solve because of its complexity—involves how to handle cross-referencing properly. Let me illustrate the problem with an example.

Suppose both Object A and Object B contain a pointer to Object C. You write Object A, and Object A writes a copy of Object C as part of this operation. You then write Object B, and Object B writes a copy of Object C. Later you read Object A and Object B. Each one allocates space for Object C and reads its copy of Object C. Object A and Object B then initialize the pointer

to the appropriate location, but now the Object A and Object B pointers refer to *different* copies of Object C rather than to the same copy. This scenario is illustrated in Figure 1.1. Although this problem is significant, I have found that it is relatively easy to avoid relying on cross-reference integrity between persistent objects.

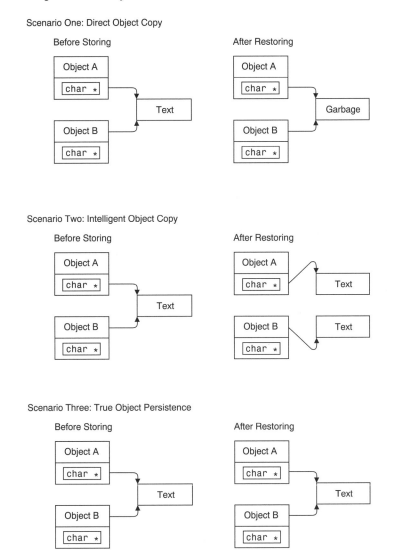

Figure 1.1. Persistence and pointers.

The second problem can be easily worked around, but it introduces a potential source of bugs because it requires that the programmer insert specific code for every streamable class. The problem arises when a class has parents—that is, uses inheritance. When you implement a Read or Write function for the child class, the child cannot read or write parent class data. The solution is for the child classes' Read and Write functions to call the Read and Write functions for all its parent classes, which should in turn call the Read and Write functions for their parents, and so on. The Read or Write function for the parent class should be called before reading or writing local class data.

Required Class Functions

I have found that it is a good idea to specify a minimum set of functions that all classes should implement. This provides consistency across classes. It also provides for common functionality that programers can count on when they use your class. These functions fall into three main categories: helper functions that enhance the ease of use for the class, functions that provide binary image persistence, and functions that provide human-readable persistence, primarily for use while debugging. The exact functions you will include for all your classes is a personal decision, based on how you intend to use the classes. I usually choose to make the functions that are listed as follows required for all classes.

Helper Functions

I include two helper functions, ClassName and ResetAll, in all classes. ClassName returns a string that defines the class name. Useful during debugging, ClassName is a method of identifying an object type if you are given just a pointer to the object. The prototype and implementation of this function for a sample class called Sample are as follows:

```
virtual WStr ClassName ();

WStr Sample::ClassName (void)
{
```

```
        return (WStr) "Sample";
}
```

NOTE: Sometimes when I declare a function with no parameters, I type the `void` keyword. This is not necessary in C++ because empty parentheses imply no parameters. However, this is a habit from C that I'm trying to break (with sporadic success).

The `ResetAll` function sets all class variables to their default state and clears any dynamic memory previously allocated by the class. This function typically is used by all the function's constructors, and it is often useful for other member functions as well. Implementation of the `ResetAll` function varies from class to class, based on the data elements present. Any descendant versions of `ResetAll` need to make sure that they call their ancestors' versions. The function prototype for `ResetAll` is

```
virtual void ResetAll (void);
```

Binary Persistence

I like to include a persistence capability in all classes so that they can be written to and read from disk. I do this by including a `Write` and `Read` function for all classes. These functions take a reference to an output or input stream (`ostream` or `istream`), respectively, and write or read all local data when called. During a write, pointers are handled by writing the data actually pointed at. During a read, pointers are handled by reading the data into dynamic memory, then initializing the pointer to point to the proper location. To handle inheritance, the `Write` and `Read` functions call the `Write` or `Read` functions for all parent classes (in left-to-right order if multiple inheritance is used) and then write all local data. The function prototypes for `Read` and `Write` are as follows:

```
virtual void Write (ostream&);
virtual void Read (istream&);
```

Human-Readable Persistence

Often it is useful to have a method of working with human-readable persistence. For example, you might want to output the object contents in human-readable form to the screen or to a file as part of your debugging. During testing it is useful to be able to generate object initiation values by using an editor, and then to use persistence to read these values into the objects. I include four functions that provide human-readable persistence for all classes. Print outputs a human-readable version of all data to an output stream; each data element is output on a separate line. Scan reads a human-readable version of all class data from an input stream, and requires that each data element appear on a separate line. The function prototypes for these two functions are as follows:

```
virtual void Print (ostream&);
virtual void Scan (istream&);
```

The other two functions are overloaded versions of Print and Scan in which the stream argument is void. These functions print the object to stdout or scan the object from stdin. Using WStr as an example, the prototypes and implementation of these functions are as follows:

```
virtual void Print (void);

void WStr::Print (void)
{
    Print (cout);
}

virtual void Scan (void);

void WStr::Scan (void)
{
    Scan (cin);
}
```

Ensuring *STRICT* Compliance

If you have the Borland C++ compiler and use the Windows 3.1 mode by defining WIN31, I recommend that you enable strict type checking for

Windows typedefs (for example, HINSTANCE and HMODULE) by defining STRICT. This helps you find errors that involve passing improper variables to Windows application programming interface (API) functions at compile time rather than at runtime. STRICT must be defined before you load WINDOWS.H, because it affects the way WINDOWS.H is compiled. Normally you accomplish this by defining STRICT globally, either on the compiler's command line or by selecting Options/Compiler/Code Generation from Borland's integrated development environment.

For existing Windows 3.0 code, you need to change some of the types you use for variables and parameters. These changes are shown in Table 1.1.

TABLE 1.1. STRICT **type changes.**

Windows 3.0 Type	Windows 3.1 Types	Description
HANDLE	HINSTANCE	Instance handle
	HMODULE	Module handle
	HLOCAL	Local handle
	HGLOBAL	Global handle
	HTASK	Task handle
	HFILE	File handle
	HRSRC	Resource handle
	HGDIOBJ	Generic GDI object
	HMETAFILE	Metafile handle
	HDWP	DeferWindowPos handle
	HACCEL	Accelerator table handle
	HDRVR	Driver handle

continues

TABLE 1.1. continued

Windows 3.0 Type	Windows 3.1 Types	Description
WORD	WORD	16-bit int
	UINT	16- or 32-bit int
	WPARAM	16- or 32-bit int
LONG	LPARAM	32-bit int
	LRESULT	32-bit int
FARPROC	WNDPROC	Window procedure
	DLGPROC	Dialog procedure
	HOOKPROC	Hook procedure

The UINT type is important when migrating your code from 16-bit Windows to 32-bit Windows. Using 32-bit UINTs is much more efficient than forcing the compiler to restrict the value to 16 bits under a native 32-bit operating system.

What About Commercial Libraries?

Eventually, you will be able to sit down with a catalog of object libraries and browse through subjects such as accounting objects, communication objects, charting objects, and so on. You will select the object libraries you need for your application, purchase them, and use them to complete the application quickly. Where it is necessary, you will extend functionality by using inheritance. We're not there yet.

Existing commercial libraries are designed primarily to simplify the development of graphical user interfaces and the use of Windows, or they provide primitive capabilities such as arrays and linked lists. Even worse than the sparse selection, most commercial libraries I'm familiar with are not well designed or implemented. Be sure to buy the source so that you can fix them.

NOTE: I would like to see an independent agency evaluate and certify the quality of function libraries in terms of their design for reuse, completeness of functionality, and robustness of implementation. This agency could then give its seal of approval, much like the Underwriters Laboratories' UL seal of approval. I do not know of any group currently performing this function.

Most of my reuse library was developed by me or someone I know. I continue to watch the commercial offerings, however, because I am convinced that this is the direction in which the industry will go.

Standard Code Structure

I've already mentioned that you should store one class in each file, and that the header file should be separate from the file containing the class body. Within the files, I recommend that you structure your header and class definitions consistently to avoid forgetting something, to simplify reading the code, and to simplify finding specific functions when maintaining the code. Chapter 2, "Efficiency and Consistency Using C++ Coding Foundations," presents my recommended standard structure. It provides you with templates that simplify your class implementation.

Efficiency and Consistency Using C++ Coding Foundations

Problem

Software reuse is greatly simplified when all your C++ classes use the same general structure and contain all the member functions you have decided should be available for all classes. These conventions are difficult to enforce when several people are developing code at the same time, especially if they are required to change their coding style to make it comply with these conventions. In addition, writing new C++ classes can become tedious as you repetitively type the basic framework of each class header file and source file.

A simple method of automating the mundane task of coding the basic structure of your classes would save considerable time and ensure consistency between classes, even when code is developed by different programmers. To be effective, the chosen approach should work with any editor, be easy to learn and use, and be easily tailored to your specific coding style and standards.

Solution

A simple way to achieve these objectives is to use C++ *foundations*. A C++ foundation is a reusable text file that can be read into your editor and used as a template for coding. To avoid confusion with C++ templates, a feature built into version 3.0 of the language, I don't use the term *template*.

TRICK: I've adopted the convention of using the keyword NEW (in all uppercase) as a placeholder for the class name. I then do a global search-and-replace within the file to replace the NEW keyword with the class name before I tailor the foundation to the specific class. Be sure to instruct your editor to do the search-and-replace in a case-sensitive mode to avoid matching on the C++ new operator.

I begin by presenting three generic foundations that are useful when you are coding a new class. One is used for the class header, one is used for the class source (implementation), and one is used for the introduction to each member function. I then present four foundations that are useful when you are implementing a new *Object Windows Library* (*OWL*) application. Two implement the header and source for your application's main window, and the other two implement the header and source for your application's main processing object.

Generic Class Foundations

The following foundations simplify the drudgery of developing new C++ classes, but they have some built-in assumptions you should be aware of and modify if necessary. First, they assume that you place the code for one, and only one, class in each file. This approach results in more files to manage, but it greatly simplifies code reuse and maintenance.

RICK: If you find that you are consistently working with a group of related files and you become tired of typing long lists of `#include` files, or if the list of files to compile on your command line or in your IDE project file becomes excessive, create a new header or source file that consists of a list of compiler `#include` directives to load the appropriate files. You then can use this filename in place of the long list of filenames.

You also will see a performance improvement as an added benefit. When you use Borland C++ and precompiled headers, the compiler must load the snapshot (.SYM file) before it compiles each .CPP file. If you include multiple .CPP files in a consolidated file, the .SYM file needs to be loaded only once, so compiles are much faster.

Second, this approach assumes that each class includes a set of standard member functions that you have decided should be present in all classes. As I discussed in the preceding chapter, you should use my list as

a guide, but feel free to add, delete, or modify the functions on my list. Table 2.1 shows the functions that I include in all classes.

TABLE 2.1. A list of suggested standard member functions.

Function	Description
ClassName	Returns the class name as a string
ResetAll	Initializes all variables to a default value and frees any allocated memory
Write	Writes a binary image of the class to an ostream
Read	Reads a binary image of the class from an istream
Print	Prints a human-readable image of the class on an ostream
Print	Overloaded Print function to print to stdout
Scan	Reads a human-readable image of the class from an istream
Scan	Overloaded Scan function to scan from stdin

Third, this approach assumes that you have the class header in one file and the class source in another file. This approach simplifies reuse and configuration control of your code by enabling other developers to include your headers in their code when they use object files (.OBJ) or library files (.LIB) rather than source code.

RICK: Instead of including short one- or two-line member functions directly in the class header for efficiency (as many books and magazine articles do), code these short member functions at the end of the header file outside the body of the class declaration, and add the keyword inline before the member function to gain the

same efficiency. In all cases, `inline` functions only if performance makes this essential. For example:

```
inline void WTest::WSet (void)
{
    Active = TRUE;
}
```

A Class Header Foundation

Listing 2.1 shows the foundation for a generic class header. To use the foundation, use your editor's `insert file` command to insert this file, then do a global search-and-replace to substitute the class name for `NEW`. You are now ready to tailor the header by adding member functions and overloaded operators unique to this class.

The initial `#ifndef` compiler directive ensures that this file is processed only once, even if it is included multiple times. The matching `#endif` is found at the very end of the file. I then specify my `#include` files, most of which are class-specific. I group my `#include` files into the ones used on all systems, followed by the ones that are system-specific, with the files grouped by system. Compiler `#ifdef` statements are used to ensure that the code compiles on multiple platforms without change.

`WStr` is a class I developed to encapsulate string functionality. You may substitute your own favorite string class (for example, the string class supplied with Borland C++ in the container library), or you may use my string classes, included on the source disk supplied with this book and in Appendix A, "Code for a Support Class."

TRICK: Borland C++ sets three useful compiler `#defines`— `__BORLANDC__`, `__MSDOS__`, and `__Windows__`. Each begins with two underscores and ends with two underscores. Most UNIX compilers define `Unix`, and many also have a hardware platform-specific

#define (for example, sun). You can use #ifdef statements to isolate operating system code and hardware-specific code. The result is code that can be compiled without change on multiple platforms.

The class introduction comment block is used to enter a one-line description of the class, a brief description of the class's purpose, and any applicable notes. Notes might include limitations on the class, intended use, closely related classes, future enhancements that may be added, and so on.

The class header itself contains a place for private data and member functions and for public data and member functions. I use protected data and member functions less often, so I add these keywords to the class header only if they are needed. The member functions within the class are grouped into constructor(s) and destructor(s), standard functions, other member functions, cast operators, and overloaded operators.

TRICK: Borland C++ enables you to put compiler directives anywhere on the line. This is convenient for indenting nested directives. Unfortunately, many UNIX compilers require compiler directives to start flush against the left margin, thus complicating the portability of your code to a new environment. I have found a solution that works with all the compilers I have tried. Always place the pound sign (#) flush-left, then use indentation for the directive itself. All the preprocessors I have worked with ignore the white space between the pound sign and the directive.

LISTING 2.1. TEMPLATE.H foundation listing.

```
// NEW.H - Header file for NEW class

#ifndef NEW_H
#    define NEW_H
```

```
// Note that the following code is executed only
// if this file has not been previously included


// #include files for both PC and SUN
#include  <WStr.h>

#ifdef __BORLANDC__
    // PC-specific #includes
#    include   <owl.h>

#endif

#ifdef Unix
    // UNIX-specific #includes

#endif

//****************************************************
// NEW -
//
//    Purpose:
//
//    Notes:
//
//    Copyright:
//            Copyright  (c) 1993, William H. Roetzheim
//            All Rights Reserved
//
//****************************************************

_CLASSDEF (NEW)
class NEW
{
    private:
        // Private data members ********************

        // Private member functions ****************

    public:
        // Public data members *********************


        // Public member functions *****************
        // Constructors and destructors
        NEW ();
        ~NEW ();
```

continues

LISTING 2.1. continued

```
        // Standard functions
        virtual void ResetAll();
        virtual WStr ClassName ();
        virtual void Write (ostream&);
        virtual void Read (istream&);
        virtual void Print (ostream&);
        virtual void Scan (istream&);
        virtual void Print ();
        virtual void Scan ();

        // Member functions

        // Cast operators supported

        // Overloaded operators

};

#endif NEW_H
```

> **TRICK:** WIN31 and STRICT should be defined for all files. WIN31 tells the compiler to use Windows 3.1 types, and STRICT enables a higher degree of type checking for Windows parameters, resulting in fewer UAEs. If you are using dynamic link libraries, including dynamic linking to Borland's runtime, container, or OWL classes, you also need to define _CLASSDLL. Normally I define these three items in the IDE's Options/Compiler dialog box so that they are in place for all code. In many examples in this book, I define them explicitly at the top of the source file for illustrative purposes.

A Class Source Foundation

Listing 2.2 shows the foundation for a generic class source file. This file is called TEMPLATE.CPP on the source disk. Incomplete sections of code are marked with the keyword TBD, meaning *to be determined.* To complete the class, you should do a global search-and-replace to substitute the class name for NEW. Do a global search for TBD, insert the appropriate class-specific code, then add member functions and overloaded operators specific to this class.

The Read and Write member functions store and retrieve binary images of the object's data elements. Typically this is accomplished by using the overloaded operators << and >>. These operators are available for all built-in Borland C++ data types, and I define them for all the classes I develop. The Read member function calls ResetAll before reading the binary data. This ensures that all internal variables are reset to a default state and frees any dynamic memory that the object might have allocated earlier.

The Print and Scan member functions store and retrieve human-readable images of the data elements of the object. Typically this is accomplished by calling the Print and Scan member functions of each data element you want to output.

> **TRICK:** For built-in types, you often can convert the data value to a WStr and call the WStr Print function when you store an object. Alternatively, you can call the WStr Read function and then convert the WStr to the appropriate data type when you retrieve an object.

I always group my member functions, cast operators, and overloaded operators as shown in the foundation. This grouping simplifies finding a function during debug and maintenance, and it greatly facilitates understanding the class when someone else is reviewing your source code.

LISTING 2.2. TEMPLATE.CPP foundation listing.

```
// NEW.CPP - Source file for NEW class

#include "NEW.h"  // ALL other #include statements
                  // are in this file
```

continues

LISTING 2.2. continued

```
//****************************************************
// Constructors and destructors for NEW
//
//     Copyright:
//             Copyright  (c) 1993, William H. Roetzheim
//             All Rights Reserved
//
//****************************************************

NEW::NEW ()
{
    TBD
}


NEW::~NEW ()
{
    TBD
}



//****************************************************
// Standard functions
//
//     Copyright:
//             Copyright  (c) 1993, William H. Roetzheim
//             All Rights Reserved
//
//****************************************************

void NEW::ResetAll ()
{
    // Reset all variables to defaults
    TBD
}


WStr NEW::ClassName ()
{
    return (WStr) "NEW";
}
```

```
void NEW::Write (ostream& os)
{
    // Use << to send all saved data elements
    // to os
    TBD
}


void NEW::Read (istream& is)
{
    ResetAll ();
    // Use >> to read all saved data elements
    // from is
    TBD
}


void NEW::Print (ostream& os)
{
    // Print ASCII representations
    // of all significant data elements to os
    TBD
}



void NEW::Scan (istream& is)
{
    ResetAll ();
    // Read ASCII representations
    // of all significant data elements from is
    TBD
}

void NEW::Print ()
{
    Print (cout);
}


void NEW::Scan ()
{
    Scan (cin);
}
```

continues

LISTING 2.2. continued

```
//****************************************************
// Member functions for class
//
//    Copyright:
//            Copyright  (c) 1993, William H. Roetzheim
//            All Rights Reserved
//
//****************************************************

TBD one header template per member function




//****************************************************
// Cast operators for NEW
//
//    Copyright:
//            Copyright  (c) 1993, William H. Roetzheim
//            All Rights Reserved
//
//****************************************************

TBD cast operators




//****************************************************
// Overloaded operators for NEW
//
//    Copyright:
//            Copyright  (c) 1993, William H. Roetzheim
//            All Rights Reserved
//
//****************************************************

TBD overloaded operators




//****************************************************
// Overloaded << and >> for simplified stream I/O
//
//    Copyright:
//            Copyright  (c) 1993, William H. Roetzheim
```

```
//          All Rights Reserved
//
//******************************************************

inline istream& operator >> (istream& is, RNEW Object)
{
    Object.Read (is);
    return is;
}


inline ostream& operator << (ostream& os, RNEW Object)
{
    Object.Write (os);
    return os;
}
```

A Member Function Introduction Foundation

Many people feel that every member function, cast operator, and over-loaded operator should begin with an introductory comment block for the function. I always followed this convention when programming in C, and I was happy with the results. In C++, I typically write many one- or two-line functions. When I include an introductory comment block for each function, my code becomes almost unreadable due to the high ratio of comment blocks to code. A compromise is in order. I've found that obeying the following rules results in a good mixture of comments and code:

➤ If a function or operator is complicated or long, it should have its own introductory comment block.

➤ If a function or operator has built-in limitations you know about, it should have its own introductory comment block, and the limitations should be documented in the comment block.

➤ If you expect future modifications to the function or operator, it should have its own introductory comment block, and the future modifications you expect should be documented in the comment block.

➤ If, during program maintenance, you find a less-than-obvious bug in a function or operator, and the function or operator does not already have an introductory comment block, add one. Then document the bug fix in the comment block.

➤ If a function or operator has many parameters, parameters that are not obvious, significant internal error processing, or an other-than-trivial return variable, it should have an introductory comment block.

➤ Often it is appropriate to have a single introductory comment block that introduces a group of related functions or operators.

Listing 2.3 shows the introductory comment block foundation I like to use. This file is called TEMPLATE (with no extension) on the source disk. The first line contains the name of the function or operator and a brief (one-line) description. The purpose of the function or operator is explained in the section labeled Purpose. Under General Notes I include anything that seems significant, including pass parameter meanings, return values, limitations, future enhancements, bug fixes, and so on. I include a subsection under General Notes called Testing Notes, where the developer of the class can make notes about things to watch for when writing the test driver for the class.

LISTING 2.3. A foundation for the introductory comment block of a function or operator.

```
//******************************************************
// class
//
//     Purpose:
//
//     General Notes:
//
//     Testing Notes:
//
//     Copyright:
//          Copyright  (c) 1993, William H. Roetzheim
//          All Rights Reserved
//
//******************************************************
```

OWL Application Foundations

All OWL applications include a class to represent the running application, and most include a class to represent the application's main window. These classes normally are named to match the name of the application. For example, an application called Tester would call its main application class `Tester` and its main window class `TesterWindow`. Because these classes are specific, the generic class foundations can be extended to enable you to implement a new OWL application quickly and easily.

A Main Processing Object Header Foundation

Listing 2.4 shows the header file foundation for your program's main application object. This file is called MAIN.H on the source disk. The foundation is similar to our generic class header, but it has been tailored by including the application main window header, using the proper variation of the constructor, and adding an `InitMainWindow` member function. Other than doing the global search to replace NEW with your application name, normally you don't need to modify this foundation before using it.

LISTING 2.4. Main application class header foundation.

```
// NEW.H - Header file for NEW application

#ifndef NEW_H
#    define NEW_H

// Note that the following code is executed only
// if this file has not been previously included


// #include files for both PC and SUN
#include   <WStr.h>
#include   <NEWWindow.h>

#ifdef __BORLANDC__
    // PC-specific #includes
#    include   <owl.h>
```

continues

LISTING 2.4. continued

```
#elseifdef Unix
     // UNIX-specific #includes

#endif

//*****************************************************
// NEW - NEW application class
//
//     Purpose:
//         This class is the overall application
//         executive for NEW.
//
//     Notes:
//         Application names should be seven characters
//         or less for this to work optimally in terms
//         of automatic code using global search-and-
//         replace.
//
//     Copyright:
//            Copyright  (c) 1993, William H. Roetzheim
//            All Rights Reserved
//
//*****************************************************
_CLASSDEF (NEW)
class NEW : public TApplication
{
     private:
         // Private data members *******************
         //   None


         // Private member functions ***************
         //   None

     public:
         // Public data members ********************
         //   None


         // Public member functions ****************
         // Constructors and destructors
         NEW (char *szName, HINSTANCE hInstance,
                 HINSTANCE hPrevInstance,
                 LPSTR lpCmdLine,
                 int nCmdShow);
         ~NEW ();
```

```
            // Standard functions
            virtual void ResetAll();
            virtual WStr ClassName ();
            virtual void Write (ostream&);
            virtual void Read (istream&);
            virtual void Print (ostream&);
            virtual void Scan (istream&);
            virtual void Print ();
            virtual void Scan ();

            // Member functions
            virtual void InitMainWindow ();

            // Cast operators supported
            // None

            // Overloaded operators
            // None
};

#endif NEW_H
```

A Main Processing Object Source Foundation

Listing 2.5 shows the source file for the main processing object foundation of your application. This file is called MAIN.CPP on the source disk. With most OWL applications, to create a fully functioning program, the only change you have to make is to do a global search-and-replace to substitute your application name for NEW. Note that PNEW becomes a pointer to your application class, and that RNEW becomes a reference to your application class because of the _CLASSDEF preprocessor directive. Similarly, PNEWWindow becomes a pointer to your application class main window, and RNEWWindow becomes a reference to your application class main window.

LISTING 2.5. MAIN.CPP: The main processing object foundation source file.

```
// NEW.CPP - Source file for NEW application

#include "NEW.h"  // ALL other #include statements
                  // are in this file
```

continues

LISTING 2.5. continued

```
//*****************************************************
// Constructors and destructors for NEW
//
//      Copyright:
//              Copyright  (c) 1993, William H. Roetzheim
//              All Rights Reserved
//
//*****************************************************

#pragma argsused  // Turn off arguments not used warning
NEW::NEW(char *szName, HINSTANCE hInstance,
            HINSTANCE hPrevInstance, LPSTR lpCmdLine,
            int nCmdShow)
            : TApplication (szName, hInstance,
            hPrevInstance, lpCmdLine, nCmdShow)
{
    return;
}



NEW::~NEW ()
{
    return;
}



//*****************************************************
// Standard functions
//
//      Copyright:
//              Copyright  (c) 1993, William H. Roetzheim
//              All Rights Reserved
//
//*****************************************************

void NEW::ResetAll ()
{
    // Reset all variables to defaults
    return;
}


WStr NEW::ClassName ()
{
```

```
        return (WStr) "NEW";
}


void NEW::Write (ostream& os)
{
    // Use << to send all saved data elements
    // to os
    ((PNEWWindow) MainWindow)->Write (os);
}


void NEW::Read (istream& is)
{
    ResetAll ();
    // Use >> to read all saved data elements
    // from is
    ((PNEWWindow) MainWindow)->Read (is);
}


void NEW::Print (ostream& os)
{
    // Print ASCII representations
    // of all significant data elements to os
    ((PNEWWindow) MainWindow)->Print (os);
}



void NEW::Scan (istream& is)
{
    ResetAll ();
    // Read ASCII representations
    // of all significant data elements from is
    ((PNEWWindow) MainWindow)->Scan (is);
}

void NEW::Print ()
{
    Print (cout);
}



void NEW::Scan ()
{
    Scan (cin);
}
```

continues

LISTING 2.5. continued

```
//****************************************************
// Member functions for class
//
//    Copyright:
//            Copyright  (c) 1993, William H. Roetzheim
//            All Rights Reserved
//
//****************************************************

void NEW::InitMainWindow ()
{
    MainWindow = new NEWWindow ("NEW");
}




//****************************************************
// Cast operators for NEW
//
//    Copyright:
//            Copyright  (c) 1993, William H. Roetzheim
//            All Rights Reserved
//
//****************************************************




//****************************************************
// Overloaded operators for NEW
//
//    Copyright:
//            Copyright  (c) 1993, William H. Roetzheim
//            All Rights Reserved
//
//****************************************************




//****************************************************
// Overloaded << and >> for simplified stream I/O
//
```

```
//    Copyright:
//            Copyright  (c) 1993, William H. Roetzheim
//            All Rights Reserved
//
//****************************************************

inline istream& operator >> (istream& is, RNEW Object)
{
    Object.Read (is);
    return is;
}


inline ostream& operator << (ostream& os, RNEW Object)
{
    Object.Write (os);
    return os;
}




// Here is the main () for the program
int PASCAL WinMain (HANDLE hInstance,
    HANDLE hPrevInstance, LPSTR lpCmdLine,
    int)
{

    // Create NEW application from class
    NEW oNEW ("NEW", hInstance,
                hPrevInstance, lpCmdLine, SW_NORMAL);

    // Start created application running
    oNEW.Run ();  // Runs till window closed

    // Return termination status when window closed
    return oNEW.Status;
}
```

A Main Window Header Foundation

Listing 2.6 shows the foundation for your application's main window header. This file is called MAINWIN.H on the source disk. Do the standard global search-and-replace to substitute your application name for the word NEW. You also need to add the prototypes for your dynamic dispatch virtual table (DDVT) functions in the appropriate section and any support functions used by your DDVT functions as public or private member functions. DDVT functions handle all message processing for your window.

LISTING 2.6. MAINWIN.H: The main window header foundation.

```
// NEWWINDOW.H - Header file for NEW main window

#ifndef NEWWindow_H
#       define NEWWindow_H

// Note that the following code is executed only
// if this file has not been previously included


// #include files for both PC and UNIX
#include  <WStr.h>

#ifdef __BORLANDC__
     // PC-specific #includes
#       include   <owl.h>

#elseifdef Unix
     // UNIX-specific #includes

#endif

//****************************************************
// NEWWindow - Main window for NEW application
//
//     Notes:
//
//     Copyright:
//           Copyright  (c) 1993, William H. Roetzheim
//           All Rights Reserved
//
//****************************************************
```

```
_CLASSDEF (NEWWindow)
class NEWWindow : public TWindow
{
    private:
        // Private data members ********************


        // Private member functions ****************

    public:
        // Public data members *********************


        // Public member functions *****************
        // Constructors and destructors
        NEWWindow (WStr Title);
        ~NEWWindow ();

        // Standard functions
        virtual void ResetAll();
        virtual WStr ClassName ();
        virtual void Write (ostream&);
        virtual void Read (istream&);
        virtual void Print (ostream&);
        virtual void Scan (istream&);
        virtual void Print ();
        virtual void Scan ();

        // Member functions

        // DDVT functions

        // Cast operators supported

        // Overloaded operators


};

#endif NEWWindow_H
```

A Main Window Source Foundation

Listing 2.7 shows the foundation for your application's main window source. This file is called MAINWIN.CPP on the source disk.

LISTING 2.7. MAINWIN.CPP: The main window source foundation.

```cpp
// NEWWINDOW.CPP - Source file for NEWWindow class

#include "NEWWindow.h"  // ALL other #include statements
                        // are in this file


//****************************************************
// Constructors and destructors for NEWWindow
//
//     Copyright:
//             Copyright  (c) 1993, William H. Roetzheim
//             All Rights Reserved
//
//****************************************************
NEWWindow::NEWWindow (WStr Title)
     : TWindow (NULL, (char *) Title)
{
     TBD;
}


NEWWindow::~NEWWindow ()
{
     TBD;
}



//****************************************************
// Standard functions
//
//     Copyright:
//             Copyright  (c) 1993, William H. Roetzheim
//             All Rights Reserved
//
//****************************************************

void NEWWindow::ResetAll ()
{
     // Reset all variables to defaults
     TBD
}
```

```cpp
WStr NEWWindow::ClassName ()
{
    return (WStr) "NEWWindow";
}


void NEWWindow::Write (ostream& os)
{
    // Use << to send all saved data elements
    // to os
    TBD
}


void NEWWindow::Read (istream& is)
{
    ResetAll ();
    // Use >> to read all saved data elements
    // from is
    TBD
}


void NEWWindow::Print (ostream& os)
{
    // Print ASCII representations
    // of all significant data elements to os
    TBD
}


void NEWWindow::Scan (istream& is)
{
    ResetAll ();
    // Read ASCII representations
    // of all significant data elements from is
    TBD
}

void NEWWindow::Print ()
{
    Print (cout);
}
```

continues

LISTING 2.7. continued

```
void NEWWindow::Scan ()
{
    Scan (cin);
}


//****************************************************
// Member functions for class
//
//    Copyright:
//            Copyright  (c) 1993, William H. Roetzheim
//            All Rights Reserved
//
//****************************************************

TBD one header template per member function




//****************************************************
// DDVT member functions for NEWWindow
//
//    Copyright:
//            Copyright  (c) 1993, William H. Roetzheim
//            All Rights Reserved
//
//****************************************************

TBD DDVT functions




//****************************************************
// cast operators for NEWWindow
//
//    Copyright:
//            Copyright  (c) 1993, William H. Roetzheim
//            All Rights Reserved
//
//****************************************************

TBD cast operators
```

```
//*****************************************************
// Overloaded operators for NEWWindow
//
//     Copyright:
//             Copyright  (c) 1993, William H. Roetzheim
//             All Rights Reserved
//
//*****************************************************

TBD overloaded operators



//*****************************************************
// Overloaded << and >> for simplified stream I/O
//
//     Copyright:
//             Copyright  (c) 1993, William H. Roetzheim
//             All Rights Reserved
//
//*****************************************************

inline istream& operator >> (istream& is, RNEWWindow Object)
{
    Object.Read (is);
    return is;
}


inline ostream& operator << (ostream& os, RNEWWindow Object)
{
    Object.Write (os);
    return os;
}
```

CHAPTER

3

Coding Dynamic Link Libraries

Problem

Suppose you write an incredibly useful class—so useful, in fact, that soon many of your coworkers incorporate it into their code. Six months later you discover a subtle bug in the code. The fix is easy, but how do you determine what other code must be relinked to incorporate the bug fix?

Suppose you write a handy compression routine that is somewhat large in size but so useful that most applications in your company incorporate it in their code. You later notice that four applications, all of which include your code, are running simultaneously. A quick mental calculation confirms that a total of 300K of memory is used by your 75K routine.

Suppose you want your application to run on computers that have a minimal amount of memory. However, you require some very bulky code to handle exception cases, such as spell checking and error processing. Although you could switch to the medium memory model and define independently loadable code segments, you're confused about how to handle these conflicting requirements without leaving the simplicity of the large memory model.

Solution

Three problems, one solution. *Dynamic link libraries*, or *DLLs*, are designed specifically to solve these problems. You might not know it, but your code already uses DLLs. Most of the Microsoft Windows application program interface (API) functions (and much of Borland C++, for that matter) are implemented as DLLs. Take a look at how they work before you learn how to build them.

NOTE: In general, you should always use `#defines` to identify your dialog box controls (as demonstrated in Chapter 6, "Implementing Large Dialog Boxes"). For the next three chapters I ignore this practice to simplify my demonstrations of some concepts that use trivial dialog boxes.

Understanding How DLLs Work

Historically, most functions have been statically linked to applications. When you use a library (denoted by the .LIB extension) or object code (denoted by the .OBJ extension), the executable versions of the functions contained in the code are brought in to your executable file (denoted by the .EXE extension). The process of bringing in executable functions and adjusting addresses and pointers is called *static linking*. You are left with a larger executable, because the actual code for the functions you use is included in your program file. This is why even a small C program that uses library functions results in a large executable file. Furthermore, because the actual code is physically present in your file, multiple versions of the same library function code almost certainly exist on disk and, sometimes, in memory. If the code is modified, perhaps to fix a bug, each application that uses that code is relinked to remove the old code and replace it with the new.

Dynamic linking occurs at runtime. Your application knows that certain functions exist, but the code for these functions is not included in your application program code. Instead, the function code is maintained in a central file called a dynamic link library. When your executing program makes a call to a dynamic link function, Windows checks to see whether the function is already in memory. If it is in memory, Windows increases the in-use counter for this library by one and passes execution to the new memory location. If the function is not already in memory, Windows tries to find a file, with a .DLL extension, that contains the desired function. Windows then loads the function into memory, sets the in-use counter for the library to 1, and passes execution to the new memory location. The places where Windows searches, and the order of search, are shown in Table 3.1. When you return from a DLL function, Windows decreases the in-use counter for that library by one. Whenever memory becomes tight, Windows searches for DLLs that have an in-use counter of 0 and frees that memory space. Take a look at how switching from static linking to dynamic linking solves the three problems mentioned at the beginning of this chapter.

TABLE 3.1. Priority Windows uses when searching for a DLL.

Priority	Search Path
1	Current directory
2	Directory where WIN.COM is located
3	Windows system directory (normally WINDOWS\SYSTEM)
4	Directory where the application .EXE was loaded from
5	All directories in the PATH
6	Any directories mapped in a network

Because linking is accomplished at runtime, you can have all your library files reside in one directory on your computer (or on your file server if you are networked). You can make any changes to the function code that don't affect the calling interface by replacing the appropriate DLL. There is no requirement to relink any of the code that uses these DLLs. Because all applications share a common instance of each function's code within a DLL, you don't have redundant code either on disk or in memory. Finally, because DLL function code is loaded only when needed, you can place bulky and seldom-used code, such as spell checking and exception handling, in a DLL and load it only when it is required.

If you're still not convinced, here's one more reason to learn how to write DLLs: Windows programmers (and people who hire Windows programmers) esteem those who are sharp enough to write DLLs. Let's learn how.

A DLL in Action

I begin with a sample program demonstrating the use of DLLs. This test program demonstrates calling a DLL to perform all processing and using the classes in a DLL to support local processing. CHPT3.EXE creates a window and uses a DLL function to display a Login dialog box. The user enters his or her name and password, and the program returns the name and password. Next, CHPT3.EXE creates a WLogin dialog object by using the code in the DLL and setting the default value to the name and password that have just been returned. Then, it displays the return values from the second Login dialog box. The code for processing the dialog box and the definition of the dialog box itself are contained within the DLL WLOGIN.DLL. Figure 3.1 shows CHPT3.EXE in action. This program is a good example of a reusable component implemented by using a DLL.

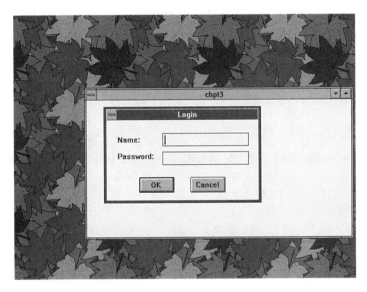

Figure 3.1. CHPT3.EXE in operation.

To run CHPT3.EXE, follow these steps:

1. Create a directory called \BOOK to be used for sample programs in this book. Copy file CHPT3.EXE from the source disk to this directory.

2. Copy file WLOGIN.DLL from the source disk to your \WINDOWS\SYSTEM directory, which is the normal location for installing DLLs, or to the \BOOK directory.

3. From Windows, run program CHPT3.EXE by giving the File/Run command from Program Manager. You also can create a new icon for this application and double-click on it to run the program.

4. When prompted, enter a name and password. This dialog box resides in the DLL and is displayed by a single call. The entered name and password are displayed in a message box. I then display the same dialog box using a different approach internally. Enter your name and password when the dialog box is redisplayed. This dialog box resides in the CHPT3.EXE resource file. It is displayed by creating a WLogin object using the class that is defined in the DLL.

In the following sections, I show you how to create and use a dynamic link library. I start by describing a DLL header file and source file, using WLOGIN.H and WLOGIN.CPP as examples. Then I step through the process of compiling the DLL. To conclude, I walk through the sample program that uses a DLL, CHPT3.CPP.

INT: A test driver is a set of code that automatically or semiautomatically tests a piece of your production code. The test driver code is used during development but normally is not delivered to the customer. Normally it is best to write and test the DLL code and test driver as an ordinary program until you are confident that the code works properly. Then you can convert the DLL portion of the code to a DLL and retest. This simplifies the compile-test-debug cycle, and it helps in tracking down any bugs that might be introduced when running the code as a DLL. Otherwise, you must compile the DLL project and the test driver project separately.

DLL Header Files

A DLL can contain both exported classes and functions and also local classes and functions. Exported classes and functions are available to other applications, whereas local classes and functions are private to the DLL code itself. An application using a DLL needs a header file that it can include to define the function prototypes for all exported functions and classes. Likewise, the DLL implementing code needs a header file that addresses exported and local functions and classes as well as external functions called from within a DLL itself. This includes functions in other DLLs. People use three different approaches to meet these two needs.

The first approach is to have a single header file that includes only the exported functions and classes of the DLL. The header information for the local functions and classes is added directly to the source code that implements the DLL. I generally disapprove of this approach for the same reason that I believe headers should contain only header information and source code should contain only implementing code. An exception would be short prototype code used to demonstrate or test a concept. In cases like this, where the code will be thrown away, saving time is more important.

The second approach is to have a single header that covers both exported and local functions and classes of the DLL and that is used by both the DLL itself and code that calls the DLL. I disapprove of this approach, too. The person using the DLL has no clear way of knowing which functions and classes are exported and, therefore, available, versus the functions and classes that are local and hence not available. Although any misuse would be caught at link time, this trial-and-error approach for seeing what is available is not efficient.

The third, and recommended, approach is to have two header files for the DLL code. One header file provides prototypes for all exported functions and classes; it is publicly distributed. The other header file provides prototypes for all local functions and classes for use by the DLL itself; it includes the first header file as well. For DLLs consisting of many classes, these two header files include the public or private header files (as appropriate) for each class in the DLL.

All the WLogin DLL's classes and functions are exported, so the single header file shown in Listing 3.1 is adequate.

 NOTE: All the code in this chapter and subsequent chapters assumes that you consistently use the large memory model for compiling all your code. This is what I recommend.

LISTING 3.1. WLOGIN.H header file.

```
#define   _CLASSDLL
#define WIN31
#define STRICT

// WLOGIN.H - Header file for WLogin class

#ifndef WLogin_H
#    define WLogin_H

// Note that the following code is executed only
// if this file has not been previously included


// #include files for both PC and SUN

#include   <owl.h>
#include <edit.h>

#ifdef __DLL__
#    define _EXPORT _export
#else
#    define _EXPORT _CLASSTYPE
#endif

//****************************************************
// WLogin - Display Login dialog box
//
//    Purpose:
//        Use a dialog box to capture a user log in
//        name and password.
//
//    Notes:
//        This code is implemented as a DLL in the
//        large memory model.
//
//    Copyright:
//            Copyright (c) 1993, William H. Roetzheim
//            All Rights Reserved
//
//****************************************************

#define MAX_NAME 80
#define MAX_PASSWORD 80

struct WLoginTransferBuffer
{
```

```
        char Name [MAX_NAME];
        char Password [MAX_PASSWORD];

        WLoginTransferBuffer ()
        {
            Name[0] = 0;
            Password [0] = 0;
        };
};

typedef WLoginTransferBuffer *PWLoginTransferBuffer;

_CLASSDEF (WLoginDialog)
class EXPORT WLoginDialog : public TDialog
{
    public:

            // Public member functions *****************
            // Constructors and destructors
            WLoginDialog (PTWindowsObject Parent, LPSTR szName,
                            PTModule Module,
                            PWLoginTransferBuffer tb);
};


extern "C"
{
    int GetLogin(PTWindowsObject ParentWnd,
        PWLoginTransferBuffer tb);
}

#endif WLogin_H
```

I'll step through the interesting portions of the code, starting with the
lines that read

```
#define   _CLASSDLL
#define WIN31
#define STRICT
```

As I mentioned earlier, all files should define WIN31 and STRICT, and all
files that use DLLs (including Borland's dynamic versions of the Borland
libraries) must define _CLASSDLL.

RICK: If you get linker errors indicating that the linker cannot find functions that you know exist (for example, the Borland runtime library, `classlib`, or OWL functions), check to be sure that `CLASSDLL` is defined.

C++ classes that are local to a DLL can be coded without any change from the way you currently code C++ classes. Classes that are exported from the DLL so that they can be accessed by other code must be `far` and must use full 32-bit pointers for the virtual table and the `this` parameter. The easiest way to accomplish this is to declare the class as `_export` when it is declared in the DLL, as in

```
class _export Test
{
    . . .
}
```

In this case, the same header file will be used by my DLL code and also by the external application code. I don't want the external application inclusion of this header to have the result that the class is declared as `_export`. Therefore, I use a compiler directive to define EXPORT conditionally either as `_export` (for the DLL) or as `_CLASSTYPE` (for the external application):

```
#ifdef __DLL__
#    define EXPORT _export
#else
#    define EXPORT _CLASSTYPE
#endif
```

`_CLASSTYPE` expands to huge when `_CLASSDLL` is defined.

INT: All virtual table pointers and `this` parameters for classes shared between application code and DLLs must be 32 bits. Classes declared as huge or `_export` automatically have 32-bit virtual table pointers and `this` parameters; classes declared using other memory models, including `far`, by default do not. Many programmers like to declare all classes as `_export`, accepting the small performance penalty for increased safety. You can force the compiler to use 32-bit values all the time if you select Options/C++ Options from the IDE menu, and check the Far Virtual Tables check box. This is handy when code must work with DLLs and you don't want to change the source code. Likewise, if your code compiles correctly but gives runtime errors or UAEs when using the DLL, select this compiler option. If the problems go away, you know that one of your shared classes is not declared as huge or export.

Because the DLL is coding a dialog box, I defined a transfer buffer in the header file. The transfer buffer is used to transfer data into and out of the dialog box during processing. For a detailed discussion of transfer buffers, refer to the OWL documentation or to my book *Programming Windows with Borland C++* (2D Press, 1992). The code that defines the transfer buffer is as follows:

```
struct WLoginTransferBuffer
{
    char Name [MAX_NAME];
    char Password [MAX_PASSWORD];

    WLoginTransferBuffer ()
    {
        Name[0] = 0;
        Password [0] = 0;
    };
};
typedef WLoginTransferBuffer *PWLoginTransferBuffer;
```

The WLoginTransferBuffer structure contains two variables used in the transfer process—Name and Password. If you use strcpy() to initialize these variables to a value before you call the dialog box, they become the default values in the dialog box. When the dialog box closes, these variables are set to the value entered by the user if the OK button was pressed, or they are left at their original values if the Cancel button was pressed. I also declare a far pointer to a WLoginTransferBuffer as PWLoginTransferBuffer using a typedef.

WLoginTransferBuffer uses a convenient technique to ensure that it is properly initialized when it is declared—a constructor. Yes, structures can

have constructors and destructors. Because the only code I normally place in a structure is a constructor and a destructor, structures are an exception to my rule of not placing inline code in the header file. The entire implementation of the WLoginTransferBuffer constructor is present in the header definition.

The class that actually handles the dialog box is called WLoginDialog. I use the _CLASSDEF macro for all my classes, as in the following:

```
_CLASSDEF (WLoginDialog)
```

This macro defines a shorthand syntax for coding a reference to a class, RWLoginDialog, and also a pointer to a class, PWLoginDialog. The class itself contains only a constructor. This constructor takes these four things as an argument:

➤ A pointer to a Windows object, PTWindowsObject, that defines the window that will own the dialog box

➤ A string that contains the dialog box name to be used

➤ A pointer to a TModule object that defines where the dialog resource should be loaded from

➤ A pointer to the WLoginTransferBuffer

```
_CLASSDEF (WLoginDialog)
class EXPORT WLoginDialog : public TDialog
{
      public:

            // Public member functions ****************
            // Constructors and destructors
            WLoginDialog (PTWindowsObject Parent, LPSTR szName,
                          PTModule Module,
                          PWLoginTransferBuffer tb);
};
```

Normally you use the WLoginDialog class when you want to define the appearance of the Login dialog box in your application but want to use the DLL code to take care of the processing. The dialog box you create using the Resource Workshop must have two edit fields: Name, with an identifier value of 101, and Password, with an identifier value of 102. The dialog box must also have at least an OK pushbutton with an identifier of IDOK, which is defined in WINDOWS.H. You'll see an example of this approach later in this chapter.

If you are content to use the Login dialog box defined within the DLL, simply call the GetLogin function. This function must be defined as an external function using the extern keyword. I also choose to define it as a C function (because doing so avoids name-mangling) so that the Login dialog box can be used easily from both C and C++ programs. The GetLogin function does not need to know the dialog box name or TModule identifier because it loads the dialog box from its own resource area in the DLL.

```
extern "C"
{
    int GetLogin(PTWindowsObject ParentWnd,
        PWLoginTransferBuffer tb);
}
```

Understanding DLL Code

Listing 3.2 shows the code that actually implements the DLL.

LISTING 3.2. WLOGIN.CPP code.

```
// WLOGIN.CPP - Source file for WLogin class

#include "WLogin.h"   // ALL other #include statements
                      // are in this file


// Create a place to store a pointer to
// a new instance to represent this DLL
PTModule DLLModule;


// Must include definition for LibMain function
// for all DLLs
int FAR PASCAL LibMain (HINSTANCE hInstance,
                               WORD /* DataSeg */,
                               WORD /* HeapSize */,
                               LPSTR lpCmdLine)
{
    DLLModule = new TModule ("DLLModule", hInstance,
        lpCmdLine);
```

continues

LISTING 3.2. continued

```
    if ((DLLModule==NULL) ¦¦ (DLLModule->Status != 0))
    {
        delete DLLModule;
        DLLModule = NULL;
      return 0;
    }
    else return 1;  // Success
}


//****************************************************
// Constructor for WLoginDialog
//
//    Copyright:
//            Copyright (c) 1993, William H. Roetzheim
//            All Rights Reserved
//
//****************************************************

#define IDD_NAME 101
#define IDD_PASSWORD 102

_export WLoginDialog::WLoginDialog (PTWindowsObject Parent,
                                    LPSTR szName,
                                    PTModule Module,
                                    PWLoginTransferBuffer tb)
                :TDialog (Parent, szName, Module)
{
// Don't need to save returned pointers because OWL
// automatically deletes all child windows when
// parent window is destroyed
    new TEdit (this, IDD_NAME, MAX_NAME);
    new TEdit (this, IDD_PASSWORD, MAX_PASSWORD);
    SetTransferBuffer (tb);
}



// Function that actually creates the Login dialog box
int _export GetLogin(PTWindowsObject ParentWnd,
            PWLoginTransferBuffer tb)
{
    PWLoginDialog TheDialog;
```

```
        TheDialog = new WLoginDialog (ParentWnd,
             "Login", DLLModule, tb);


        return DLLModule->ExecDialog (TheDialog);
}
```

DLLs often need to display a Windows object or load a resource. Both actions require you to know the instance handle for the running application—in this case, the DLL itself. This information is stored in a pointer to a `TModule` object that is declared as a variable global to this module:

`PTModule DLLModule;`

All DLLs must include a function called `LibMain`. This function is automatically called whenever the DLL is loaded into memory and executed, but not when the DLL is accessed while still in memory. I use `LibMain` to create a new `TModule` instance and to initialize `DLLModule` to point to this instance. `LibMain` returns 1 for success and 0 for failure.

The implementation of the `WLoginDialog` class is accomplished in the single constructor. This function begins by calling the `TDialog` constructor. It creates two new objects that correspond to the two edit fields in the dialog box; this process is necessary for the transfer mechanism to work. Then the function sets the dialog transfer buffer to point to `tb`.

The `GetLogin` function is equally simple. It declares a pointer to a `WLoginDialog` object and initializes that pointer with the `WLoginDialog` constructor. The dialog box resource is created with the Resource Workshop and is named `Login`. Then, `GetLogin` executes the dialog box, causing it to be displayed. When the dialog box is closed, `GetLogin` returns the value of the key that was used to close the dialog box—either `IDOK` or `IDCANCEL`, as defined in WINDOWS.H. The transfer buffer is updated automatically by the `TDialog` object when `IDOK` is used to close the dialog.

Compiling the DLL Code

To compile the `WLogin` DLL successfully, perform the following steps:

1. Copy file WLOGIN.H from the source disk to the \BOOK directory you created earlier.

2. Copy file WLOGIN.CPP from the source disk to the \BOOK directory.

3. Copy file WLOGIN.PRJ from the source disk to the \BOOK directory.

4. Copy file WLOGIN.RC from the source disk to the \BOOK directory.

5. Run Borland C++ for Windows. From the main menu, select Project/Open. Choose the WLOGIN.PRJ project (see Figure 3.2).

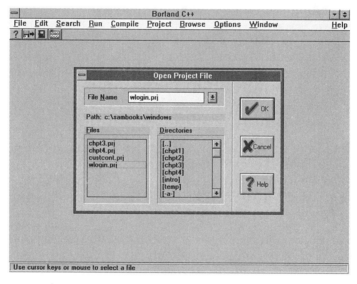

Figure 3.2. Opening the WLogin *project.*

6. From the main menu, select Compile/Make. The DLL is built, and a .DLL file is the result. If you have problems, the most likely cause is that your directories are different from the ones I used. Change the directories in the IDE by selecting Options/Directories. Also change the directories in the project file by selecting Window/ Project. Delete any files with invalid directory locations, and add the same filenames with the proper location.

The file WLOGIN.RC contains the dialog box definition. To view this dialog box, load the Borland Resource Workshop, then select File/Open. Select the WLOGIN.RC file to display the screen shown in Figure 3.3. Double-click on the WLogin dialog resource to display the WLogin dialog itself (see Figure 3.4). The dialog box contains four controls, not counting the static text:

➤ An edit field labeled Name with an identifier of 101

➤ An edit field labeled Password with an identifier of 102

➤ A pushbutton labeled OK with an identifier of IDOK

➤ A pushbutton labeled Cancel with an identifier of IDCANCEL

Normally you would use #defines to define all identifiers, then store these #defines in a header file used by both the DLL and the calling application. I chose to hard-code these values in this example for simplicity.

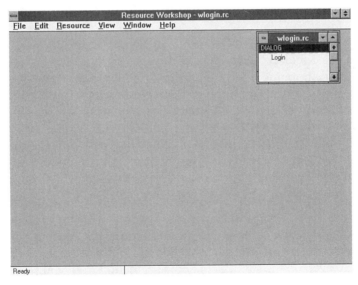

Figure 3.3. The initial Resource Workshop screen.

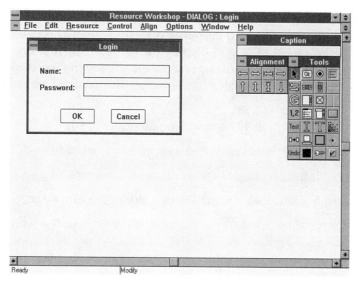

Figure 3.4. The WLogin *dialog box.*

Now take a look at the contents of the WLogin project file. Close the Resource Workshop and open the Borland C++ window. Load the WLogin project, if necessary. Open the project window by selecting Window/Project. The screen shown in Figure 3.5 is displayed. The reason for the inclusion of files WLOGIN.CPP and WLOGIN.RC is obvious. The file OWLDLL.DEF (found in BORLAND\OWL\LIB) is a module definition file provided by Borland that is appropriate for DLLs. Including this file is optional, but if you don't include it, a linker warning results.

Finally, take a look at the IDE settings contained in the project file. You need to use these settings when you create a project file for your own DLL. Table 3.2 lists the IDE settings I use when I build a DLL. Most options were discussed earlier or are obvious. For code in a DLL, the stack segment will seldom, if ever, be the same as the data segment. When you set all functions as exportable, special prolog code is included so that you can export any function you want. If this option isn't selected, exported functions must be explicitly listed in the .DEF file—a common source of runtime errors. By setting all libraries to dynamic, you avoid including copies of the Borland libraries in your code, relying on the equivalent DLLs instead.

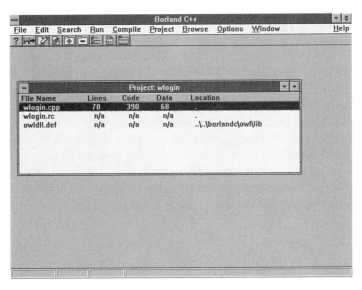

Figure 3.5. WLogin *project files.*

TABLE 3.2. IDE settings used when building a DLL.

IDE Location	Settings That Matter
Options/Application	Windows DLL
Options/Compiler/Code Generation	Memory model: large Assume SS=DS: never
Options/Compiler/Entry Exit Code	Prolog/epilog: Windows DLL All functions exportable
Option/Compiler/C++ Options	Options: far virtual tables
Options/Messages/Display	Warnings: display all
Options/Linker/Settings	Output: DLL Options: default libraries
Options/Linker/Libraries	Dynamic for all

Using IMPLIBW

You've created a dynamic link library with a .DLL extension, and you have a header file that provides prototypes for all classes and functions that are exported from the DLL. Now you can write code that includes this header file and uses these classes and functions, right? Not quite. At this point, the code compiles properly, but it doesn't link because the linker is looking for static code it can link in. You must tell the linker that these functions and classes are dynamic. Use a special library file (with a .LIB extension) that contains no code but does have linker instructions for each exported function and class. You create this file by using the program IMPLIBW, short for Import Library for Windows, that Borland supplies with the C++ compiler.

Run IMPLIBW. Then select File/File Select. Select the DLL you want—in this case, WLOGIN.DLL. IMPLIBW creates a library file with the same filename as the DLL file—in this case, WLogin—but with a .LIB extension. Figure 3.6 shows the result. You can add this library file to any application that uses the DLL classes or functions.

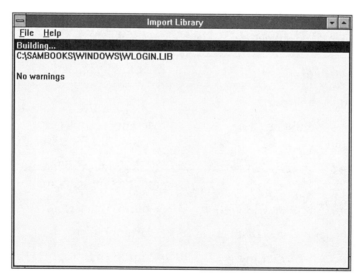

Figure 3.6. IMPLIBW in action.

You might wonder why you don't need to include a library file to tell your application about the DLL functions that are built into Windows itself. These functions are defined in a file called IMPORT.LIB, which Borland provides in the BORLANDC\LIB directory. The compiler includes the file automatically when you compile your program.

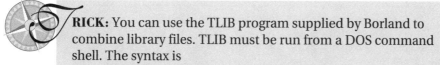 **RICK:** You can use the TLIB program supplied by Borland to combine library files. TLIB must be run from a DOS command shell. The syntax is

```
TLIB LibraryName Commands
```

Commands can be any sequence shown in Table 3.3. *LibraryName* is the name of your DLL .LIB file that includes the .LIB extension.

TABLE 3.3. TLIB commands.

Command	Function
+FileName	Adds the file to the library
-FileName	Deletes the file from the library
-+FileName	Replaces the file in the library

The Test Application

Listing 3.3 shows the code used to test the new DLL. To load and compile this code, follow these steps:

1. Copy file CHPT3.CPP from the source disk to the \BOOK directory you created.

2. Copy file CHPT3.PRJ from the source disk to the \BOOK directory.

3. Run Borland C++ for Windows. Select Project/Open. Choose the
   CHPT3.PRJ project.

4. Select Compile/Make.

LISTING 3.3. chpt3 **test driver code.**

```
#define _CLASSDLL  // Needed if you use a DLL class
#define WIN31  // Windows 3.1
#define STRICT  // Strict type checking
#include  <owl.h>
#include  "Wlogin.h"


//*****************************************************
// chpt3 - chpt3 application class
//
//    Purpose:
//        This class is the overall application
//        executive for chpt3.
//
//    Notes:
//        None
//
//    Copyright:
//        Copyright (c) 1993, William H. Roetzheim
//        All Rights Reserved
//
//*****************************************************

_CLASSDEF (chpt3)
class chpt3 : public TApplication
{
    public:
        // Public member functions *****************
        // Constructors and destructors
        chpt3 (LPSTR szName, HINSTANCE hInstance,
                HINSTANCE hPrevInstance, LPSTR lpCmdLine,
                int nCmdShow);

        // Member functions
        virtual void InitMainWindow ();
};
```

```
//*****************************************************
// chpt3Window - Main window for chpt3 application
//
//     Notes:
//
//     Copyright:
//             Copyright (c) 1993, William H. Roetzheim
//             All Rights Reserved
//
//*****************************************************


_CLASSDEF (chpt3Window)
class chpt3Window : public TWindow
{
    protected:
        virtual void WMSize(RTMessage);

    public:
        // Public member functions ****************
        // Constructors and destructors
        chpt3Window (char *Title);
};




//*****************************************************
// Constructors and destructors for chpt3
//
//     Copyright:
//             Copyright (c) 1993, William H. Roetzheim
//             All Rights Reserved
//
//*****************************************************


#pragma argsused  // Turn off arguments not used warning
chpt3::chpt3(LPSTR szName, HINSTANCE hInstance,
         HINSTANCE hPrevInstance, LPSTR lpCmdLine,
         int nCmdShow)
         : TApplication (szName, hInstance,
         hPrevInstance, lpCmdLine, nCmdShow)
{
    return;
}
```

continues

LISTING 3.3. continued

```
//***************************************************
// Member functions for class chpt3
//
//      Copyright:
//              Copyright (c) 1993, William H. Roetzheim
//              All Rights Reserved
//
//***************************************************

void chpt3::InitMainWindow ()
{
    MainWindow = new chpt3Window ("chpt3");
}




//***************************************************
// Constructors and destructors for chpt3Window
//
//      Copyright:
//              Copyright (c) 1993, William H. Roetzheim
//              All Rights Reserved
//
//***************************************************

chpt3Window::chpt3Window (char *Title)
    : TWindow (NULL, Title)
{
    return;
}




//***************************************************
// Member functions for class chpt3Window
//
//      Copyright:
//              Copyright (c) 1993, William H. Roetzheim
//              All Rights Reserved
//
//***************************************************

void chpt3Window::WMSize(RTMessage)
{
    TWindow::WMSize(RTMessage);
    PWLoginTransferBuffer tb = new WLoginTransferBuffer;
    PWLoginDialog TheDialog;
```

```
        // Call dialog password routine using dialog box in DLL
        GetLogin(this, tb);
        MessageBox (HWindow, tb->Name, tb->Password, MB_OK);

        // Call dialog password routine using dialog box in our .EXE
        TheDialog = new WLoginDialog (this,
            "Login", GetModule (), tb);
        // Note that ExecDialog automatically deletes the
        // dialog object when the dialog box is closed
        GetModule()->ExecDialog (TheDialog);
        MessageBox (HWindow, tb->Name, tb->Password, MB_OK);

        delete tb;
        Destroy ();
}


// Here is the main () for the program
int PASCAL WinMain (HINSTANCE hInstance,
    HINSTANCE hPrevInstance, LPSTR lpCmdLine,
    int nCmdShow)
{

        // Create chpt3 application
        chpt3 ochpt3 ("chpt3", hInstance,
                    hPrevInstance, lpCmdLine, nCmdShow);

        // Start created application running
        ochpt3.Run ();  // Runs till window closed

        // Return termination status when window closed
        return ochpt3.Status;
}
```

The bulk of the code in CHPT3.CPP is standard code that creates a Windows application and main window. For this purpose, I use the foundations described in the previous chapter without any change. Because this is simply a test driver, I combine the header files and the source files into one file for the sake of simplicity.

The only code unique to this application is found in the WMSize member function. I overload the WMSize virtual function simply because this is a convenient place to create the sample dialog box.

Within this function, I begin by allocating a `WLoginTransferBuffer` structure used for transferring data into and out of the dialog box. I declare a `WLoginDialog` pointer, which is needed when I use the `WLoginDialog` class to operate directly on a dialog resource in this application. If you use only the `GetLogin` function, you don't need to include this variable.

Then I demonstrate the use of the `GetLogin` function. The following code uses the DLL to display the library, then it tests the return values in the transfer buffer. For the sake of simplicity, I use just a message box to display the name and password entered.

```
GetLogin(this, tb);
MessageBox (HWindow, tb->Name, tb->Password, MB_OK);
```

Next I demonstrate the use of the `WLoginDialog` class that operates on a dialog box resource local to this application. For the sake of simplicity, I use the same LOGIN.RC resource file used by the DLL.

```
TheDialog = new WLoginDialog (this,
    "Login", GetModule (), tb);
GetModule()->ExecDialog (TheDialog);
MessageBox (HWindow, tb->Name, tb->Password, MB_OK);
```

Finally, I free the transfer buffer memory I allocated, and I use the `Destroy` function to close the application's main window and terminate the test program.

Take a look at the IDE settings contained in the test driver project file. Table 3.4 lists the IDE settings I use when I build a file that accesses a DLL.

TABLE 3.4. IDE settings used when accessing a DLL.

IDE Location	Settings That Matter
Options/Application	Windows executable
Options/Compiler/Code Generation	Memory model: large Assume SS=DS: default for memory model
Options/Compiler/Entry Exit Code	Prolog/epilog: Windows smart callbacks

IDE Location	Settings That Matter
Options/Compiler/C++ Options	Options: `far` virtual tables
Options/Messages/Display	Warnings: display all
Options/Linker/Settings	Output: Windows .EXE Options: default libraries
Options/Linker/Libraries	Dynamic for all

Restrictions, Cautions, and Hints

This section presents some restrictions, cautions, and hints pertaining to the use of DLLs.

Delays in Loading a DLL

There is a noticeable wait when you load a DLL from disk. In some cases, such as exception-processing routines and help routines, this is not a problem, but in other cases, delays aren't desirable. You can use the `LoadLibrary` function to force a DLL to be loaded into memory if it isn't already present. The syntax is

```
HINSTANCE ReturnValue;
ReturnValue = LoadLibrary ("LibraryName");
```

ReturnValue is either the instance handle of the loaded DLL or an error code. Refer to the Windows API reference manual for the error codes. Every successful call to `LoadLibrary` must have a matching call to `FreeLibrary`, or the DLL will be left in memory until you exit Windows.

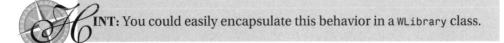

HINT: You could easily encapsulate this behavior in a `WLibrary` class.

Shared Global Memory

All global data in a DLL is shared by every application using that library. This means that you cannot rely on the data to remain unchanged as you use it. If you need data to be private for a certain caller of a DLL, you must dynamically allocate the data and manually manage the access to that data. Of course, if a DLL implements a class, but the class is actually allocated by the calling application, the internal, nonstatic data within the class is unique to that particular instance of the class.

 RICK: Because the global data within a DLL is shared by all applications using the DLL, this is a fast mechanism for passing data between applications. This trait of DLLs enables you to implement a semaphore by using a value stored in a DLL.

Adding a Windows Exit Procedure

If your DLL allocates memory dynamically when it is created with `LibMain`, you need to deallocate that memory when the DLL is deleted. To accomplish this, add a procedure named `WEP` (which stands for Windows Exit Procedure) to your DLL, and add the exit code in this procedure. The function prototype for `WEP` is

```
int FAR PASCAL WEP (int nParameter);
```

`nParameter` is either `WEP_SYSTEMEXIT`, which means that Windows itself is shutting down, or `WEP_FREE_DLL`, which means that this DLL is being unloaded. If you program a `WEP()` function, you must be sure to return 1 to indicate success. However, Windows currently does not use this value.

Missing Start-Up Code

Normally, the linker adds start-up code to all Windows programs during linking. This is not done for DLLs. Among other things, this start-up code sets the global variables in the program's data segment and allows the program to access the DOS environment. Because this code is not present, the functions `getenv` and `putenv` don't work, and most of the predefined Borland global variables aren't available.

CHAPTER

4

Implementing
Custom Controls

Problem

Most Windows programs make heavy use of controls that enable user interaction. Microsoft Windows includes many control types that simplify the coding of this interaction. Borland's OWL extends this concept further by adding a wealth of Borland custom controls, most of which work like their Microsoft equivalents but with an enhanced appearance. But what if the predefined controls don't completely fulfill your requirements? What if you want controls that look different, or act differently, or were never envisioned by the designers of Microsoft Windows and OWL?

In traditional Windows programming, this required designing an entirely new Windows class and implementing considerable code to provide the class with the desired functionality. Custom controls were difficult to design and implement and, therefore, were few and far between.

Solution

Several features of C++ greatly simplify developing custom controls that are based on existing control types. Inheritance enables you to design your new control around an existing control, modifying the behavior of the existing control only where it is necessary. Virtual functions, a component of polymorphism, enable you to override existing behavior where you desire. In addition, Borland designed the Resource Workshop to smooth the integration of user-developed custom controls into the Resource Workshop Dialog editor. This chapter shows you how to modify the appearance and behavior of an existing control and how to implement a completely new type of control. To demonstrate these concepts, I implement two new control types:

➤ A WEditNumber control that is similar to an Edit control but designed to allow only numeric entry

➤ A WFlyn control that works like a little yellow Post-it™ Note within a dialog box. The WFlyn control is empty if it contains no text. If it contains a text note, it is colored, and the text can be displayed by clicking on the control.

The usefulness of the WEditNumber custom control is obvious. The approach can be applied easily to a wide variety of custom edit fields, such as WEditSSN, WEditPhone, and WEditDate. A sample application for the WFlyn control is a dialog box with an expert system type function that scans the entered data and identifies actual or potential errors. The fields in question can be flagged, using color or another method, and the problem with each field can be written to the WFlyn controls next to the field. Then the user can click on each WFlyn and correct the fields one by one. Because no text is written to the WFlyns next to fields that are correct, these WFlyns remain empty and do not distract or confuse the user.

Figure 4.1 shows a simple dialog box illustrating these two controls. Figure 4.2 shows the results of clicking on the WFlyn control. The program CHPT4.EXE is used to test these two sample controls. The custom controls are implemented in a DLL called CUSTCNTL.DLL. To use the program, copy these two files to your hard disk and run CHPT4.EXE. The rest of this chapter shows you how to implement custom controls.

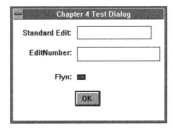

Figure 4.1. A dialog box illustrating WEditNumber *and* WFlyn *custom controls.*

Modifying the Appearance of a Standard Control

There are three ways to modify the appearance of a standard control. Each is progressively more powerful but also more difficult to implement. You should become familiar with all three approaches.

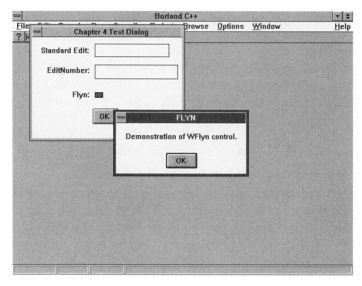

Figure 4.2. The response by the WFlyn *class when it is clicked on.*

Modifying Attribute Bits

The first approach is simply to modify the control's attributes. This approach doesn't require you to implement a derived class, but it does offer limited customization. For example, to remove a border from an edit control, you could use the following code:

```
PTEdit    Edit;

Edit = new TEdit (Parent, ID_EDIT, "Text", 100, 100, 100, 25, 10,
                  FALSE);
Edit->Attr.Style &= WS_BORDER;
```

You can modify the attribute bits from within the Dialog editor in the Resource Workshop by double-clicking on the control to be modified.

Modifying the *window* Class

The second approach is to modify the window class. (Borland refers to the *window* style to avoid confusion with a C++ class.) Almost as simple as modifying the attribute bits, this approach requires you to derive a new class from an existing class. For example, to create an edit control with a different background color, use the following approach.

First, derive a new class from the TEdit class:

```
class TNewEdit : public TEdit
{
    . . . Add constructors that just call the equivalent TEdit
        constructors
    virtual LPSTR GetClassName ();
    virtual void GetWindowClass (WNDCLASS _FAR & WndClass);
};
```

Next, override the GetClassName function to return the name of your new window class:

```
LPSTR TNewEdit::GetClassName ()
{
    return "TNewEdit";
}
```

Finally, override the GetWindowClass function to change the background color. This is also where you can change other aspects of the window class, such as the cursor.

```
void TNewEdit::GetWindowClass (WNDCLASS _FAR & WndClass)
{
    TEdit::GetWindowClass (WndClass);  // Set to default
                                       // values for TEdit
    WndClass.hbrBackground = (HBRUSH) (COLOR_ACTIVECAPTION + 1);
}
```

HINT: For the sake of simplicity, I set the background to the color that the system uses for active caption bars. To set the background color to a specific color of your choice, you must create a brush. Use a Windows API function such as CreateSolidBrush or CreateBrushIndirect; normally this is done in the constructor for your class. Store the brush in the private data area of your class, and set hbrBackground to the brush in the GetWindowClass function. Then, delete the brush by using the Windows API function DeleteObject in the class destructor.

Making the Control Owner-Drawable

In the third approach, you modify the appearance of a control within the limits of its predefined shape by making the control owner-drawable. Again, you must derive a new class from an existing class and set the style to owner-drawable. For example, OR `Attr.Style` with `BS_OWNERDRAW` for a button control. Then override the three member functions shown in Table 4.1.

TABLE 4.1. Owner-draw related member functions (from the `TControl` class).

Function to Override	When Called
ODADrawEntire	The control needs to be redrawn
ODAFocus	The control has gained or lost the focus, and its appearance may be updated
ODASelect	The control has been selected, and its appearance may be updated

If you don't want to worry about modifying the appearance of a control when it is selected or has the focus, an alternative and often easier approach is to override the OWL `DrawItem` function, which is called by `ODADrawEntire`, `ODAFocus`, and `ODASelect` by default.

Modifying the Behavior of a Standard Control

Modifying the appearance of a standard control is fun, but the changes are purely aesthetic. You often need a control with modified behavior, not just a modified appearance. The `WEditNumber` custom control, a control that accepts only numeric entries, is an example. I've implemented `WEditNumber` as a DLL to facilitate its use by other programmers and because custom controls are usable by Borland's Resource Workshop only if they are resident in a DLL.

Listing 4.1 shows the header file for the WEditNumber class. As you should expect, the class is derived from Borland's TEdit class. The class definition is not surprising if you read the preceding chapter on implementing a DLL. The only significant member function is a dynamic dispatch virtual table (DDVT) function that intercepts and processes WM_CHAR messages.

LISTING 4.1. WEditNumber **header file.**

```
#define    _CLASSDLL
#define    WIN31
#define STRICT


// WEDITNUMBER.H - Header file for WEditNumber class

#ifndef WEditNumber_H
#    define WEditNumber_H

// Note that the following code is executed only
// if this file has not been previously included


// #include files for both PC and SUN
#include    <owl.h>

#ifdef __BORLANDC__
    // PC-specific #includes
#    include   <Edit.h>

#endif

#ifdef Unix
    // UNIX-specific #includes

#endif

#ifdef __DLL__
#    define EXPORT _export
#else
#    define EXPORT _CLASSTYPE
#endif
```

continues

LISTING 4.1. continued

```cpp
//*******************************************************
// WEditNumber - Edit control that takes numbers only
//
//     Purpose:
//         Customized edit control that does not enable
//         the user to enter anything but a digit,
//         a plus, a minus, or a decimal.
//
//     Notes:
//
//     Copyright:
//             Copyright (c) 1993, William H. Roetzheim
//             All Rights Reserved
//
//*******************************************************


_CLASSDEF (WEditNumber)
class EXPORT WEditNumber : public TEdit
{
    private:
        // Private data members *******************
        // None


        // Private member functions ****************
        // None

    public:
        // Public data members ********************
        // None


        // Public member functions *****************
        // Constructors and destructors
        WEditNumber (PTWindowsObject Parent,
                    int ID,
                    LPSTR Text,
                    int X,
                    int Y,
                    int Width,
                    int Height,
                    WORD TextLen,
                    BOOL Multiline,
                    PTModule Module = NULL);
```

```
WEditNumber (PTWindowsObject Parent,
                int ResourceID,
                WORD TextLen,
                PTModule Module = NULL);

        // Member functions
        virtual void WMChar (RTMessage Msg) =
            [WM_FIRST + WM_CHAR];
};


#endif WEditNumber_H
```

Listing 4.2 shows the source file for the WEditNumber class. The WMChar member function watches for numeric entries—including values such as '+' and '-'—and passes them on to DefWndProc for normal processing. Other WM_CHAR messages result in a MessageBeep and are discarded.

LISTING 4.2. WEditNumber source file.

```
// WEDITNUMBER.CPP - Source file for WEditNumber class

#include "WEditNumber.h"  // ALL other #include statements
                          // are in this file

//****************************************************
// Constructors and destructors for WEditNumber
//
//    Copyright:
//          Copyright (c) 1993, William H. Roetzheim
//          All Rights Reserved
//
//****************************************************

far _export WEditNumber::WEditNumber (PTWindowsObject Parent,
            int ID,
            LPSTR Text,
            int X,
            int Y,
            int Width,
            int Height,
            WORD TextLen,
            BOOL Multiline,
```

continues

LISTING 4.2. continued

```
                PTModule Module)
                :
                TEdit (Parent, ID, Text, X, Y,
                    Width, Height, TextLen, Multiline,
                    Module)
{
    return;
}

#pragma argsused
far _export WEditNumber::WEditNumber (PTWindowsObject Parent,
                int ResourceID,
                WORD TextLen,
                PTModule Module)
                :
                TEdit (Parent, ResourceID, TextLen, Module)
{
    return;
}


//****************************************************
// Member functions for class
//
//     Copyright:
//             Copyright (c) 1993, William H. Roetzheim
//             All Rights Reserved
//
//****************************************************


void far _export WEditNumber::WMChar (RTMessage Msg)
{
    switch (Msg.WParam)
    {
        case '0':
        case '1':
        case '2':
        case '3':
        case '4':
        case '5':
        case '6':
        case '7':
        case '8':
        case '9':
        case '+':
```

```
      case '-':
      case '.':
      case 8:   // Backspace
      case 9:   // Tab and Shift-Tab
    case 13:    // Return
          DefWndProc (Msg);
          break;

      default:
          MessageBeep (0);
        break;
    }
}
```

Implementing a New Type of Control

Thanks to Borland's OWL, implementing a completely new control is not much more difficult than modifying the behavior of an existing control. OWL includes a TControl class that serves as a parent class for your own custom controls. To illustrate how to implement a custom control, I implement the WFlyn class discussed earlier. Listing 4.3 shows the WFlyn header file. The WFlyn class contains

> One private data element

> A pointer to WFlyn's text called Text

> Two constructors

> The five member functions shown in Table 4.2

TABLE 4.2. WFlyn **member functions.**

Function	Purpose
Transfer	Provides transfer buffer support for the custom control
Paint	Controls the appearance of the control

continues

85

TABLE 4.2. continued

Function	Purpose
SetText	Sets the text to be displayed by the control
WMLButtonUp	Responds to a left mouse button release over the control by displaying the text stored in the control
GetClassName	Returns WFlyn

LISTING 4.3. WFLYN.H file.

```
#define    _CLASSDLL
#define    WIN31
#define    STRICT

// WFLYN.H - Header file for WFlyn class

#ifndef WFlyn_H
#    define WFlyn_H

// Note that the following code is executed only
// if this file has not been previously included

// #include files for both PC and SUN

#ifdef __BORLANDC__
    // PC-specific #includes
#    include   <owl.h>
#    include <button.h>

#endif

#ifdef Unix
    // UNIX-specific #includes
#endif

#ifdef __DLL__
#    define EXPORT _export
#else
#    define EXPORT _CLASSTYPE
#endif
```

```
//*****************************************************
// WFlyn - Little yellow note custom control
//
//     Purpose:
//         This class can be added to a dialog box
//         to make notes available to the dialog box
//         user.
//
//     Notes:
//         1.    If the FLYN contains no note, it
//               is not visible.
//         2.    The pointer to text for the WFlyn
//               class must be far, and must remain
//               valid as long as the FLYN is displayed.
//         3.    The pointer to the FLYN text must be
//               deallocated by the calling application.
//
//     Copyright:
//         Copyright (c) 1993, William H. Roetzheim
//         All Rights Reserved
//
//*****************************************************


_CLASSDEF (WFlyn)
class EXPORT WFlyn : public TControl
{
    private:
        // Private data members *******************
        char far *Text;


        // Private member functions ***************
        // None


    public:
        // Public data members ********************
        // None


        // Public member functions ****************
        // Constructors and destructors
        WFlyn (PTWindowsObject Parent,
                    int ID,
                    LPSTR Text,
                    int X,
                    int Y,
                    int Width,
```

continues

LISTING 4.3. continued

```
                        int Height,
                        PTModule Module = NULL);
        WFlyn (PTWindowsObject Parent,
                        int ResourceID,
                        PTModule Module = NULL);

        // Member functions
        virtual WORD Transfer (Pvoid Data, WORD TransferFlag);
        virtual void Paint (HDC, PAINTSTRUCT _FAR &);
        void SetText (char *Text);
        void WMLButtonUp (RTMessage) =
            [WM_FIRST + WM_LBUTTONUP];
        LPSTR GetClassName ();
};

#endif WFlyn_H
```

Listing 4.4 shows the implementation of the WFlyn class. The constructors set the private variable Text to NULL to indicate that no text is stored in the control. This causes the control to be blank until text is inserted. The class has the five member functions discussed in Table 4.2: Transfer, Paint, SetText, WMLButtonUp, and GetClassName. I discuss each in turn.

LISTING 4.4. WFLYN.CPP file.

```
// WFLYN.CPP - Source file for WFlyn class

#include "WFlyn.h"  // ALL other #include statements
                     // are in this file


//*****************************************************
// Constructors and destructors for WFlyn
//
//      Copyright:
//              Copyright (c) 1993, William H. Roetzheim
//              All Rights Reserved
//
//*****************************************************
```

```
#pragma argsused
far _export WFlyn::WFlyn (PTWindowsObject Parent,
                int ID,
                LPSTR Text,
                int X,
                int Y,
                int Width,
                int Height,
                PTModule Module)
                :
                TControl (Parent, ID, Text, X, Y,
                    Width, Height, Module)
{
    SetText (NULL);
}

#pragma argsused
far _export WFlyn::WFlyn (PTWindowsObject Parent,
                int ResourceID,
                PTModule Module)
                :
                TControl (Parent, ResourceID, Module)
{
    SetText (NULL);
}




//****************************************************
// Member functions for class
//
//    Copyright:
//            Copyright (c) 1993, William H. Roetzheim
//            All Rights Reserved
//
//****************************************************

//****************************************************
// WFlyn::Transfer - WFlyn transfer buffer support
//
//    Purpose:
//        Provide transfer buffer capabilities for the
//        WFlyn class.
//
//    General Notes:
//        The transfer buffer entry for a WFlyn class
//        consists of a far char * that should be
```

continues

LISTING 4.4. continued

```
//        initialized to point to the text to be
//        displayed or to NULL if no text is available.
//
//    Testing Notes:
//        Test with both NULL and valid pointer.
//
//    Copyright:
//        Copyright (c) 1993, William H. Roetzheim
//        All Rights Reserved
//
//*****************************************************

WORD far _export WFlyn::Transfer (Pvoid Data, WORD TransferFlag)
{
    switch (TransferFlag)
    {
        case TF_SIZEDATA:  // Requests size of transfer
        break;

        case TF_GETDATA:  // From control to transfer
            break;

        case TF_SETDATA:  // From transfer to control
            Text = (char *) Data;
            break;
    }
    return sizeof (char *);
}


//*****************************************************
// WFlyn::Paint - Paint the WFlyn control
//
//    Purpose:
//        Paints a yellow box on the screen if the
//        WFlyn has text available to display.
//
//    General Notes:
//        None
//
//    Testing Notes:
//        Test with Text set to text and to NULL.
//
```

```
//     Copyright:
//             Copyright (c) 1993, William H. Roetzheim
//             All Rights Reserved
//
//********************************************************

void WFlyn::Paint (HDC PaintDC, PAINTSTRUCT _FAR &)
{
    if (Text != NULL)
    {
        RECT Rect;
        HBRUSH NewBrush;
      HBRUSH OldBrush;

        GetClientRect (HWindow, &Rect);
        NewBrush = CreateSolidBrush (RGB (125, 125, 0));
      OldBrush =(HBRUSH) SelectObject (PaintDC, NewBrush);
        Rectangle (PaintDC, Rect.left, Rect.top,
                        Rect.right, Rect.bottom);
      SelectObject (PaintDC, OldBrush);
        DeleteObject (NewBrush);
    }
}


//********************************************************
// WFlyn::SetText - Set new text
//
//     Purpose:
//         Reset the object with a new text message.
//
//     General Notes:
//         1.    The using application is responsible for
//               keeping the pointer valid while the WFlyn
//               object is alive, and for deallocating
//               the space when it is no longer needed.
//         2.    To hide a WFlyn, call SetText and pass
//               it a NULL.
//
//      Testing Notes:
//               Test going from a NULL text to a valid
//               text and from a valid text to a NULL text.
//
//     Copyright:
//             Copyright (c) 1993, William H. Roetzheim
//             All Rights Reserved
//
//********************************************************
```

continues

LISTING 4.4. continued

```
void far _export WFlyn::SetText (char *NewText)
{
    Text = NewText;
    InvalidateRect (HWindow, NULL, TRUE);
}


//****************************************************
// WFlyn::WMLButtonUp - Display WFlyn text
//
//      Purpose:
//          Display WFlyn text if present.
//
//      General Notes:
//          None
//
//       Testing Notes:
//          None
//
//      Copyright:
//              Copyright (c) 1993, William H. Roetzheim
//              All Rights Reserved
//
//****************************************************

void far _export WFlyn::WMLButtonUp (RTMessage)
{
    char far *Flyn = "FLYN";
    // Display the text, if present
    if (Text != NULL)
    {
        MessageBox (HWindow,Text, Flyn, MB_OK);
    }
}


LPSTR WFlyn::GetClassName ()
{
    return "WFlyn";
}
```

The Transfer member function allows WFlyn to use a transfer buffer in the same way in which other OWL controls operate. A transfer buffer is used to initialize the control at start-up, and it is updated by the `TDialog` class with the control's final status and values when the OK pushbutton is pressed.

To add transfer buffer support, the `Transfer` function accepts a void pointer to a block of memory and a transfer flag, takes an action specific to the flag's parameter, then returns the size of the transfer area for this specific control. For the `WFlyn` control, the transfer area consists simply of a character pointer, so the return value is `sizeof (char *)`. The transfer flag can take on any of three values. Table 4.3 shows the valid values, their meanings, and the `WFlyn` response.

TABLE 4.3. Transfer flag values and meanings.

Transfer Flag Value	Meaning	`WFlyn` Action
TF_SIZEDATA	Returns the size of the transfer area for this control	Returns `sizeof (char *)`
TF_GETDATA	Transfers data from the from control to the transfer buffer, and returns the size of the data transferred	No data goes out the control, so no action is taken—except returning `sizeof (char *)`
TF_SETDATA	Transfers data from the transfer buffer to the control, and returns the size of the data transferred	Copies the character pointer stored in the transfer buffer to `Text`, and returns `sizeof (char *)`

The `Paint` member function is called when the control needs to be drawn on-screen. If the member data variable `Text` is `NULL`, `Paint` returns without drawing anything. Otherwise, `Paint` creates a solid brush and fills the client area of the control with the color of the brush.

INT: When you create a GDI (graphical device interface) object (for example, a brush) and use SelectObject to select the object into a device context, be sure to save the old GDI object. You need to select the old GDI object back into the device context before you delete the newly created object. If you don't delete the newly created GDI object, your application will use Windows internal resources even after it terminates. Deleting the GDI object while it is still selected into a device context can cause a UAE.

The SetText member function sets the data variable Text to the value passed as a parameter. If NULL is passed, Text is set to NULL. Then, InvalidateRect is called to force the control to update itself. NULL is passed as the region parameter to force an update of the entire control client area, and TRUE is passed to indicate that the control must be erased before painting. Notice that if FALSE is passed (the control shouldn't be erased before painting), the control won't disappear when it is set to NULL, because the Paint member function returns when Text == NULL without performing any action. Notice also that the memory used to store the text itself belongs to the application that calls SetText, not to this control.

The WMLButtonUp function simply uses a message box to display the WFlyn text, if any exists.

GetClassName returns "WFlyn". I didn't need to write a GetClassName function for the WEditNumber class because that class can use the standard TEdit class, "EDIT", without any change. The WFlyn class is an entirely new class. If you look at a resource file created by the Resource Workshop (for example, CHPT4.RC), you will find that the edit number control (102) is specified to be of class EDIT, and that all special processing occurs because I attach a special class, WEditNumber, to that control after the dialog box is executed. In the same resource file, the Flyn control is specified to be of class "WFlyn". This makes the control truly unique.

Making a New Control Usable from the Resource Workshop

Using just the code in WEDITNUM.H, WEDITNUM.CPP, WFLYN.H, and WFLYN.CPP, you have two custom controls that can be created and used from your application. For example, the following code works from within a window:

```
PWEditNumber NumberEdit;
PWFlyn Flyn;

NumberEdit = new WEditNumber (this,      // Parent
                              101,       // ID
                              "123",     // Text
                              50, 100,   // x, y
                              100, 25,   // Width, height
                              10,        // Text length
                              FALSE);    // Multiline flag
Flyn = new WFlyn (this,      // Parent
                  102,       // ID
                  "Flyn",    // Text
                  50, 150,   // x,y
                  15, 10);   // Width, height

Flyn->SetText ("Test");
```

Unfortunately, that's not good enough. If you're like me, you would rather draw your controls onto a dialog box by using the Resource Workshop, then incorporate their handling into a dialog class. Luckily, Borland designed the Resource Workshop to enable you to add custom controls to the Workshop. The controls appear directly on the tools palette. They can be used just like other controls. The steps involved are as follows:

1. Design and code your custom controls as part of a DLL.

2. Create an icon for each control, and store the icon as a resource in the DLL. This is the icon that the Resource Workshop adds to the tools palette.

3. Create a cursor for each control, and store the cursor as a resource in the DLL. This is the cursor that the Resource Workshop uses when your control is selected from the tools palette.

4. If your control is not based on an existing Resource Workshop control, create a style dialog box that will appear whenever the user double-clicks on your control from within the Resource Workshop. In my case, the WEditNumber control doesn't require a style dialog box, but the WFlyn control does. At a minimum, this dialog box should enable the user to enter the control ID. Captions, status bits, and so on often are set by the user in this dialog box. Creating a style dialog box requires that you develop the dialog resource and a dialog-handling class.

5. For each new control, create the three functions shown in Table 4.4. Controls derived from existing Resource Workshop control classes need only the Info function.

6. For each new control, create a function to register the control class.

7. Create a single ListClasses function somewhere in the DLL.

TABLE 4.4. Resource Workshop support functions for each control.

Function	Purpose
Info	Tells the Resource Workshop which string to add to the Control menu, as well as which default style, tools palette icon, and cursor to use
Flag	Tells the Resource Workshop the text string that represents the control's style bits. (This text string is added to the .RC file.)
Style	Displays a style dialog box that enables the user to enter the control ID (among other things)

In the remainder of this section, I go over each step in detail. I use the code for WEditNumber and WFlyn as an example. The code that provides support specific to the Resource Workshop for WEditNumber and WFlyn is found in CUSTCONT.H, CUSTCONT.CPP, and CUSTCONT.RC. I also cover some advanced aspects of writing DLLs that I avoided in Chapter 3, "Coding

Dynamic Link Libraries," for the sake of simplicity. Brace yourself: the rest of this section is a bit complicated. It's worth the effort, however. It is critical that you thoroughly understand these concepts so that you can add custom controls to the Resource Workshop and write DLLs that don't cause UAEs.

Designing and Coding Custom Controls as Part of a DLL

Custom controls accessed by the Resource Workshop must be part of a DLL. As with all classes, implement each control in its own pair of files (for example, WFLYN.H and WFLYN.CPP). Test the controls thoroughly until you are convinced that they operate properly. Then combine the controls into a single DLL and test them again until you are satisfied that they continue to operate as expected. Now you are ready to make this DLL Resource Workshop-compatible.

Creating a Tools Palette Icon for Each Control

For each control, design an icon that represents the control on the Resource Workshop tools palette. The icon will be represented in a 16-color bitmap that is 24-by-24. The bitmap should include a 2-pixel-wide white border on the left and top edges and a 2-pixel-wide black border on the right and bottom edges. Table 4.5 shows the icons for the WEditNumber and WFlyn controls. These icons were drawn as bitmaps with the Resource Workshop, as Figure 4.3 shows.

TABLE 4.5. The WEditNumber and WFlyn tools palette icons.

Control	*Icon*
WEditNumber	123
WFlyn	Flyn

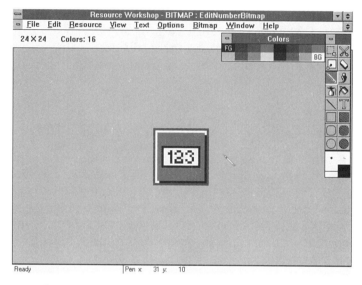

Figure 4.3. The Resource Workshop Bitmap editor.

HINT: For professional-looking icons, it is often best to use an external paint program, such as CorelDRAW! with its sophisticated drawing utilities and predrawn icons. You can copy the images to the clipboard then paste them into your bitmap within the Resource Workshop.

HINT: If you ever get confused about which edges of a button or group area to make white and which to make black, remember that "the sun always shines on the Borland display from the upper-left corner." If you think about it, this implies that for raised surfaces, the left and top edges are brighter, whereas the right and bottom edges are in the shadow and, therefore, darker. For depressed surfaces, such as Borland group boxes, the right and bottom edges are bright, and the left and top edges are in the shadow and, therefore, darker.

Creating a Cursor for Each Control

When the user selects your control from the Resource Workshop tools palette, the cursor shape changes into a shape representative of your control until the control is placed in the dialog box. This cursor shape is called the *drop cursor* for your control. Drop cursors should be black-and-white. Normally they are created with the cursor tool in the Resource Workshop. Table 4.6 shows the drop cursors for WEditNumber and WFlyn. These cursors are created with the Resource Workshop cursor editor, as Figure 4.4 shows.

TABLE 4.6. WEditNumber and WFlyn.

Control	*Drop Cursor*
WEditNumber	
WFlyn	

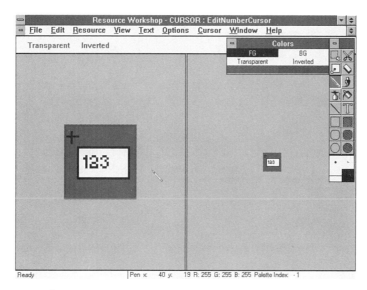

Figure 4.4. The Resource Workshop cursor editor.

HINT: Don't forget to set the cursor hot spot to a visually obvious location on your cursor.

Creating a Style Dialog Box

You should already be familiar with the Dialog editor within the Resource Workshop. When you double-click on a control, a dialog box is displayed that enables you to edit the control's attributes. This dialog box is called a style dialog box. Look at the style dialog boxes for some Microsoft standard and Borland custom controls to review the types of information that can be entered. You must implement your own style dialog box for each custom control that is not based on an existing control type.

HINT: If your resource is similar to a Microsoft or Borland control, you can use the Resource Workshop to open the Workshop executable file with WORKSHOP.EXE or the Borland custom control DLL BWCC.DLL. Load the dialog box you want, modify it, and save it as a new file. WORKSHOP.EXE normally is found in your \BORLANDC\BIN directory, and BWCC.DLL in your \WINDOWS\SYSTEM directory.

At a minimum, your style dialog box must enable the user to enter an ID for your control. For the sake of simplicity, this is the only functionality I incorporate into the sample style dialog box. Figure 4.5 shows the dialog box I use. Listing 4.5 shows the dialog-handling portion of the code. The complete listing for CUSTCONT.CPP is found near the end of this chapter. The code is straightforward and does not require further explanation.

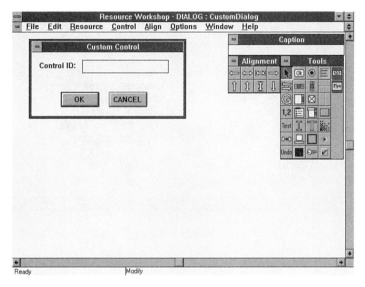

Figure 4.5. A sample dialog box for my custom controls.

LISTING 4.5. The dialog-handling portion of CUSTCONT.CPP.

```
#define MAX_CONTROL_ID_LENGTH 10

struct TransferBuffer
{
    char Id [MAX_CONTROL_ID_LENGTH];
};

_CLASSDEF (WCustomControlDialog)
class WCustomControlDialog : public TDialog
{
    public:

        // Public member functions *****************
        // Constructors and destructors
        WCustomControlDialog (PTWindowsObject Parent,
                              LPSTR szName,
                              PTModule Module,
                              struct TransferBuffer *tb);
};
```

continues

LISTING 4.5. continued

```
#define IDD_ID 101

WCustomControlDialog::WCustomControlDialog (
                                  PTWindowsObject Parent,
                                  LPSTR szName,
                                  PTModule Module,
                                  struct TransferBuffer *tb)
                  :TDialog (Parent, szName, Module)
{
    new TEdit (this, IDD_ID, MAX_CONTROL_ID_LENGTH -1, DLLModule);
    SetTransferBuffer (tb);
}
```

> **INT:** You can use the same dialog box and dialog-handling routine for all controls that require identical data input from the user. This approach is used for the two custom controls in this chapter.

Creating *info*, *flags*, and *style* Functions

You need to create three *callback functions* for each new type of control: an `info` function, a `flags` function, and a `style` function. A callback function is a function that is called by routines external to your program (for example, Windows itself). Controls such as `WEditNumber` that are derived from existing controls need only an `info` function. The CALLBACK macro, defined in WINDOWS.H, expands to `far pascal`.

> **INT:** Because callback functions are called from non-C++ programs, you cannot use an ordinary member function as a callback function. Remember that ordinary member functions are passed a hidden `this` parameter as their first parameter from within C++, and that the parameter is not passed when the function is called from a non-C++ program. You can, however, use a static member

function as a callback function, because static member functions don't receive a hidden `this` parameter. Because your callback functions are written in a C++ environment, they can create objects and call their member functions with impunity.

The *info* Function

The info function is used by the Resource Workshop to obtain information about the class. The function returns a global memory handle that is freed by the Resource Workshop. It should not be freed within the DLL. Listing 4.6 shows the `info` function for the `WFlyn` class.

LISTING 4.6. `WEditNumberInfo` **function definition.**

```
HGLOBAL CALLBACK WFlynInfo ()
{
    HANDLE     hInfo = GlobalAlloc
                    (GMEM_SHARE ¦ GMEM_ZEROINIT,
                     sizeof(RWCTLINFO));

    if ( hInfo )
    {
        LPRWCTLINFO Info = (LPRWCTLINFO)
                    GlobalLock(hInfo);

        Info->wVersion =    0x0100;  // Version 1.00
        Info->wCtlTypes =   1;  // One control type
        strcpy(Info->szClass, szControlClassName);
        strcpy(Info->szTitle, "");

        Info->Type[0].wWidth  = 15 ¦ 0x8000;  // High bit to 1
        Info->Type[0].wHeight = 10 ¦ 0x8000;  // High bit to 1
        strcpy(Info->Type[0].szDescr, "FLYN");
        Info->Type[0].dwStyle = WS_VISIBLE ¦
                                WS_BORDER ¦
                                WS_CHILD;

        Info->Type[0].hToolBit = LoadBitmap(
                    DLLModule->hInstance,
                    "FlynBitmap");
```

continues

LISTING 4.6. continued

```
        Info->Type[0].hDropCurs = LoadCursor(
                        DLLModule->hInstance,
                        "FlynCursor");

        GlobalUnlock(hInfo);
    }

    return hInfo;
}
```

The global memory area is used to store a RWCTLINFO structure. The structure should be zero-initialized; GMEM_ZEROINIT does this. The structure consists of five fixed fields followed by an array that contains a variable number of RWCTLTYPE structures. The format of the RWCTLINFO structure is

```
typedef struct
{
        UINT wVersion;              // Control version
        UINT wCtlTypes;             // Control types
        char szClass[CTLCLASS];     // Control class name
        char szTitle[CTLTITLE];     // Control title
        char szReserved[10];        // Reserved for future use
        RWCTLTYPE Type[CTLTYPES];   // Control type list
} RWCTLINFO;
typedef RWCTLINFO *RWPCTLINFO;
typedef RWCTLINFO FAR *LPRWCTLINFO;
```

wVersion is for your own use. Borland recommends that you use the major version in the high-order byte and the minor version in the low-order byte. wCtlTypes tells the number of control subtypes. szClass is the control class name as it is registered with Windows. The szReserved field is reserved for future expansion.

Each RWCTLTYPE structure defines a control subtype. Control subtypes are controls that use the same window class but have different characteristics. A pushbutton and default pushbutton are examples of two subtypes appropriate for a single control. I define my controls to have a single type.

The RWCTLTYPE structure has the following format:

```
typedef struct
{
        UINT wType;                 // Type style
        UINT wWidth;                // Suggested width
        UINT wHeight;               // Suggested height
        DWORD dwStyle;              // Default style
        char  szDescr[CTLDESCR];    // Menu name
        HBITMAP hToolBit;           // Toolbox bitmap
        HCURSOR hDropCurs;          // Drag and drop cursor
} RWCTLTYPE, FAR * LPRWCTLTYPE;
```

The wType field is user-defined. The wWidth and wHeight fields indicate the default width for the control. These fields are in units of dialog coordinates unless the high bit is set. When the high bit is set, the units are pixels. It's more convenient to use pixels for controls that contain bitmaps, which normally are considered in terms of pixels. Usually it's more convenient to use dialog units for other controls because dialog units are independent of display mode and resolution. (In other words, the control will have the same dimensions on a wide variety of displays.) For example, wWidth = 100 is in dialog units, whereas wWidth = 100 ¦ 0x8000 is in pixels. dwStyle is the style value that the Resource Workshop assigns to this control class. szDescr is the name of the control to be added to the menu within the Resource Workshop. CTLDESCR is defined to 22. hToolBit is a handle to the bitmap that represents this control on the Resource Workshop tool palette. hDropCurs is a handle to the cursor used by the Resource Workshop when you add one of these controls to a dialog box. Create the bitmap and cursor with the Resource Workshop, and include them as resources in this DLL.

The *flags* Function

The Resource Workshop uses the flags function to translate the style of a control into a text string for insertion into the .RC file. The control's style is passed as the first parameter. For each valid control style, you must provide a valid string representing that style. For the WFlyn control, the style cannot be changed within the Resource Workshop, so this function is of little importance. Listing 4.7 shows the WFlynFlag function.

LISTING 4.7. WEditNumberFlag **function.**

```
UINT CALLBACK WFlynFlag (DWORD /* Style */,
        LPSTR Buff, UINT BuffLength)
{
    char *StyleString = "WS_VISIBLE ¦ WS_BORDER ¦
                            WS_CHILD";
    if (BuffLength > strlen (StyleString))
    {
        strcpy(Buff, StyleString);
        return strlen (StyleString);
    }
    else return 0;
}
```

INT: When you deal with more complex controls, look at each bit individually and build an appropriate style string one item at a time. Don't be concerned about the standard Windows style bits (WS_VISIBLE and so on) stored in the upper 16 bits of DWORD. They are handled automatically.

The *style* Function

The Resource Workshop calls the style function to display your style dialog box. If multiple controls use the same style dialog box, you need only one style function. This function is shown in Listing 4.8. It receives the four parameters shown in Table 4.7. Within the function, I need to associate an OWL window with the window handle passed as the first parameter. I have no guarantee that this window handle points to an OWL window at all; it might, for example, be a window created with C code.

As a solution, I use TModule's GetParentObject member function. If GetParentObject is passed a window handle to an OWL window, it returns a pointer to the OWL window. If it is passed a window handle to a non-OWL window, it creates an OWL window object, associates the two windows, and returns a pointer to the newly created OWL window.

INT: This approach is appropriate if you want any of your OWL DLL functions to support ordinary C code. For instance, in the WLogin example in Chapter 3, "Coding Dynamic Link Libraries," you could use this approach with the GetLogin function (passing in an HWND rather than a PTWindowsObject) to make the Login dialog box in the DLL accessible from ordinary C code.

TABLE 4.7. Style function parameters.

Parameter Type	Parameter Name	Description
HWND	hWnd	A handle to the Resource Workshop window that owns the dialog box
HGLOBAL	hCtlStyle	A global memory handle that points to a structure that contains the control's style. The format of this structure is

```
typedef struct tagCTLSTYLE {
    UINT    wX;
    UINT    wY;
    UINT    wCx;
    UINT    wCy;
    UINT    wId;
    DWORD   dwStyle;
    char    szClass[CTLCLASS];
    char    szTitle[CTLTITLE];
} CTLSTYLE;
```

continues

TABLE 4.7. continued

Parameter Type	Parameter Name	Description
LPFNSTRTOID	lpfnStrToId	A pointer to a function in the Resource Workshop that converts a string to a valid control ID. For example, the string might be "IDD_TEST" and the corresponding ID might be 101. This function and the lpfnIdToStr function are aware of things such as identifiers defined in a header file included with the project.
LPFNIDTOSTR	lpfnIdToStr	A pointer to a function in the Resource Workshop that converts a control ID to a string

LISTING 4.8. The style function.

```
BOOL CALLBACK ControlStyle (HWND hWnd, HGLOBAL hCtlStyle,
        LPFNSTRTOID lpfnStrToId, LPFNIDTOSTR lpfnIdToStr)
{
    LPCTLSTYLE Style = (LPCTLSTYLE) GlobalLock(hCtlStyle);
    PWCustomControlDialog TheDialog;
    PTWindowsObject AParentAlias;
    BOOL Result = FALSE;

    TransferBuffer *tb = new TransferBuffer;

    lpfnIdToStr (Style->wId,
        tb->Id, MAX_CONTROL_ID_LENGTH);


    // Save the old window procedure
    WNDPROC wp = (WNDPROC) GetWindowLong
```

```
                    (hWnd, GWL_WNDPROC);

    AParentAlias = DLLModule->GetParentObject (hWnd);

    TheDialog = new WCustomControlDialog (AParentAlias,
        "CustomDialog", DLLModule, tb);


    if (DLLModule->ExecDialog (TheDialog) == IDOK)
    {
        Result = TRUE;
        Style->wId = (WORD) lpfnStrToId (tb->Id);
    }

    // Restore the old window procedure
    SetWindowLong (hWnd, GWL_WNDPROC, (DWORD) wp);

    GlobalUnlock (hCtlStyle);
    delete tb;

    return Result;
}
```

HINT: I bracket the `GetParentObject` code with new code to save the old window's `window` procedure prior to calling `GetParentObject`, and I restore the old window's `window` procedure after the function call. This corrects a subtle bug that most DLL code contains. The `GetParentObject` actually subclasses the window passed as a parameter. In doing this, it installs its own `window` procedure in the parent window so that any messages to the parent window now go through the DLL window. If the DLL is unloaded but the parent window still exists, a UAE results the next time a message comes for that window. This error results because the message is routed to the window procedure in the DLL, which no longer exists. The solution is to restore the `window` procedure of the calling window after the call to `GetParentObject`.

Creating a *register* Function for the Control Class

If your control is a new class, you must register the class with Windows
before you use it. If you are creating controls directly in your application,
the OWL does this automatically as each control is created. Unfortunately,
things are not so simple when the Resource Workshop creates an instance
of your control to place on a dialog template. The Resource Workshop assumes that your control is already registered with Windows. To register
your control, you need to write a window procedure and a register function for the control. Listing 4.9 shows both functions for the WFlyn class.

LISTING 4.9. WFlyn register functions.

```
LONG FAR PASCAL _export WFlynWndProc(HWND HWindow,
                         WORD wMsg,
                         WORD wParam,
                         LONG lParam)
{    // This function is called only if the control was created
     // by a nonOWL application, because OWL overrides a window's
     // window procedure. We are concerned only with WM_CREATE
     // messages for nonOWL usage.
     if (wMsg == WM_CREATE)  // If called by
                             // non-OWL application (RW)
     {
         PTWindowsObject ParentAlias;

         // Save the old window procedure
         WNDPROC wp = (WNDPROC)
             GetWindowLong (HWindow, GWL_WNDPROC);

         ParentAlias = DLLModule->GetParentObject
                           GetParent (HWindow));
         PWFlyn Flyn = new WFlyn
             (
                 ParentAlias,
                 GetWindowWord (HWindow, GWW_ID),
                 DLLModule
             );
             DLLModule->MakeWindow (Flyn);

         // Restore the old window procedure
         SetWindowLong (HWindow, GWL_WNDPROC, (DWORD) wp);
     }
     return DefWindowProc(HWindow, wMsg, wParam, lParam);
}
```

```
BOOL RegisterWFlynClass()
{
  WNDCLASS  wc;
  wc.style          = CS_HREDRAW | CS_VREDRAW;
  wc.lpfnWndProc    = (WNDPROC)WFlynWndProc;
  wc.cbClsExtra     = 0;
  wc.cbWndExtra     = 0;
  wc.hInstance      = DLLModule->hInstance;
  wc.hIcon          = NULL;
  wc.hCursor        = LoadCursor(NULL, IDC_ARROW);
                     //(Clear Background);
  wc.hbrBackground  = (HBRUSH)(NULL_BRUSH);
  wc.lpszMenuName   = NULL;
  wc.lpszClassName  = szControlClassName;
  return RegisterClass(&wc);
}
```

Creating a *ListClasses* Function

You need to include and export a ListClasses function in your DLL. It must
be a C function. This function, shown in Listing 4.10, uses GlobalAlloc to
allocate enough memory for an integer plus one RWCTLCLASS for each custom control in the DLL. The integer contains the number of custom controls. Each RWCTLCLASS contains a pointer to the control's info, flags, and
style functions and to the name of the class. The integer and array of
RWCTLCLASSes are stored in a CTLCLASSLIST structure. The global memory
handle is returned by the ListClasses function for use by the Resource
Workshop.

INT: If you attempt to load your DLL into the Resource Workshop,
and it tells you that the DLL is invalid, the reason is that the Resource Workshop cannot find the ListClasses function. If the
Resource Workshop informs you that it cannot tell whether the
DLL is a valid control library, then the Resource Workshop cannot
find the ListClasses function, but there are four or more exported functions in the DLL. The Resource Workshop will try to use
an older convention of looking for required functions based on
ordinal number (that is, the number in the DLL export table). In
either case, fix your ListClasses function declaration.

LISTING 4.10. ListClasses function.

```
extern "C" HGLOBAL CALLBACK _export  ListClasses
        (
                LPSTR,          // szApplication
                UINT,           // wVersion
                LPFNLOADRES,    // fnLoad
                LPFNEDITRES     // fnEdit
        )
{
    const NumberOfControls = 2;
    HGLOBAL hClasses = GlobalAlloc(GMEM_SHARE |
                GMEM_ZEROINIT, sizeof(int) +
                (NumberOfControls *
                sizeof(RWCTLCLASS)));


    if ( hClasses )
    {
        LPCTLCLASSLIST      Controls = (LPCTLCLASSLIST)
                            GlobalLock(hClasses);

        Controls->nClasses = NumberOfControls;

        Controls->Classes[0].fnRWInfo  = WEditNumberInfo;
        Controls->Classes[0].fnRWStyle = NULL;
        Controls->Classes[0].fnFlags   = NULL;
        strcpy(Controls->Classes[0].szClass, "EDIT");


        Controls->Classes[1].fnRWInfo  = WFlynInfo;
        Controls->Classes[1].fnRWStyle = ControlStyle;
        Controls->Classes[1].fnFlags   = WFlynFlag;
        strcpy(Controls->Classes[1].szClass,
                        szControlClassName);

        GlobalUnlock(hClasses);
    }

    return hClasses;
}
```

The ListClasses function must list all controls, including both the unique ones and the ones similar to existing controls. For those that are similar to existing controls, the ListClasses function must set the szClass variable to the control class name (EDIT, BUTTON, and so on). These names are documented in the GetClassName for each corresponding OWL class (TEdit, TButton, and so on). For functions in which you use the style and flags functions of the existing class, you can set the corresponding function pointers in this data structure to NULL.

Fixing the *LibMain* Function

There is only one difference between a LibMain function in a custom control DLL and a LibMain function in a standard DLL. The custom control DLL must call the register function for all classes that need to be registered. I choose to modify the LibMain function even more. I make it use a class derived from TModule that corrects another potential DLL bug.

If your DLL is a server for more than one executable program, and both programs might run simultaneously, the standard TModule creates a problem. When a DLL calls GlobalAlloc, the memory is owned by the executable task that called the DLL. When the calling task is terminated, the memory it allocated is freed.

Suppose Application A calls the DLL and causes LibMain to be executed, and that LibMain allocates memory that is owned by Application A. Then, Application B starts up and begins to use the DLL. Application A terminates, and all its memory, including the memory used by the DLL, is released. Application B then accesses a function in the DLL. The function tries to access the released memory, causing a UAE.

In one solution, the DLL ensures that TModule and the saved command-line string within TModule are allocated from the DLL's local heap. You do this by overloading the new and delete operator for TModule and by reallocating the storage for the command line, as Listing 4.11 shows.

LISTING 4.11. A new TModule class that fixes a DLL bug.

```
_CLASSDEF (TDLLModule);
class TDLLModule : public TModule
{
    public:
        TDLLModule (LPSTR, HMODULE, LPSTR);
        ~TDLLModule ();
        void *operator new (unsigned);
```

continues

113

LISTING 4.11. continued

```
            void operator delete (void *);
};

#pragma argsused

TDLLModule::TDLLModule (LPSTR n, HMODULE m, LPSTR Command)
    : TModule (n, m, Command)
{
    // Free the TModule constructor allocated memory
    farfree (lpCmdLine);
    if (Command)
    {
        lpCmdLine = (LPSTR) (void *) LocalAlloc (LPTR,
                             strlen (Command) + 1);
        strcpy (lpCmdLine, Command);
    }
    else
    {
        lpCmdLine = (LPSTR) (void *) LocalAlloc (LPTR, 1);
        lpCmdLine[0] = 0;
    }
}

TDLLModule::~TDLLModule ()
{
    LocalFree ((HLOCAL) FP_OFF (lpCmdLine));
    lpCmdLine = NULL;
}

void *TDLLModule::operator new (unsigned n)
{
    return (void *) LocalAlloc (LPTR, n);
}

void TDLLModule::operator delete (void *p)
{
    LocalFree ((HLOCAL) FP_OFF (p));
}
```

Notice that the offset portion of a `far` pointer, `FP_OFF`, can be treated as a local memory handle.

INT: If your application uses a DLL and crashes, the reference count for the DLL remains incremented. This tells Windows that the DLL is still in use and cannot be unloaded. This can cause disturbing behavior when you iteratively debug a DLL you are writing. After you modify and recompile your DLL, you typically return to your test application and test the modified DLL. Unfortunately, you might be testing the previous version of the DLL still buffered in RAM! To solve this problem, you must either obtain a third-party program to unload a DLL explicitly, or exit Windows and then return to it after you have modified the DLL. (A third-party program is included on the source disk.)

INT: When you debug OWL applications, occasionally you will receive a message box with an error message from the OWL. This message box typically provides you with the OWL class in which the error occurred and an error code. The most common error codes are shown in the following table.

Error Code	Meaning
–1	One or more of the window's children has become invalid
–2	MDI client window cannot be created
–3	Main window cannot be created
–4	Window is invalid because the `Module` object wasn't set
–5	Window is invalid because `Create` didn't succeed
–6	A memory allocation ate into the safety pool

Using Your Custom Controls Within the Resource Workshop

As soon as you have successfully created your DLL with custom controls and the Resource Workshop's required support functions (ListClasses and the info, flags, and style functions for each unique control), you are ready to import the DLL controls into the Resource Workshop.

Run the Resource Workshop, then either start a new project or load an existing one. Run the Dialog editor by selecting Resource/New and then Dialog from the list box. Select Dialog Editor/Options/Install Control Library (see Figure 4.6). From the displayed dialog box, select your new DLL. The custom controls are installed and the tools palette is updated.

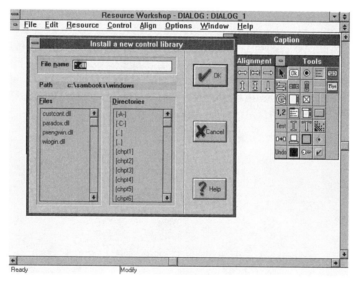

Figure 4.6. Installing a new control library.

HINT: I haven't discovered an easy way to delete a control library after it has been installed. One approach that works is to rename the DLL so that the Resource Workshop is unable to find it, then run the Resource Workshop Dialog editor. When it can't find the DLL, it removes the custom controls from the tools palette and appears to remove the custom control library. Then you can rename the DLL with its original name.

CustCont and *chpt4* Listings

Listing 4.12 contains the CUSTCONT.H file, and Listing 4.13 contains the complete CUSTCONT.CPP file. To compile the CustCont DLL project, you need the files shown in Table 4.8.

TABLE 4.8. Files needed to compile CUSTCONT.DLL.

File	Description
WFLYN.H	Header file for WFlyn class
WFLYN.CPP	Source file for WFlyn class
WEDITNUMBER.H	Header file for WEditNumber class
WEDITNUMBER.CPP	Source file for WEditNumber class
CUSTCONT.H	Header file for the custom control DLL. Used to include other header files.
CUSTCONT.CPP	Source file for the custom control DLL. Contains all the DLL-specific code, such as LibMain, and all code specific to the Resource Workshop for both WEditNumber and WFlyn.
CUSTCONT.RC	Contains resources (dialog, tools palette icon, cursor) needed by the Resource Workshop for the custom controls
CUSTCONT.PRJ	Project file for the custom control DLL

Included in Listing 4.14 is the CHPT4.CPP test file listing. This file demonstrates how to use a dialog box as the main window for your application. I designed CHPT4.CPP so that you can use it without change to test either the dialog version of the two custom controls (by defining DIALOG_VERSION) or a window version in which they operate as stand-alone controls (by defining WINDOW_VERSION). In addition, if you define SET_TEXT in the file, the WFlyn control is initialized with sample text. To compile the Chapter 4 test program, you need CUSTCONT.LIB, which you create using ImpLib from CUSTCONT.DLL; CHPT4.CPP; and CHPT4.RC, which contains the test dialog box.

LISTING 4.12. CUSTCONT.H file.

```
#define      _CLASSDLL
#define      WIN31
#define      STRICT

#include   <string.h>
#include   <custcntl.h>
#include   <alloc.h>
#include   "WFlyn.h"
#include   "WEditNum.h"
```

LISTING 4.13. CUSTCONT.CPP file.

```
// CUSTCONT.CPP - Source file for custom controls DLL

#include "CustCont.h"   // ALL other #include statements
                        // are in this file


// Create place to store new instance to represent this DLL


// We need to create a derived class from TModule to
// support proper memory allocation if multiple applications
// are simultaneously using our DLL.
```

```
_CLASSDEF (TDLLModule);
class TDLLModule : public TModule
{
    public:
        TDLLModule (LPSTR, HMODULE, LPSTR);
        ~TDLLModule ();
        void *operator new (unsigned);
        void operator delete (void *);
};

#pragma argsused

TDLLModule::TDLLModule (LPSTR n, HMODULE m, LPSTR Command)
    : TModule (n, m, Command)
{
    // Free the TModule constructor allocated memory
    farfree (lpCmdLine);
    if (Command)
    {
        lpCmdLine = (LPSTR) (void *) LocalAlloc (LPTR,
                                        strlen (Command) + 1);
        strcpy (lpCmdLine, Command);
    }
    else
    {
        lpCmdLine = (LPSTR) (void *) LocalAlloc (LPTR, 1);
        lpCmdLine[0] = 0;
    }
}

TDLLModule::~TDLLModule ()
{
    LocalFree ((HLOCAL) FP_OFF (lpCmdLine));
    lpCmdLine = NULL;
}

void *TDLLModule::operator new (unsigned n)
{
    return (void *) LocalAlloc (LPTR, n);
}

void TDLLModule::operator delete (void *p)
{
    LocalFree ((HLOCAL) FP_OFF (p));
}

PTDLLModule DLLModule;
```

continues

LISTING 4.13. continued

```c
// Class name for TControl class
char szControlClassName [35];

/********************************************************/
// Callback and Windows functions for WEditNumber class
/********************************************************/
HGLOBAL CALLBACK WEditNumberInfo (void)
{
    HGLOBAL hInfo =      GlobalAlloc(GMEM_SHARE ¦ GMEM_ZEROINIT,
        sizeof(RWCTLINFO));

    if ( hInfo )
    {
        LPRWCTLINFO     Info =     (LPRWCTLINFO) GlobalLock(hInfo);

        Info->wVersion =    0x0100;  // Version 1.00
        Info->wCtlTypes =   1;  // One type
        strcpy(Info->szClass, "EDIT");
        strcpy(Info->szTitle, "");

        Info->Type[0].wWidth  = 100 ¦ 0x8000;
        Info->Type[0].wHeight = 25 ¦ 0x8000;
        strcpy(Info->Type[0].szDescr, "Edit Number");
        Info->Type[0].dwStyle = WS_VISIBLE ¦ ES_AUTOHSCROLL ¦
                    ES_LEFT ¦ WS_TABSTOP ¦ WS_BORDER ¦
                    WS_CHILD;

        Info->Type[0].hToolBit = LoadBitmap(DLLModule->hInstance,
            "EditNumberBitmap");
        Info->Type[0].hDropCurs = LoadCursor(DLLModule->hInstance,
            "EditNumberCursor");

        GlobalUnlock(hInfo);
    }

    return hInfo;
}


/********************************************************/
// Callback and Window functions for WFlyn class
/********************************************************/
```

```
HGLOBAL CALLBACK WFlynInfo (void)
{
    HANDLE    hInfo =        GlobalAlloc(GMEM_SHARE | GMEM_ZEROINIT,
        sizeof(RWCTLINFO));

    if ( hInfo )
    {
        LPRWCTLINFO    Info =     (LPRWCTLINFO) GlobalLock(hInfo);

        Info->wVersion =    0x0100;  // Version 1.00
        Info->wCtlTypes =   1;  // One type
        strcpy(Info->szClass, szControlClassName);
        strcpy(Info->szTitle, "");

        Info->Type[0].wWidth  = 15 | 0x8000;
        Info->Type[0].wHeight = 10 | 0x8000;
        strcpy(Info->Type[0].szDescr, "FLYN");
        Info->Type[0].dwStyle = WS_VISIBLE | WS_BORDER | WS_CHILD;

        Info->Type[0].hToolBit = LoadBitmap(DLLModule->hInstance,
            "FlynBitmap");
        Info->Type[0].hDropCurs = LoadCursor(DLLModule->hInstance,
            "FlynCursor");

        GlobalUnlock(hInfo);
    }

    return hInfo;
}

UINT CALLBACK WFlynFlag (DWORD /* Style */,
        LPSTR Buff, UINT BuffLength)
{
    char *StyleString = "WS_VISIBLE | WS_BORDER | WS_CHILD";
    if (BuffLength > strlen (StyleString))
    {
        strcpy(Buff, StyleString);
        return strlen (StyleString);
    }
    else return 0;
}


LONG FAR PASCAL _export WFlynWndProc(HWND HWindow,
                        WORD wMsg,
```

continues

LISTING 4.13. continued

```
                            WORD wParam,
                            LONG lParam)
{
    if (wMsg == WM_CREATE)  // If called by non-OWL
                            // application (RW)
    {
        PTWindowsObject ParentAlias;

        // Save the old window procedure
        WNDPROC wp = (WNDPROC) GetWindowLong (HWindow,
                                              GWL_WNDPROC);

        ParentAlias = DLLModule->GetParentObject (GetParent
                                                  (HWindow));
        PWFlyn Flyn = new WFlyn
                (
                ParentAlias,
                    GetWindowWord (HWindow, GWW_ID),
                    DLLModule);
        DLLModule->MakeWindow (Flyn);

        // Restore the old window procedure
        SetWindowLong (HWindow, GWL_WNDPROC, (DWORD) wp);
    }
    return DefWindowProc(HWindow, wMsg, wParam, lParam);
}

BOOL RegisterWFlynClass()
{
  WNDCLASS  wc;
  wc.style         = CS_HREDRAW | CS_VREDRAW;
  wc.lpfnWndProc   = (WNDPROC)WFlynWndProc;
  wc.cbClsExtra    = 0;
  wc.cbWndExtra    = 0;
  wc.hInstance     = DLLModule->hInstance;
  wc.hIcon         = NULL;
  wc.hCursor       = LoadCursor(NULL, IDC_ARROW);
  wc.hbrBackground = (HBRUSH)(NULL_BRUSH);  //(Clear Background);
  wc.lpszMenuName  = NULL;
  wc.lpszClassName  = szControlClassName;
  return RegisterClass(&wc);
}

/******************************************************/
// Custom Control style and Dialog object
/******************************************************/
```

```
#define MAX_CONTROL_ID_LENGTH 10

struct TransferBuffer
{
     char Id [MAX_CONTROL_ID_LENGTH];
};

_CLASSDEF (WCustomControlDialog)
class WCustomControlDialog : public TDialog
{
     public:

          // Public member functions *****************
          // Constructors and destructors
          WCustomControlDialog (PTWindowsObject Parent,
                              LPSTR szName,
                              PTModule Module,
                              struct TransferBuffer *tb);

};



#define IDD_ID 101

WCustomControlDialog::WCustomControlDialog (
                                PTWindowsObject Parent,
                                LPSTR szName,
                                PTModule Module,
                                struct TransferBuffer *tb)
                    :TDialog (Parent, szName, Module)
{
     new TEdit (this, IDD_ID, MAX_CONTROL_ID_LENGTH -1, DLLModule);
     SetTransferBuffer (tb);
}


BOOL CALLBACK ControlStyle (HWND hWnd, HGLOBAL hCtlStyle,
        LPFNSTRTOID lpfnStrToId, LPFNIDTOSTR lpfnIdToStr)
{
     LPCTLSTYLE    Style   =   (LPCTLSTYLE) GlobalLock(hCtlStyle);
     PWCustomControlDialog TheDialog;
     PTWindowsObject AParentAlias;
    BOOL Result = FALSE;

     TransferBuffer *tb = new TransferBuffer;

     lpfnIdToStr (Style->wId, tb->Id, MAX_CONTROL_ID_LENGTH);
```

continues

LISTING 4.13. continued

```
    // Save the old window procedure
    WNDPROC wp = (WNDPROC) GetWindowLong (hWnd, GWL_WNDPROC);

    AParentAlias = DLLModule->GetParentObject (hWnd);

    TheDialog = new WCustomControlDialog (AParentAlias,
        "CustomDialog", DLLModule, tb);


    if (DLLModule->ExecDialog (TheDialog) == IDOK)
    {
        Result = TRUE;
        Style->wId = (WORD) lpfnStrToId (tb->Id);
    }

    // Restore the old window procedure
    SetWindowLong (hWnd, GWL_WNDPROC, (DWORD) wp);

    GlobalUnlock (hCtlStyle);
    delete tb;

    return Result;
}


// Must include definition for ListClasses for all custom
// controls that will be used by the Resource Workshop.
// The Resource Workshop expects this to be a C function,
// so we must prevent name-mangling from confusing it.


extern "C" HGLOBAL CALLBACK _export  ListClasses(LPSTR,
                                        //szApplication
                                UINT,          // wVersion
                                LPFNLOADRES,   // fnLoad
                                LPFNEDITRES)   // fnEdit
{
    const NumberOfControls = 2;
    HGLOBAL hClasses = GlobalAlloc(GMEM_SHARE | GMEM_ZEROINIT,
        sizeof(int) + (NumberOfControls * sizeof(RWCTLCLASS)));


    if ( hClasses )
    {
        LPCTLCLASSLIST Controls =
        (LPCTLCLASSLIST) GlobalLock(hClasses);
```

```
        Controls->nClasses = NumberOfControls;

        Controls->Classes[0].fnRWInfo  = WEditNumberInfo;
        Controls->Classes[0].fnRWStyle = NULL;
        Controls->Classes[0].fnFlags   = NULL;
        strcpy(Controls->Classes[0].szClass, "EDIT");


        Controls->Classes[1].fnRWInfo  = WFlynInfo;
        Controls->Classes[1].fnRWStyle = ControlStyle;
        Controls->Classes[1].fnFlags   = WFlynFlag;
        strcpy(Controls->Classes[1].szClass, szControlClassName);

        GlobalUnlock(hClasses);
    }

    return hClasses;
}



// Must include definition for LibMain function
// for all DLLs
int FAR PASCAL LibMain (HINSTANCE hInstance,
                        WORD /* DataSeg */,
                        WORD /* HeapSize */,
                        LPSTR lpCmdLine)
{
    DLLModule = new TDLLModule ("DLLModule", hInstance,
        lpCmdLine);

    if (DLLModule->Status != 0)
    {
        delete DLLModule;
        DLLModule = NULL;
      MessageBeep (0);
      return 0;
    }
    else
    {
        // Initialize szControlClassName
        strcpy (szControlClassName, "WFlyn");
        RegisterWFlynClass ();
        return 1;  // Success
    }
}
```

LISTING 4.14. CHPT4.CPP file.

```cpp
#define DIALOG_VERSION
#define SET_TEXT

#define        _CLASSDLL
#define  WIN31
#define  STRICT
#include <owl.h>
#include <edit.h>
#include "CustCont.h"


//****************************************************
// chpt4 - chpt4 application class
//
//      Purpose:
//           This class is the overall application
//           executive for chpt4.
//
//      Notes:
//           None
//
//      Copyright:
//               Copyright (c) 1993, William H. Roetzheim
//               All Rights Reserved
//
//****************************************************

_CLASSDEF (chpt4)
class chpt4 : public TApplication
{
    public:
           // Public member functions ****************
           // Constructors and destructors
           chpt4 (LPSTR szName, HINSTANCE hInstance,
                    HINSTANCE hPrevInstance, LPSTR lpCmdLine,
                    int nCmdShow);

           // Member functions
           virtual void InitMainWindow ();
};


#ifdef WINDOW_VERSION
```

```
_CLASSDEF (chpt4Window)
class chpt4Window : public TWindow
{
    public:
        PTEdit Edit;
        PWEditNumber EditNumber;
      PWFlyn Flyn;
        chpt4Window (PTModule);
};

chpt4Window::chpt4Window (PTModule Module)
    :
    TWindow (NULL, "Chapter Four Test Window", Module)
{   // You shouldn't hard-code the control sizes in a
    // real-world application
    Edit = new TEdit (this, 101, "Edit Test", 10, 10, 100, 25, 10,
                      FALSE);
    EditNumber = new WEditNumber (this, 102, "123", 10, 40, 100,
                                  25, 10, FALSE);
    Flyn = new WFlyn (this, 103, NULL, 10, 80, 25, 25);
#ifdef SET_TEXT
    Flyn->SetText ("Demonstration of WFlyn control.");
#endif SET_TEXT
}

#endif


#ifdef DIALOG_VERSION

_CLASSDEF (WTestDialog)
class WTestDialog : public TDialog
{
    public:
        PWEditNumber EditNumber;
        PWFlyn Flyn;
      PTEdit Edit;

        WTestDialog (PTWindowsObject Window, LPSTR Dialog,
                     PTModule Module = NULL);
};


WTestDialog::WTestDialog (PTWindowsObject Window, LPSTR Dialog,
                          PTModule Module)
                              :
                          TDialog (Window, Dialog, Module)
{
```

continues

LISTING 4.14. continued

```
        Edit = new TEdit (this, 101, 10);
        EditNumber = new WEditNumber (this, 102, 10);
        Flyn = new WFlyn (this, 103);
#ifdef SET_TEXT
        Flyn->SetText ("Demonstration of WFlyn control.");
#endif SET_TEXT
}


#endif


//****************************************************
// Constructors and destructors for chpt4
//
//      Copyright:
//                Copyright (c) 1993, William H. Roetzheim
//                All Rights Reserved
//
//****************************************************

#pragma argsused  // Turn off arguments not used warning
chpt4::chpt4(LPSTR szName, HINSTANCE hInstance,
            HINSTANCE hPrevInstance, LPSTR lpCmdLine,
            int nCmdShow)
            : TApplication (szName, hInstance,
            hPrevInstance, lpCmdLine, nCmdShow)
{
    return;
}




//****************************************************
// Member functions for class chpt4
//
//      Copyright:
//                Copyright (c) 1993, William H. Roetzheim
//                All Rights Reserved
//
//****************************************************

void chpt4::InitMainWindow ()
{
#ifdef WINDOW_VERSION
    MainWindow = new chpt4Window (this);
```

```
#endif

#ifdef DIALOG_VERSION
    MainWindow = new WTestDialog (NULL, "DemoDialog", this);
#endif

}


// Here is the main () for the program
int PASCAL WinMain (HINSTANCE hInstance,
    HINSTANCE hPrevInstance, LPSTR lpCmdLine,
    int)
{

    // Ensure that CUSTCONT dynamic link library is loaded
    HINSTANCE hDLL = LoadLibrary ("CUSTCONT.DLL");

    // Create chpt4 application from class
    chpt4 ochpt4 ("chpt4", hInstance,
                  hPrevInstance, lpCmdLine, SW_NORMAL);

    // Start created application running
    ochpt4.Run ();   // Runs till window closed

    // Free the CUSTCONT dynamic link library
    if (hDLL>31) FreeLibrary (hDLL);

    // Return termination status when window closed
    return ochpt4.Status;

}
```

Implementing
Custom
Style Dialog
Boxes

Problem

Your application works great, but it looks boring and just like everyone else's application. You need pizazz! You need sizzle! You need flair! With their steel gray background and shading, Borland's dialog boxes look pretty good. Borland's custom controls, especially the bitmapped buttons, look great. It would be ideal to give your dialog boxes that level of sophistication. But how?

Solution

When you run CHPT5.EXE, included on the source disk, you see a sample dialog box that illustrates the use of Borland's background and custom controls, including two bitmapped buttons (see Figure 5.1). In this chapter, I begin by showing you how to implement this dialog box quickly and easily. To demonstrate the full power and convenience of the WLogin DLL, which I showed you in Chapter 3, "Coding Dynamic Link Libraries," I start with a version of the dialog box that does not implement the Beep button. I then show you how to extend the WLogin class to process new controls—in this case, the Beep button—properly. Finally, I provide a brief overview of the full suite of Borland custom controls.

Implementing a Borland-Style Dialog Box

In Chapter 3, I showed you how to implement a reusable login dialog box in a dynamic link library. You might recall that I built in two ways to use the dialog box—by calling a DLL function that displayed the dialog box resource included in the DLL, and by using the DLL's dialog handler with your own application-specific dialog box resource. I use the second method to demonstrate the use of Borland's style of dialog box.

The first step is to create a Borland-style custom dialog box with a Name field ID of 101, a Password field ID of 102, a bitmapped pushbutton that causes a beep, and an OK pushbutton that closes the dialog box. Start the Resource Workshop and load the file CHPT5.RC from the source disk. Open the dialog box BCPassword to display the screen shown in Figure 5.2.

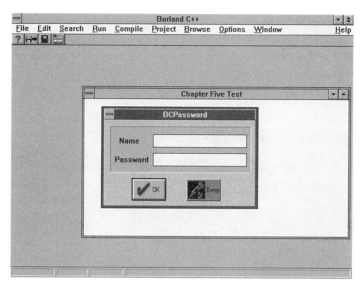

Figure 5.1. CHPT5.EXE demonstrating a Borland-style dialog box.

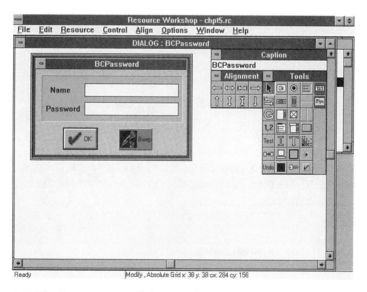

Figure 5.2. The Resource Workshop dialog editor working on BCPassword.

To give the dialog box the Borland-style steel gray background, I double-clicked on the caption bar of the dialog box to display the Window style dialog box (see Figure 5.3). The Class field was then set to "B or Dlg." This gave the box the Borland-style appearance and improved its performance over the standard dialog box class. (See the discussion in Borland's online documentation.)

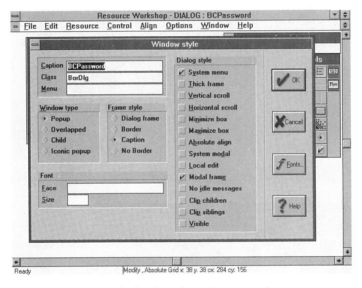

Figure 5.3. Window style dialog box for BCPassword.

Borland provides several custom controls that can be used on your Borland-style dialog box (see Table 5.1). I discuss each control in more detail later in this chapter. For now, I'll describe how I added the bitmapped Beep button to the Login dialog box.

TABLE 5.1. Borland custom dialog controls.

Borland Custom Control	Resource Workshop Icon
Bitmapped pushbuttons (BORBTN)	

Borland Custom Control	Resource Workshop Icon
Better-looking radio buttons (BORRADIO)	
Better-looking check boxes (BORCHECK)	
Horizontal dips and bumps	
Vertical dips and bumps	
Borland-style group box	
Borland bitmap (splash panel)	

When you add the bitmapped Beep button to the dialog box, the initial step is no different from when you add any other button, except that you should select the bitmapped pushbutton icon from the tools palette. The button added to your dialog box will be 64 pixels wide by 40 pixels high. I recommend that you don't change the size of these buttons. The size is good to begin with, and it simplifies production of the required bitmaps, which are discussed next.

> **HINT:** When you work with bitmapped images on a dialog box, it is best to set the dialog box status line units to pixels rather than to dialog units. To do this, select Options/Preferences from the Resource Workshop's main menu. Set the Status Line Units to Screen on the resulting dialog box.

Each bitmapped button has as many as three bitmaps associated with it—six if you need compatibility with EGA monitors. The bitmaps are created as a bitmap within the Resource Workshop by using its paint tool. They are included in your resource file along with the dialog box. The linking

between a bitmapped button and its associated bitmaps is based on the control ID of the button, as shown in Table 5.2.

TABLE 5.2. The relationship between button ID and associated bitmaps.

Bitmap ID Number	Used For
Control ID + 1000	Normal VGA resolution image
Control ID + 3000	Pressed VGA resolution image
Control ID + 5000	Focused VGA resolution image
Control ID + 2000	Normal EGA resolution image
Control ID + 4000	Pressed EGA resolution image
Control ID + 6000	Focused EGA resolution image

To create an appropriate bitmap in the Resource Workshop, select Resource/New/Bitmap. Specify a 64-by-40 16-color bitmap on the resulting dialog box (see Figure 5.4). The Resource Workshop paint tool appears, ready for you to design your bitmap (see Figure 5.5).

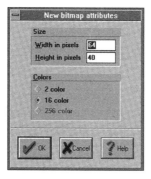

Figure 5.4. A new bitmap definition dialog box.

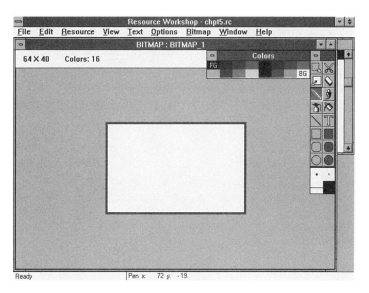

Figure 5.5. The Resource Workshop paint tool.

The button's normal bitmap should have a white border on the left and top sides and a black border on the right and bottom sides. The remainder of your button contains your bitmapped image, including any text you want displayed. The Borland `button` class doesn't display text except for what is included in the bitmap itself. The button's pressed bitmap often is the same as the normal bitmap, except that the white border is on the right and bottom sides, and the black border is on the left and top sides.

INT: You can derive a class from the Borland `button` class that enables you to add text to the button at runtime. Make the derived class owner drawable. Have it first call the appropriate parent class function to draw the bitmap, then have it use `TextOut` to display the desired text on the bitmap.

INT: If you're not artistic, you can use the Windows clipboard to clip images from a commercial drawing program into your bitmap in the Resource Workshop. You also can use the clipboard to copy images from existing applications into your application.

To do this, use the Resource Workshop to open the executable version of the application (or the DLL, if appropriate). Select the bitmaps—and icons, if desired—one-by-one until you find the one that interests you. Use Select All to select the entire bitmap, then select Copy to copy it into the clipboard. Return to your own project file and open the bitmap you are working on (or create a new bitmap resource). Use Paste to insert the transferred image.

ARNING: Be careful when copying images. Some companies have copyrighted or otherwise protected their icons and bitmapped images. You might want to get permission to use the image, talk to a lawyer, or get liability insurance.

Finally, you should rename your bitmap to an appropriate number based on the control ID of the bitmapped button.

The Borland Windows Custom Control (BWCC) dynamic link library includes appropriate bitmap images for eight standard button IDs. These are shown in Table 5.3. Avoid numbering your own custom bitmap buttons with any of these numbers lest they conflict with the standard Borland buttons.

TABLE 5.3. Borland predefined bitmapped buttons.

Identifier	Button	Image
1 (IDOK)	OK	Green check mark
2 (IDCANCEL)	Cancel	Red X
3 (IDABORT)	Abort	Panic button

Identifier	Button	Image
4 (IDRETRY)	Retry	Slot machine
5 (IDIGNORE)	Ignore	55 mph speed-limit sign
6 (IDYES)	Yes	Green check mark
7 (IDNO)	No	Red circle with a slash
998 (IDHELP)	Help	Blue question mark

The other trick to using Borland custom controls is to ensure that the BWCC dynamic link library is available to the user of your application. (You can distribute the library with your code without paying Borland any royalties.) Also make sure that it is loaded and available when your application is loaded. Remember that parts of this DLL need to be available as soon as a dialog box is displayed—potentially before you call any BWCC function that would force the operating system to load BWCC. To force the operating system to load BWCC, include the following code in your WinMain function:

```
HINSTANCE hDLL = LoadLibrary ("BWCC.DLL");

. . . Create and run your application class

if (hDLL>31) FreeLibrary (hDLL);

. . . Return from WinMain
```

Also, it is good practice to check for return LoadLibrary() values less than 32, because these indicate an error.

HINT: Be very careful here. If you forget to include this code, your application probably will appear to work properly on your computer because BWCC is already loaded by Borland C++ or the Resource Workshop. However, it won't work on a customer's machine, because that person hasn't run an application that forced BWCC to be loaded.

To use my new Login dialog box, BCPassword, I can use the WLogin class defined in Chapter 3, "Coding Dynamic Link Libraries," as part of my WLogin DLL. Here is the code for using the newly defined Borland-style dialog box:

```
PWLoginTransferBuffer tb = new WLoginTransferBuffer;
PWLogin TheDialog;

TheDialog = new WLogin (this, "BCPassword", GetModule (), tb);
GetModule()->ExecDialog (TheDialog);
```

In this example, I use the standard WLogin dialog-handling class to handle my BCPassword dialog with its custom appearance. Unfortunately, the WLogin class doesn't know anything about the Beep button that I've added to the dialog box, so it ignores it. To make this button functional, I must derive a class from the WLogin class.

Extending *WLogin* Processing to Handle New Controls

Because C++ supports inheritance, I can easily extend the WLogin class to recognize my new custom control, the Beep button. I simply created a new class, derived from WLogin, that includes a message-response function for the control of interest:

```
#define IDD_BEEP 103

_CLASSDEF (WBCLogin)
class WBCLogin : public WLoginDialog
{
    public:

            // Public member functions ***************
            // Constructors and destructors
            WBCLogin (PTWindowsObject Parent, LPSTR szName,
                            PTModule Module = NULL,
                            PWLoginTransferBuffer tb);

            virtual void Beep (RTMessage) =
                [ID_FIRST + IDD_BEEP];
};
```

The constructor doesn't need to do anything but call the `WLogin` constructor:

```
WBCLogin::WBCLogin (PTWindowsObject Parent, LPSTR szName,
                               PTModule Module,
                               PWLoginTransferBuffer tb)
                               :
                               WLoginDialog (Parent, szName,
                               Module, tb)
{
    return;
}
```

This particular control-handling function is trivial:

```
void WBCLogin::Beep (RTMessage Msg)
{
    MessageBeep (0);
    DefChildProc (Msg);
}
```

> **HINT:** Notice that `WBCLogin` calls the `WLogin` constructor, even though I know that the `WLogin` constructor does nothing except call the `TDialog` constructor. I don't call the `TDialog` constructor directly from `WBCLogin`. Later on, I might decide to add additional processing to the `WLogin` constructor, and I would then have a bug because the `WBCLogin` constructor couldn't take advantage of this additional processing.
>
> Two rules of thumb should guide you in this area. First, unless you know exactly what you are doing, always call the parent's version of a member function either before or after you perform your processing. Second, when you use scope resolution, always go up only one level; let the immediate parent call higher levels if appropriate.

Listing 5.1 shows the complete source code for the CHPT5 source file. Be sure to include the file CHPT5.RC when you compile this code. This resource file contains the dialog box template and the bitmapped image for the Beep button. You also need to use WLOGIN.H and include WLOGIN.LIB in your project file.

LISTING 5.1. CHPT5.CPP file.

```
#define _CLASSDLL  // Needed if you use a DLL class
#define WIN31  // Windows 3.1
#define STRICT  // Strict type checking
#include  <owl.h>
#include  <dialog.h>
#include  <Button.h>
#include  "Wlogin.h"


//*****************************************************
// chpt5 - chpt5 application class header
//
//     Purpose:
//         This class is the overall application
//         executive for chpt5.
//
//     Notes:
//         None
//
//     Copyright:
//             Copyright (c) 1993, William H. Roetzheim
//             All Rights Reserved
//
//*****************************************************

_CLASSDEF (chpt5)
class chpt5 : public TApplication
{
     public:
             // Public member functions ****************
             // Constructors and destructors
             chpt5 (LPSTR szName, HINSTANCE hInstance,
                     HINSTANCE hPrevInstance, LPSTR lpCmdLine,
                     int nCmdShow);

             // Member functions
             virtual void InitMainWindow ();
};


//*****************************************************
// chpt5Window - Main window for chpt5 application
//
//     Notes:
//
```

```
//      Copyright:
//              Copyright (c) 1993, William H. Roetzheim
//              All Rights Reserved
//
//****************************************************


_CLASSDEF (chpt5Window)
class chpt5Window : public TWindow
{
    public:
            // Public member functions ****************
            // Constructors and destructors
            chpt5Window (char *Title, PTModule Module = NULL);

            virtual void WMSize(RTMessage);
};




//****************************************************
// BCLogin - BCLogin dialog header and code
//
//      Notes:
//
//      Copyright:
//              Copyright (c) 1993, William H. Roetzheim
//              All Rights Reserved
//
//****************************************************


#define IDD_BEEP 103

_CLASSDEF (WBCLogin)
class WBCLogin : public WLoginDialog
{
    public:

            // Public member functions ****************
            // Constructors and destructors
            WBCLogin (PTWindowsObject Parent, LPSTR szName,
                            PTModule Module = NULL,
                            PWLoginTransferBuffer tb);
```

continues

LISTING 5.1. continued

```
            virtual void Beep (RTMessage) =
                [ID_FIRST + IDD_BEEP];
};




//*****************************************************
// Constructors and destructors for chpt5
//
//     Copyright:
//            Copyright (c) 1993, William H. Roetzheim
//            All Rights Reserved
//
//*****************************************************

#pragma argsused  // Turn off arguments not used warning
chpt5::chpt5(LPSTR szName, HINSTANCE hInstance,
            HINSTANCE hPrevInstance, LPSTR lpCmdLine,
            int nCmdShow)
            : TApplication (szName, hInstance,
            hPrevInstance, lpCmdLine, nCmdShow)
{
    return;
}




//*****************************************************
// Member functions for class chpt5
//
//     Copyright:
//            Copyright (c) 1993, William H. Roetzheim
//            All Rights Reserved
//
//*****************************************************

void chpt5::InitMainWindow ()
{
    MainWindow = new chpt5Window ("Chapter Five Test",
                                            this);
}




//*****************************************************
// Constructors and destructors for chpt5Window
//
```

```
//     Copyright:
//             Copyright (c) 1993, William H. Roetzheim
//             All Rights Reserved
//
//*****************************************************

chpt5Window::chpt5Window (char *Title, PTModule Module)
                    : TWindow (NULL, Title, Module)
{
    return;
}



//*****************************************************
// Member functions for class chpt5Window
//
//     Copyright:
//             Copyright (c) 1993, William H. Roetzheim
//             All Rights Reserved
//
//*****************************************************

void chpt5Window::WMSize(RTMessage)
{
    PWLoginTransferBuffer tb = new WLoginTransferBuffer;
    PWBCLogin TheDialog;

    // Call dialog password routine using dialog box in our .EXE
    TheDialog = new WBCLogin (this,
        "BCPassword", GetModule (), tb);
    GetModule()->ExecDialog (TheDialog);
    MessageBox (HWindow, tb->Name, tb->Password, MB_OK);

    delete tb;
    Destroy ();
}



//*****************************************************
// Constructors and destructors for BCLogin
//
//     Copyright:
//             Copyright (c) 1993, William H. Roetzheim
//             All Rights Reserved
//
//*****************************************************
```

continues

145

LISTING 5.1. continued

```
WBCLogin::WBCLogin (PTWindowsObject Parent, LPSTR szName,
                               PTModule Module,
                               PWLoginTransferBuffer tb)
                               :
                               WLoginDialog (Parent, szName,
                               Module, tb)
{
    return;
}




//*****************************************************
// Member functions for class chpt5
//
//      Copyright:
//              Copyright (c) 1993, William H. Roetzheim
//              All Rights Reserved
//
//*****************************************************

void WBCLogin::Beep (RTMessage Msg)
{
    MessageBeep (0);
   DefChildProc (Msg);
}


// Here is the main () for the program
int PASCAL WinMain (HINSTANCE hInstance,
    HINSTANCE hPrevInstance, LPSTR lpCmdLine,
    int nCmdShow)
{

    // Ensure that BWCC dynamic link library is loaded
    HINSTANCE hDLL = LoadLibrary ("BWCC.DLL");

    // Create chpt5 application from class
    chpt5 ochpt5 ("chpt5", hInstance,
                hPrevInstance, lpCmdLine, nCmdShow);

    // Start created application running
    ochpt5.Run ();  // Runs till window closed
```

```
    // Free the BWCC dynamic link library
    if (hDLL>31) FreeLibrary (hDLL);

    // Return termination status when window closed
    return ochpt5.Status;
}
```

An Overview of Borland Custom Controls

In this section, I present a brief overview of the Borland custom controls included in BWCC.DLL. I cover bitmapped pushbuttons, radio buttons, check boxes, horizontal and vertical dips and bumps, Borland-style group boxes, and splash panels. I focus on what is unique about each control, while ignoring behavior identical to Microsoft's equivalent controls, such as buttons, radio buttons, check boxes, and static.

Bitmapped Pushbuttons

Borland's bitmapped pushbuttons are similar to Microsoft's button controls, except for the addition of their bitmapped visual appearance and the new message responses, shown in Table 5.4. If a bitmap maps to the button—that is, if it is named with the button ID plus 1000, 2000, 3000, 4000, 5000, or 6000—the bitmap must contain the button text. If no bitmap is defined for the button, the button displays its caption just like the Microsoft equivalent.

TABLE 5.4. Borland bitmap button extensions to standard button messages.

Message	Description
BBS_PARENTNOTIFY	Causes the control to generate the following notification messages at runtime:

continues

147

TABLE 5.4. continued

Message	Description
	BBN_SETFOCUS BBN_SETFOCUSMOUSE BBN_GOTATAB BBN_GOTABTAB WParam and LParam are not used.
BBS_OWNERDRAW	Causes the control to send WM_DRAWITEM messages to the parent at runtime. WParam and LParam are not used.
BBM_SETBITS	Sets the control's three bitmaps from within an application, as opposed to using the Resource Workshop numbering convention. This message is needed when using a bitmap button as a stand-alone control, not in a dialog box. WParam is not used. LParam is a pointer to an array of three bitmap handles. It represents the normal, pressed, and focused bitmaps.
BBN_SETFOCUS	The button has gained the focus from something other than a mouse click. WParam and LParam are not used.
BBN_SETFOCUSMOUSE	The button has gained the focus from a mouse click. WParam and LParam are not used.
BBN_GOTATAB	The Tab key was pressed while this control had the focus. WParam and LParam are not used.
BBN_GOTABTAB	The Shift-Tab key combination was pressed while this control had the focus. WParam and LParam are not used.

Here is an example of code that uses the `BBM_SETBITS` message from a descendant of `TDialog`:

```
#define BUTTON 101  // Replace with your actual button ID
HBITMAP Bits [3];

Bits [0] = . . . Load or initialize your normal bitmap handle
Bits [1] = . . . Load or initialize your pressed bitmap handle
Bits [2] = . . . Load or initialize your focus bitmap handle

SendDlgItemMessage (BUTTON, BBM_SETBITS, 0, (DWORD) Bits);
```

Radio Buttons and Check Boxes

Borland defines radio buttons and check boxes that are more attractive than their Microsoft equivalents. These two control types support the same list of new messages as the bitmapped button messages shown in Table 5.4, except for the `BBM_SETBITS` messages, which are not supported.

Horizontal and Vertical Dividers

Borland includes static controls. These are basically horizontal and vertical lines used as separators within a dialog box. Lines appearing as depressions, called *dips,* are used to divide the main dialog box into various areas. Lines appearing as ridges, called *bumps,* are used to divide the gray Borland group box into sections.

The Borland-Style Group Box

The Borland-style group box is a gray shaded area that appears depressed into the surface of the dialog box. Its behavior and characteristics are identical to those of a standard group box.

Splash Panels

You can specify the type of a Borland button as a bitmap rather than as a default or ordinary pushbutton. The button then behaves exactly like an ordinary bitmapped button: it displays bitmaps based on number, and so on. It cannot, however, be pressed by the user.

149

This control, often called a *splash panel,* is used to display static bitmaps easily. Of course, when you work with splash panels, normally you want to resize the bitmap image from the default 64-by-40 pixels to a size appropriate for your needs. A large splash panel is used to display a start-up logo when either Borland C++ or the Resource Workshop starts (see Figure 5.6).

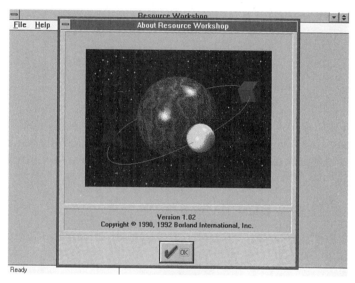

Figure 5.6. An example of a splash panel.

The Next Step

Chapter 6, "Implementing Large Dialog Boxes," applies what you've learned about Borland-style dialog boxes to a dialog box that is too large to fit on one screen.

CHAPTER

6

Implementing Large Dialog Boxes

Problem

By this time, I'm sure you've discovered the pleasure of using the Dialog Editor in the Resource Workshop to put together impressive dialogs quickly. These dialog boxes are great for short data entry tasks. Recently, when I was asked to implement an application for the California Employment Development Department, my inclination was to turn to this tried-and-true tool. I needed to put a full-page unemployment application form online. This required a dialog box with more controls than would fit on the screen at any one time. It seems as though this task would be simple, but neither Windows nor OWL is designed to handle dialog boxes larger than a single screen. Even the OWL TScroller class, a natural solution to the problem, works only for classes derived from TWindow. (TDialog is not a descendant of TWindow.)

Solution

There are three basic approaches to solving this problem. The easiest and most common is to break the data entry form into smaller pieces. Each piece is implemented as its own dialog box. The user completes each piece separately, normally in response to a series of menu choices. This is often the best choice, but for many applications it is less than satisfactory. The user must select each menu choice to complete the form properly. Cross-checking among fields (controls) on different forms is difficult. If the user must look at many dialog boxes just to find the right one, completing and modifying a specific field can be difficult. Many times I have been forced to open a series of dialog boxes using Borland's Options/Compiler menu selection just to find the dialog box with the specific field I wanted to change.

The second alternative is to use a single dialog box that brings up additional dialog boxes in response to user button selections. Because bringing up one dialog box from within another is no different from bringing up a dialog box at any other time, this approach is easy to implement. It might still be difficult for the user to complete a form and find specific fields, but cross-checking among fields is simplified.

Cross-checking is easily accomplished within the master dialog box, because it has all the transfer buffers from support dialog boxes. Within a support dialog box, you can cross-check to fields in other support dialog boxes by passing the required data to the support dialog box in the constructor. Then make all the transfer buffers public within the master dialog box. Otherwise, make the support dialog classes friends of the master dialog class so that they can directly access its transfer buffers.

The third option is to implement a single, very large dialog box—larger than what can fit on a computer screen—and to make the dialog box scrollable. The user can complete something that has a visual appearance simulating familiar paper forms. Because the window within the Resource Workshop Dialog Editor is scrollable, using this tool you can create a dialog box as large as you want. When you run out of room, use the scroll bars to scroll the Dialog Editor window, then resize the dialog box to expand into the space created, and continue to add controls. Figure 6.1 shows the CHPT6.EXE application running, with the Unemployment Insurance dialog box displayed. The rest of this chapter demonstrates how to implement scrollable dialog boxes.

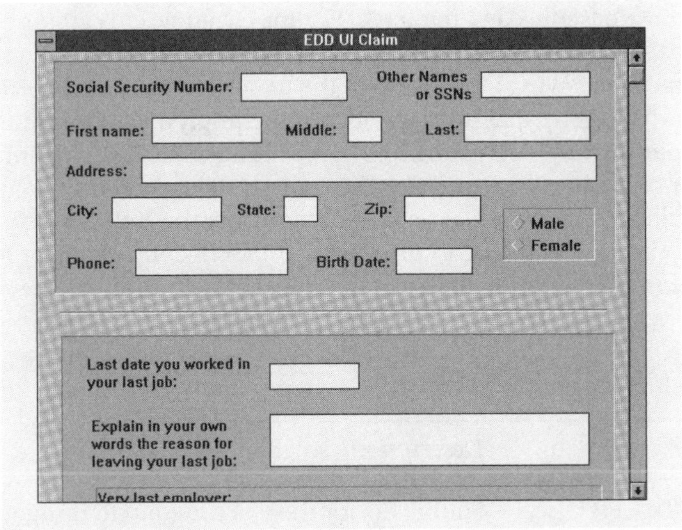

Figure 6.1. The chpt6 *application with the Unemployment Insurance dialog box displayed.*

HINT: I find that it is better to confine the width of a dialog box to one screen, then let the length of the dialog box extend beyond one screen if necessary. That way, you and the user just need to scroll the dialog box vertically.

HINT: When you add a scroll bar to a dialog, be sure to turn off the Modal Frame check box in the dialog's style so that the dialog will be drawn properly.

The *chpt6* Code

The chpt6 project consists of the files shown in Table 6.1. CHPT6.CPP is unremarkable. The program ensures that the BWCC DLL is loaded using LoadLibrary (described in Chapter 3, "Coding Dynamic Link Libraries"), and executes WEmpAppDialog as the application's main window. Then the program frees the BWCC DLL. None of the data is actually transferred to or from the dialog box; that routine code would simply add more clutter without imparting any interesting knowledge. The actual application uses a transfer buffer to move the data. The process requires defining the buffer itself, calling the SetTransferBuffer function after the dialog is created, and creating inside the dialog's constructor an OWL control object for each dialog control that participates in the transfer operation.

TABLE 6.1. chpt6 **project files.**

File	Description
CHPT6.CPP	Source file for the test program to bring up the scrollable dialog box
CHPT6.PRJ	Project file for the chpt6 test application

File	Description
WEMPAPPD.H	Header file for the scrollable dialog class to handle the Unemployment application dialog box
WEMPAPPD.CPP	Source file for the scrollable dialog class to handle the Unemployment application dialog box
EMPAPP.RC	Resource file containing the definition of the Unemployment application dialog box itself
DEMPAPP.H	Header file containing #defines for all controls in the Unemployment application dialog box

INT: When you use #define statements to make dialog control IDs mnemonic, it is best to define these mnemonics in a separate file before you run the Resource Workshop. After you start the Resource Workshop, use the File/Add To Project command to add the header file. Now, the Resource Workshop and any application that uses the dialog box can use this header file. I like to name this header file to match the .RC filename, so I prefix it with D for *defines.*

The *WEmpAppDialog* Scrollable Dialog Class

Listing 6.1 shows the WEmpAppDialog header file. Three private data members are used within the class. PositionOffset and PreviousPosition are of type POINT. POINT is defined in WINDOWS.H as a struct consisting of two integers labeled x and y. The WMVScroll function uses PositionOffset to tell the MoveControl function how far to move each child control in the x and y

directions. PreviousPosition is used to store the position of all controls—relative to their original positions—following each move. VertSBRange stores the total range of the vertical scroll bar.

MoveControl is a private callback function used by Windows to iterate through a list of child controls. This type of function is called an enum function because the Windows procedures that use them begin with the word enum. The function is declared static because Windows itself will not pass it a this pointer. Remember that because static functions do not expect or receive a hidden this parameter, they cannot access data that is internal to their class.

The function returns either 1, which allows Windows to continue iterating until Windows has called MoveControl for every child control, or 0, which stops the iteration. The function must be exported by using the _export keyword or by including it in the export section of the .DEF file. The first parameter is a handle to a specific child window that is set by Windows for each iteration, and the second parameter is an application, defined as LPARAM, that is set once for all iterations.

Handling the actual scrollbar messages is accomplished by redefining the WMVScroll function. (The V stands for *vertical scroll bar*.) Handling horizontal scrollbar messages requires that the WMHScroll function be overloaded.

LISTING 6.1. WEMPAPPD.H file listing.

```
#define WIN31
#define STRICT
#define _CLASSDLL

// WEMPAPPDIALOG.H - Header file for WEmpAppDialog class

#ifndef WEmpAppDialog_H
#     define WEmpAppDialog_H

// Note that the following code is executed only
// if this file has not been previously included


// #include files for both PC and SUN
```

```
#include    <owl.h>

//*****************************************************
// WEmpAppDialog - Employment application dialog
//
//      Purpose:
//          Process a California unemployment application
//          dialog box.
//
//      Notes:
//
//      Copyright:
//              Copyright (c) 1993, William H. Roetzheim
//              All Rights Reserved
//
//*****************************************************

_CLASSDEF (WEmpAppDialog)
class WEmpAppDialog : public TDialog
{
    private:
            // Private data members ********************
            POINT PositionOffset;
            POINT PreviousPosition;
        int VertSBRange;

            // Private member functions ***************
            static BOOL CALLBACK _export MoveControl
                                            (HWND, LPARAM);

    public:
            // Public data members ********************


            // Public member functions ****************
            // Constructors and destructors
            WEmpAppDialog (PTWindowsObject, LPSTR, PTModule);

            // Member functions
        virtual void SetupWindow ();
            virtual void WMVScroll (RTMessage Msg);
};

#endif WEmpAppDialog_H
```

SetupWindow

SetupWindow, shown in Listing 6.2, calls the TDialog version of the function, then performs two functions. First, it resizes the dialog box to fit comfortably on the screen and centers the resized dialog box. If this step is skipped, the dialog will extend past the lower part of the display. This results in an unattractive dialog box: the scroll bar lacks the lower thumb button because it is off the bottom of the screen. The code is relatively straightforward if you remember the purpose of each function:

➤ GetClientRect is used to obtain the dimensions, in pixels, of a window's client area.

➤ GetWindowRect is used to obtain the screen coordinate position, in pixels, of a window.

➤ GetDesktopWindow returns the window handle that represents the entire screen.

➤ MoveWindow moves and resizes a window.

The second function performed by SetupWindow is to initialize the scroll bar and the PreviousPosition variable. The top is left at zero, which represents the initial position of all dialog child controls. The bottom position of the scroll bar is set to be the number of pixels that the dialog must be scrolled in order to make the bottom of the dialog visible with 50 pixels to spare. PreviousPosition's x and y coordinates are initialized to 0 to show that the dialog is positioned at its initial position.

LISTING 6.2. The SetupWindow function.

```
void WEmpAppDialog::SetupWindow ()
{
    TDialog::SetupWindow();

    RECT OriginalClientRect;    // Dialog client rect
    RECT Screen;                // Full display screen
    RECT OriginalDialog;        // Dialog complete area

    GetClientRect (HWindow, &OriginalClientRect);
    GetClientRect (GetDesktopWindow(), &Screen);
```

```
// Determine new size of dialog box
GetWindowRect (HWindow, &OriginalDialog);
int Width = OriginalDialog.right - OriginalDialog.left;
int height = OriginalDialog.bottom - OriginalDialog.top;

// See if dialog is too large. 50 is arbitrary for aesthetics.
if (Width > (Screen.right - 50)) Width = Screen.right - 50;
if (height > (Screen.bottom - 50)) height = Screen.bottom - 50;

// Move and resize the dialog
MoveWindow
    (
        HWindow,
        (Screen.right - Width) / 2,    // Left
        (Screen.bottom - height) / 2,  // Top
        Width,
        height,
        TRUE   // Redraw
    );

// Initialize the scroll bar(s)
VertSBRange = OriginalClientRect.bottom - height + 50;
SetScrollRange (HWindow, SB_VERT, 0,
    VertSBRange, FALSE);
PreviousPosition.x = 0;
PreviousPosition.y = 0;
}
```

MoveControl

MoveControl, shown in Listing 6.3, is a callback function that is called itera-tively—once for every child control in the dialog box. It is passed the num-ber of pixels that each control must be moved in the LPARAM parameter. To calculate the new position for each control, MoveControl uses GetWindowRect to obtain the current screen coordinates of the control. It then uses ScreenToClient with the parent window of the control—the dialog window itself—to convert from screen coordinates to client coordinates. MoveWindow is then called to move the child window. Finally, MoveControl returns 1, which allows the iteration to continue through all the child windows.

LISTING 6.3. The `MoveControl` callback function.

```
BOOL CALLBACK _export WEmpAppDialog::MoveControl
                        (HWND hWnd, LPARAM lp)
{
    POINT *ps = (POINT *) lp;
    RECT CurrentPos;
    POINT WindowPos;

    GetWindowRect (hWnd, &CurrentPos);   // In screen coordinates
    WindowPos.x = CurrentPos.left;
    WindowPos.y = CurrentPos.top;
    // Convert to client coordinates
    ScreenToClient (GetParent (hWnd), &WindowPos);

    MoveWindow
        (
            hWnd,
            WindowPos.x - ps->x,   // New x
            WindowPos.y - ps->y,   // New y
            CurrentPos.right - CurrentPos.left,   // Width
            CurrentPos.bottom - CurrentPos.top,   // Height
            FALSE  // Don't bother redrawing now
        );
    return 1;
}
```

WMVScroll

The WMVScroll function, included in Listing 6.4, uses GetScrollPos to determine the current position of the scroll bar, then it adjusts this position
based on the user's action. If the new position would be out of range (for
example, if the down-arrow button is selected from the bottom of the
range), the position is adjusted to equal the maximum or minimum al-
lowed value. The scroll bar thumb track (the small square) is set to the
proper location using SetScrollPos, and the PositionOffset structure is initialized with the number of pixels that each control must be moved in the
x and y directions. EnumChildWindows is then used to enumerate through all
child windows, calling MoveControl for each window. Finally, the dialog box
is invalidated to force it to redraw with the controls in the new position.
Listing 6.5 shows the CHPT6.CPP file listing.

LISTING 6.4. WEMPAPPD.CPP file listing.

```cpp
// WEMpAPPDIALOG.CPP - Source file for WEmpAppDialog class

#include "WEmpAppDialog.h"  // ALL other #include statements
                            // are in this file

//*****************************************************
// Constructors and destructors for WEmpAppDialog
//
//    Copyright:
//            Copyright (c) 1993, William H. Roetzheim
//            All Rights Reserved
//
//*****************************************************

WEmpAppDialog::WEmpAppDialog (PTWindowsObject Parent,
                                   LPSTR szDialog,
                                   PTModule Module = NULL) :
    TDialog (Parent, szDialog, Module)
{
    return;
}



//*****************************************************
// Member functions for class
//
//    Copyright:
//            Copyright (c) 1993, William H. Roetzheim
//            All Rights Reserved
//
//*****************************************************

void WEmpAppDialog::SetupWindow ()
{
    TDialog::SetupWindow();

    RECT OriginalClientRect;  // Dialog client rect
    RECT Screen;              // Full display screen
    RECT OriginalDialog;      // Dialog complete area

    GetClientRect (HWindow, &OriginalClientRect);
    GetClientRect (GetDesktopWindow(), &Screen);

     // Determine new size of the dialog box
    GetWindowRect (HWindow, &OriginalDialog);
```

continues

LISTING 6.4. continued

```
    int Width = OriginalDialog.right - OriginalDialog.left;
    int height = OriginalDialog.bottom - OriginalDialog.top;

    // See if dialog is too large. 50 is arbitrary for aesthetics.
    if (Width > (Screen.right - 50)) Width = Screen.right - 50;
    if (height > (Screen.bottom - 50)) height = Screen.bottom - 50;

    // Move and resize the dialog
    MoveWindow
        (
            HWindow,
            (Screen.right - Width) / 2,     // Left
            (Screen.bottom - height) / 2,   // Top
            Width,
            height,
            TRUE  // Redraw
        );

    // Initialize the scroll bar(s)
    VertSBRange = OriginalClientRect.bottom - height + 50;
    SetScrollRange (HWindow, SB_VERT, 0,
        VertSBRange, FALSE);
    PreviousPosition.x = 0;
    PreviousPosition.y = 0;
}


BOOL CALLBACK _export WEmpAppDialog::MoveControl (HWND hWnd,
                                                  LPARAM lp)
{
    POINT *ps = (POINT *) lp;
    RECT CurrentPos;
    POINT WindowPos;

    GetWindowRect (hWnd, &CurrentPos);  // In screen coordinates
    WindowPos.x = CurrentPos.left;
    WindowPos.y = CurrentPos.top;
    // Convert to client coordinates
    ScreenToClient (GetParent (hWnd), &WindowPos);

    MoveWindow
        (
            hWnd,
            WindowPos.x - ps->x,  // New x
            WindowPos.y - ps->y,  // New y
```

```
                    CurrentPos.right - CurrentPos.left,  // Width
                    CurrentPos.bottom - CurrentPos.top,  // Height
                    FALSE  // Don't bother redrawing now
            );
        return 1;
}


void WEmpAppDialog::WMVScroll (RTMessage Msg)
{
    TDialog::WMVScroll (Msg);

    int Vertical = GetScrollPos (HWindow, SB_VERT);

    switch (Msg.WParam)
    {
        case SB_BOTTOM:
            Vertical = VertSBRange;
          break;

        case SB_LINEDOWN:
            Vertical += 5;
            break;

        case SB_LINEUP:
            Vertical -= 5;
          break;

        case SB_PAGEDOWN:
            Vertical += 100;
            break;

        case SB_PAGEUP:
            Vertical -= 100;
          break;

        case SB_THUMBPOSITION:
            Vertical = Msg.LP.Lo;
          break;

        case SB_TOP:
            Vertical = 0;
            break;
    }
    if (Vertical > VertSBRange) Vertical = VertSBRange;
    if (Vertical < 0) Vertical = 0;
```

continues

LISTING 6.4. continued

```
    if (Vertical != GetScrollPos (HWindow, SB_VERT))
    {
          SetScrollPos (HWindow, SB_VERT, Vertical, TRUE);

          //Scroll the dialog box itself

          PositionOffset.x = 0;   // Haven't implemented horiz scroll
          PositionOffset.y = Vertical - PreviousPosition.y;
          PreviousPosition.y = Vertical;   // x is unused

          EnumChildWindows (HWindow, MoveControl,
                               (LPARAM) &PositionOffset);
          InvalidateRect (HWindow, NULL, TRUE);
    }

}
```

LISTING 6.5. CHPT6.CPP file listing.

```
#define          _CLASSDLL
#define     WIN31
#define     STRICT
#include    <owl.h>
#include    "WEmpAppD.h"


//******************************************************
// chpt6 - chpt6 application class
//
//     Purpose:
//          This class is the overall application
//          executive for chpt6.
//
//     Notes:
//          None
//
//     Copyright:
//          Copyright (c) 1993, William H. Roetzheim
//          All Rights Reserved
//
//******************************************************
```

```
_CLASSDEF (chpt6)
class chpt6 : public TApplication
{
    public:
        // Public member functions ******************
        // Constructors and destructors
        chpt6 (LPSTR szName, HINSTANCE hInstance,
                HINSTANCE hPrevInstance, LPSTR lpCmdLine,
                int nCmdShow);

        // Member functions
        virtual void InitMainWindow ();
};


//****************************************************
// Constructors and destructors for chpt6
//
//      Copyright:
//              Copyright (c) 1993, William H. Roetzheim
//              All Rights Reserved
//
//****************************************************

#pragma argsused  // Turn off arguments not used warning
chpt6::chpt6(LPSTR szName, HINSTANCE hInstance,
            HINSTANCE hPrevInstance, LPSTR lpCmdLine,
            int nCmdShow)
            : TApplication (szName, hInstance,
            hPrevInstance, lpCmdLine, nCmdShow)
{
    return;
}




//****************************************************
// Member functions for class chpt6
//
//      Copyright:
//              Copyright (c) 1993, William H. Roetzheim
//              All Rights Reserved
//
//****************************************************

void chpt6::InitMainWindow ()
```

continues

LISTING 6.5. continued

```
{
    MainWindow = new WEmpAppDialog (NULL, "EmpApp", this);
}



// Here is the main () for the program
int PASCAL WinMain (HINSTANCE hInstance,
    HINSTANCE hPrevInstance, LPSTR lpCmdLine,
    int)
{
    // Ensure that BWCC dynamic link library is loaded
    HINSTANCE hDLL = LoadLibrary ("BWCC.DLL");

    // Create chpt6 application from class
    chpt6 ochpt6 ("chpt6", hInstance,
                    hPrevInstance, lpCmdLine, SW_NORMAL);

    // Start created application running
    ochpt6.Run ();   // Runs till window closed

    // Free the BWCC dynamic link library
    if (hDLL>31) FreeLibrary (hDLL);

    // Return termination status when window closed
    return ochpt6.Status;
}
```

CHAPTER

7

Interfacing with Paradox

Problem

You've started designing your application, and you realize that a database management system is in order. Your users will need the ability to write custom reports, and you certainly don't have the time or inclination to develop custom report capability yourself. You consider something powerful like Oracle, but the runtime royalties can't be justified for your application. Royalty-free database management code that can be incorporated into your code is available, but the interactive reporting tools aren't. What you need is the ability to tie your code into a popular, low-end database management system. You want your software to operate properly and free of royalties, yet you want your users to be able to purchase a low-end product easily and economically if they require custom reports or other user interaction with the database.

Solution

Borland's Paradox DBMS, combined with the Paradox Engine, gives you exactly what you're looking for. Paradox is a low-end database management system that is very popular in the PC marketplace. Low-end DBMSs generally are inexpensive and relatively easy to use. Examples include Paradox, FoxPRO, and dBASE. High-end DBMSs are more expensive and more difficult to use, but they offer more features and support more hardware and operating systems. Examples include Oracle, Informix, and Sybase. Paradox is a relational DBMS that includes features such as network support, password protection using encryption, binary large objects (BLOBs), multiple indexes, and composite indexes. Paradox comes with the Paradox Application Language (PAL), which end-users can use to write custom reports (as well as perform other database interaction). The only significant drawback of Paradox is its lack of support for the industry standard SQL. (I cover access to SQL servers in the Chapter 8, "Using Windows with SQL Databases in Client-Server Architecture.")

The Paradox Engine is an API containing more than 90 functions accessible from a C, C++, or Pascal program. The Engine enables you to create database tables and indexes and to perform all database-related operations—such as `find`, `read`, and `write`—on tables. The Engine provides functions that convert data between Paradox internal data formats and ASCII. Higher-level functions, such as report writing, are not included in the Paradox Engine, but Paradox itself can be used instead. The Paradox Engine is implemented as a DLL that can be distributed royalty-free. Of course, users who need Paradox itself must purchase the software.

Although I provide a set of simple C++ classes to demonstrate the use of the Paradox Engine in a C++ environment, you should use the Borland Paradox Application Framework classes for most real-world applications.

Figure 7.1 shows a simple application that uses the Paradox objects defined in this chapter. This application is on the source disk in the file CHPT7.EXE. You must install SHARE.EXE before running this application. You also must copy the files PARADOX.DLL, PXENGWIN.DLL, and VIDEO.DB from the source disk to your hard disk. PARADOX.DLL is my own object-oriented version of the Engine (developed in this chapter). PXENGWIN.DLL is the Paradox Engine DLL supplied by Borland. This file should be distributed royalty-free with your applications. The file VIDEO.DB is the Paradox database file.

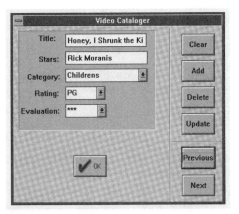

Figure 7.1. A sample Paradox application.

Paradox names all files that are related to a table with the name of the table and a file type specific extension. Table 7.1 shows the relationship between Paradox database file extensions and file type. (Not all types are required by the Video application.) The sample application is a program that catalogs a videotape collection. The chpt7 application relies on the

Paradox Engine for all database-related activities. It is important to recognize that the files produced by the Paradox classes described in this chapter—and, ultimately, by the Engine itself—are completely compatible with Paradox. For example, you could write a PAL report that accesses the Video database.

TABLE 7.1. Paradox filename extensions.

Extension	Description
.DB	Table
.F or .F??	Form
.G	Graph specification
.R or .R??	Report format
.SET	Image settings
.VAL	Validity checks
.PX	Primary index
.X?? or .Y??	Secondary indexes
.MB	Master BLOB file

INT: The Paradox Engine comes with a utility called PXENGCFG.EXE that enables you to modify the Window initialization parameters stored in WIN.INI. These parameters are used by the Paradox DLL. You can configure the Paradox network control file path; this file needs to be located on the server. Other configurable parameters are swap buffer size and the maximum number of open tables, open files, record buffers, and record locks per table.

Paradox Class Overview

I've encapsulated the core Paradox Engine functionality into three classes. The `WParadoxEngine` class is used to initialize, control, and shut down the Paradox Engine itself. A valid `WParadoxEngine` object must exist in order for the remaining objects to function properly. The `WParadoxTable` encapsulates the core capabilities of a Paradox table. The `WParadoxRecord` class represents a single record, or a *tuple*, within a Paradox table. To support BLOBs, you need to define a `WBlob` class yourself. Tables 7.2, 7.3, and 7.4 summarize the data members and member functions of each of these objects.

TABLE 7.2. `WParadoxEngine` **data member.**

Data Member

Name	Access	Description
Status	Public	Status of Engine; 0 = OK

TABLE 7.3. `WParadoxTable` **data members and member functions.**

Data Members

Name	Access	Description
Status	Public	Status of table; 0 = OK
Record	Public	Pointer to `WParadoxRecord`, a buffer used to store a single table row (tuple)
HTable	Public	Paradox table handle for this table

continues

TABLE 7.3. continued

Member Functions

Name	Access	Description
DeleteAll	Public	Deletes all records in the database
TotalRecords	Public	Returns the total number of records in the table
CurrentRecord	Public	Returns the internal pointer indicating the current table record
RecordUpdate	Public	Copies the record buffer into the database as an update of the current record
RecordDelete	Public	Deletes the current record
RecordAdd	Public	Adds the record buffer to the database. (The record is appended if the database doesn't have a primary key that requires the database to be kept in sorted order.)
ReadFirst	Public	Moves the database pointer to the first record and reads the record into the record buffer
ReadLast	Public	Moves the database pointer to the last record and reads the record into the record buffer
ReadNext	Public	Moves the database pointer to the next record and reads the record into the record buffer

Name	Access	Description
ReadPrev	Public	Moves the database pointer to the previous record and reads the record into the record buffer
ReadRecord	Public	Moves the database pointer to a specified record and reads the record into the record buffer
IndexDelete	Public	Deletes the index from a specified field
IndexAdd	Public	Adds an index for a specified field
Find	Public	Finds the first database record that matches specified criteria

TABLE 7.4. WParadoxRecord **data members and member functions.**

Data Members

Name	Access	Description
ParentTable	Public	Pointer to the WParadoxTable object that owns this record object
HRecord	Public	Paradox record handle for this record
Status	Public	Status of this record; (0 = OK)

continues

TABLE 7.4. continued

Member Functions

Name	Access	Description
RawGet	Public	Does a raw copy of the data in this record buffer to the specified memory location
RawPut	Public	Does a raw copy of the data in a specified memory location to the record buffer
GetField	Public	Returns the contents of a specified field from this record buffer
PutField	Public	Puts data into a specified field in this record buffer
Update	Public	Copies data from the record buffer over the existing data at the current database location
Add	Public	Adds data from the record buffer to the database. (Either appended for databases with no primary key or inserted if a primary key is present.)
Read	Public	Reads the data from the current location in the database into the record buffer

Before I describe these three classes in detail, I demonstrate them by using the chpt7 sample program.

The *chpt7* Application

Table 7.5 describes the files you must have in order to compile the `chpt7` sample application. The file CHPT7.CPP, shown in Listing 7.1, is virtually identical to the code you saw in earlier chapters, with the addition of one line to load the Paradox DLL and another to free the DLL. The Paradox DLL referred to here is the object-oriented version of the Engine I've developed in this chapter. My code forces the Paradox Engine DLL itself, called PXENGWIN.DLL, to load.

TABLE 7.5. `chpt7` sample application files.

File	Description
CHPT7.CPP	Source file for the `chpt7` main application
WVIDEODI.H and WVIDEODI.CPP	Header and source files for the dialog handler that encapsulates all functionality specific to the video application
WPARADOX.H	Header file that loads other header files required for my object-oriented version of the Paradox Engine
WPDOXENG.H, WPDOXTAB.H, and WPDOXREC.H	Header files for my classes that encapsulate the Paradox Engine itself, a Paradox table, and a Paradox record
CHPT7.RC	Resource file containing the video application dialog box, which also serves as the application's main window

continues

TABLE 7.5. continued

File	Description
PARADOX.LIB	Library file for my object-oriented version of Paradox
WPARADOX.DLL	DLL for my object-oriented version of Paradox
PXENGWIN.DLL	Borland's DLL of the actual Paradox Engine
DVIDEO.H	Header file containing symbolic #defines for controls in the video dialog box

LISTING 7.1. CHPT7.CPP source code listing.

```
#define      _CLASSDLL
#define   WIN31
#define   STRICT
#include  <owl.h>
#include  "DVideo.h"
#include  "WVideoDialog.h"


//*****************************************************
// chpt7 - chpt7 application class
//
//    Purpose:
//        This class is the overall application
//        executive for chpt7.
//
//    Notes:
//        None
//
//    Copyright:
//            Copyright (c) 1993, William H. Roetzheim
//            All Rights Reserved
//
//*****************************************************
```

```
_CLASSDEF (chpt7)
class chpt7 : public TApplication
{
    public:
        // Public member functions *****************
        // Constructors and destructors
        chpt7 (LPSTR szName, HINSTANCE hInstance,
                HINSTANCE hPrevInstance, LPSTR lpCmdLine,
                int nCmdShow);

        // Member functions
        virtual void InitMainWindow ();
};


//****************************************************
// Constructors and destructors for chpt7
//
//     Copyright:
//              Copyright (c) 1993, William H. Roetzheim
//              All Rights Reserved
//
//****************************************************

#pragma argsused  // Turn off arguments not used warning
chpt7::chpt7(LPSTR szName, HINSTANCE hInstance,
            HINSTANCE hPrevInstance, LPSTR lpCmdLine,
            int nCmdShow)
            : TApplication (szName, hInstance,
            hPrevInstance, lpCmdLine, nCmdShow)
{
    return;
}




//****************************************************
// Member functions for class chpt7
//
//     Copyright:
//              Copyright (c) 1993, William H. Roetzheim
//              All Rights Reserved
//
//****************************************************

void chpt7::InitMainWindow ()
{
```

continues

LISTING 7.1. continued

```
    MainWindow = new WVideoDialog (NULL, "VideoDialog", this);
}



// Here is the main () for the program
int PASCAL WinMain (HINSTANCE hInstance,
    HINSTANCE hPrevInstance, LPSTR lpCmdLine,
    int)
{
    // Ensure that the dynamic link libraries are loaded
    HINSTANCE hBWCCDLL = LoadLibrary ("BWCC.DLL");
   HINSTANCE hParadoxDLL = LoadLibrary ("Paradox.DLL");

    // Create chpt7 application from class
    chpt7 ochpt7 ("chpt7", hInstance,
                    hPrevInstance, lpCmdLine, SW_NORMAL);

    // Start created application running
    ochpt7.Run ();  // Runs till window closed

    // Free the BWCC dynamic link library
    if (hBWCCDLL) FreeLibrary (hBWCCDLL);
   if (hParadoxDLL) FreeLibrary (hParadoxDLL);

    // Return termination status when window closed
    return ochpt7.Status;
}
```

The code to handle the actual video dialog box (see Listings 7.2 and 7.3) is more interesting. First, the constructor creates an OWL object for each control in the dialog box I'll be dealing with. Then, I create a new `WParadoxTable` object to represent the relational table that will be used to store data from the Video application. For existing tables that are opened using the primary index only—if one is present—you pass just the table name to the constructor.

If you want, you can add the index to use (use 0 for primary) and initialization data. If the initialization data is present, the `WParadoxTable` constructor creates a table if one doesn't already exist. The initialization data consists of the number of fields in the table, the name of each field, and the type for each field. Valid field types are shown in Table 7.6.

TABLE 7.6. Valid Paradox field types.

Type	Storage Size in Bytes	Description
N	8	Floating-point number with 15 significant digits in the range of $\pm 10^{-307}$ to $\pm 10^{308}$. (More than 15 significant digits are rounded and stored in scientific notation.)
S	2	Integer in the range of –32,767 to 32,767
$	8	Same as floating-point, but fixed at two digits to the right of the decimal. (Used to represent currency.)
D	4	The date (stored internally as the number of days since 01/01/100, and valid through 12/31/9999)
A*nnn*	1 to 255	NULL-terminated string of length *nnn*, where *nnn* is ≤ 255.
M*n*	*n* + 10, where *n* is in the range of 0 to 240	Unformatted text BLOB. (The parameter *n* represents BLOB-related header information, and the actual data is stored in a separate file pointed to by the filename stored in Paradox.)
B*n*	*n* + 10, where *n* is in the range of 0 to 240	Same as the preceding, but for unformatted binary information
F*n*	*n* + 10, where *n* is in the range of 0 to 240	Same as the preceding, but for formatted text
O*n*	*n* + 10, where *n* is in the range of 0 to 240	Same as the preceding, but for Windows OLE objects
G*n*	*n* + 10, where *n* is in the range of 0 to 240	Same as the preceding, but for graphics data

The `SetupWindow` function initializes the three combo boxes with the appropriate values. I then call the `RecordToDialog` function, which is defined later in this file. `RecordToDialog` moves the data from the record buffer that is initialized by the `VideoTable` object to the dialog box itself. `DialogToRecord` is a sister function to move data from the dialog box fields to the record buffer.

`Reset` is a helper function that is used simply to clear the fields on the dialog box. The record buffer and the data in the database are not affected. The edit controls are cleared by calling their `Clear` function. The combo box controls are cleared by setting their current selection to invalid (–1).

The `Add`, `Delete`, `Update`, `Next`, and `Previous` functions move data between the dialog box fields, the record buffer, and the database itself. `DialogToRecord` or `RecordToDialog` is called, as appropriate, to move data between the dialog box and the record buffer. Then, the appropriate function of the `WParadoxTable` class is called to move data between the record buffer and the database itself. Finally, for many functions the `Reset` function is called to clear the dialog box fields.

The `DialogToRecord` function reads each dialog field, then uses the `WParadoxRecord` class `PutField` function to copy the string into the record buffer. The `RecordToDialog` function uses the `WParadoxRecord` class `GetField` function to obtain a string from the record buffer, then uses `SetWindowText` (edit controls) or `SetSelString` (combo box controls) to initialize the dialog box fields. Listings 7.2 and 7.3 contain the header file and source code for these functions.

LISTING 7.2. WVIDEODIALOG.H header listing.

```
// WVIDEODIALOG.H - Header file for WVideoDialog class

#ifndef WVideoDialog_H
#     define WVideoDialog_H

// Note that the following code is executed only
// if this file has not been previously included


// #include files for both PC and SUN
#include  "WStr.h"
#include  "DVideo.h"
```

```
#include   "WParadox.h"

#ifdef __BORLANDC__
    // PC-specific #includes
#    include   <owl.h>
#    include <edit.h>
#    include <combobox.h>

#endif

#ifdef Unix
    // UNIX-specific #includes

#endif



//*****************************************************
// WVideoDialog - Handler for Video dialog box
//
//    Purpose:
//        Demonstrates the use of Paradox from a dialog
//        handling class.
//
//    Notes:
//
//    Copyright:
//            Copyright (c) 1993, William H. Roetzheim
//            All Rights Reserved
//
//*****************************************************

_CLASSDEF (WVideoDialog)
class WVideoDialog : public TDialog
{
    private:
        // Private data members *******************
        PTEdit Title;
        PTEdit Stars;
        PTComboBox Category;
        PTComboBox Rating;
        PTComboBox Evaluation;
        PWParadoxTable VideoTable;
        int  nFields;
        LPSTR Names[5];
        LPSTR Types[5];
```

continues

LISTING 7.2. continued

```
                // Private member functions ****************
                virtual void DialogToRecord ();
            virtual void RecordToDialog ();

    public:
                // Public data members ********************


                // Public member functions ****************
                // Constructors and destructors
                WVideoDialog (PTWindowsObject, LPSTR, PTModule);
            ~WVideoDialog ();

                // Member functions
                virtual void SetupWindow ();
                virtual void Reset () =
                    [ID_FIRST + IDD_Clear];
                virtual void Add () =
                    [ID_FIRST + IDD_Add];
                virtual void Delete () =
                    [ID_FIRST + IDD_Delete];
                virtual void Update() =
                    [ID_FIRST + IDD_Update];
                virtual void Next () =
                    [ID_FIRST + IDD_Next];
                virtual void Previous () =
                    [ID_FIRST + IDD_Previous];
    };


#endif WVideoDialog_H
```

LISTING 7.3. WVIDEODIALOG.CPP source code listing.

```
// WVIDEODIALOG.CPP - Source file for WVideoDialog class

#include "WVideoDialog.h"  // ALL other #include statements
                           // are in this file

//****************************************************
// Constructors and destructors for WVideoDialog
//
//      Copyright:
```

```
//              Copyright (c) 1993, William H. Roetzheim
//              All Rights Reserved
//
//*****************************************************

WVideoDialog::WVideoDialog (PTWindowsObject Parent,
              LPSTR Name, PTModule Module)
          : TDialog (Parent, Name, Module)
{
    Title = new TEdit (this, IDD_Title, 35, Module);
    Stars = new TEdit (this, IDD_Stars, 76, Module);
    Category = new TComboBox (this, IDD_Category, 21, Module);
    Rating = new TComboBox (this, IDD_Rating, 6, Module);
    Evaluation = new TComboBox (this, IDD_Evaluation, 6, Module);


    nFields = 5;
    Names[0] = "Title";
    Names[1] = "Stars";
    Names[2] = "Category";
    Names[3] = "Rating";
    Names[4] = "Evaluation";
    Types[0] = "A35";
    Types[1] = "A76";
    Types[2] = "A21";
    Types[3] = "A6";
  Types[4] = "A6";

    VideoTable = new WParadoxTable ("Video", 0, nFields,
    Names, Types);

    if (VideoTable->Status != 0)
    {
        MessageBox (NULL, GetParadoxError (VideoTable->Status),
                    "WVideoDialog", MB_OK);
        Destroy ();
    }

}



WVideoDialog::~WVideoDialog ()
{

    delete VideoTable;

}
```

continues

183

LISTING 7.3. continued

```
//****************************************************
// Member functions for class
//
//     Copyright:
//             Copyright (c) 1993, William H. Roetzheim
//             All Rights Reserved
//
//****************************************************

void WVideoDialog::SetupWindow ()
{
    TDialog::SetupWindow ();

    // Initialize combo boxes
    char *Categories [] =
        {
            "Action/Adventure",
            "Childrens",
            "Comedy",
            "Drama",
            "Home Movie",
            "Horror",
            "Musical",
            "Science Fiction",
            "Western",
            ""
        };
    char *Ratings [] =
        {
            "G",
            "PG",
            "PG 13",
            "R",
            "X",
            ""
        };
    char *Evaluations [] =
        {
            "*",
            "**",
            "***",
            "****",
            "*****",
            ""
        };
```

```
        int i = 0;
        while (Categories [i][0] != 0)
            Category->AddString (Categories [i++]);
        i = 0;
        while (Ratings [i][0] != 0)
            Rating->AddString (Ratings [i++]);
        i = 0;
        while (Evaluations [i][0] != 0)
            Evaluation->AddString (Evaluations [i++]);

        RecordToDialog ();
}


void WVideoDialog::Reset ()
{

        Title->Clear();
        Stars->Clear();
        Category->SetSelIndex (-1);
        Rating->SetSelIndex (-1);
        Evaluation->SetSelIndex (-1);

}


void WVideoDialog::Add ()
{
        DialogToRecord ();
        VideoTable->RecordAdd ();
        Reset ();
}


void WVideoDialog::Delete ()
{
        VideoTable->RecordDelete ();
        Reset ();
}


void WVideoDialog::Update ()
{
        DialogToRecord ();
        VideoTable->RecordUpdate ();
        Reset ();
}
```

continues

LISTING 7.3. continued

```
void WVideoDialog::Next ()
{
    VideoTable->ReadNext ();
    RecordToDialog ();
}


void WVideoDialog::Previous ()
{
    VideoTable->ReadPrev ();
    RecordToDialog ();
}


void WVideoDialog::DialogToRecord ()
{

    int i;
    char Buffer [76];
    for (i = 0; i < nFields; i++)
    {
        GetWindowText
        (
            GetItemHandle (IDD_Title + i),
            Buffer,
            76
        );

        VideoTable->Record->PutField (Names [i], (WStr) Buffer);
    }

}


void WVideoDialog::RecordToDialog ()
{

    int i;
    WStr Buffer;
    for (i = 0; i < nFields; i++)
    {
        Buffer = VideoTable->Record->GetField (Names [i]);
        switch (IDD_Title + i)
        {
```

```
            case IDD_Title:
            case IDD_Stars:
                SetWindowText
                (
                        GetItemHandle (IDD_Title + i),
                        (char *) Buffer
                );
             break;

            case IDD_Category:
                Category->SetSelString ((char *) Buffer, -1);
                break;

            case IDD_Rating:
                Rating->SetSelString ((char *) Buffer, -1);
                break;

            case IDD_Evaluation:
                Evaluation->SetSelString ((char *) Buffer, -1);
             break;
        }
    }
}
```

The WParadox DLL

The WParadox DLL consists of DLL-specific header and source files (see
Listings 7.4 and 7.5), along with the files that make up the WParadoxEngine,
WParadoxTable, and WParadoxRecord classes. The WParadox header file is used
to include other header files. It defines the prototype for a function called
GetParadoxError, which takes a class Status variable (from the
WParadoxEngine, WParadoxTable, or WParadoxRecord classes) that represents
an error condition (some value other than 0) and returns a string representing the error condition. The possible error conditions and their
representative strings are included at the end of this chapter. They match
the error codes used internally by the Paradox Engine itself.

Most of the code in WPARADOX.CPP deals with defining a Windows
3.1-compatible TModule class, as discussed in Chapter 4, "Implementing
Custom Controls." The GetParadoxError function is exported so that it can
be used by calling applications. Code to initialize the Paradox Engine was

added to the `LibMain` function so that it is called every time the DLL is loaded. This approach is simple, and it guarantees that the Paradox Engine will be initialized before any of my Paradox objects are accessed. One disadvantage of this approach is that the Engine is always initialized with the same string (`ParadoxDLL`), as opposed to the name of a specific application. (This string is displayed to the user during file conflicts.) The other disadvantage is that if the Engine is unloaded for any reason other than the DLL's being unloaded (for example, if an error is encountered), the DLL must be removed from memory. An alternative approach is to remove the code so that you can initialize the Paradox Engine from the DLL `LibMain` procedure and require that any application using the Engine create a `ParadoxEngine` object itself.

HINT: Notice that the dynamic memory allocated in `LibMain` by the DLL is not freed. At first, you might think you should implement a WEP function to perform this function. (Recall that a WEP function in a DLL is where exit code is placed.) In fact, however, dynamically allocated memory within a DLL is automatically freed by Windows when the DLL is unloaded. Therefore, this code is not necessary.

LISTING 7.4. WPARADOX.H header listing.

```
#ifndef WPARADOX_H
#    define WPARADOX_H
#    include <alloc.h>
#    include <string.h>
#    include "WPdoxEngine.h"
#    include "WPdoxTable.h"
#    include "WPdoxRecord.h"

char *GetParadoxError (int nError);
#endif
```

LISTING 7.5. WPARADOX.CPP source code listing.

```
// WPARADOX.DLL - Source file for Paradox support DLL

#include "WParadox.h"  // ALL other #include statements
                       // are in this file


// Create place to store pointer to Paradox Engine
PWParadoxEngine ParadoxEngine;

// Create place to store new instance to represent this DLL


// We need to create a derived class from TModule to
// support proper memory allocation if multiple applications
// are simultaneously using our DLL.

_CLASSDEF (TDLLModule)
class TDLLModule : public TModule
{
    public:
        TDLLModule (LPSTR, HMODULE, LPSTR);
        ~TDLLModule ();
        void *operator new (unsigned);
        void operator delete (void *);
};

#pragma argsused

TDLLModule::TDLLModule (LPSTR n, HMODULE m, LPSTR Command)
    : TModule (n, m, Command)
{
    // Free the TModule constructor allocated memory
    farfree (lpCmdLine);
    if (Command)
    {
        lpCmdLine = (LPSTR) (void *) LocalAlloc (LPTR,
                                         strlen (Command) + 1);
        strcpy (lpCmdLine, Command);
    }
    else
    {
        lpCmdLine = (LPSTR) (void *) LocalAlloc (LPTR, 1);
        lpCmdLine[0] = 0;
    }
}
```

continues

LISTING 7.5. continued

```
TDLLModule::~TDLLModule ()
{
    LocalFree ((HLOCAL) FP_OFF (lpCmdLine));
    lpCmdLine = NULL;
}

void *TDLLModule::operator new (unsigned n)
{
    return (void *) LocalAlloc (LPTR, n);
}

void TDLLModule::operator delete (void *p)
{
    LocalFree ((HLOCAL) FP_OFF (p));
}

PTDLLModule DLLModule;


LPSTR _export GetParadoxError (int nError)
{
    return PXErrMsg (nError);
}


// Must include definition for LibMain function
// for all DLLs
int FAR PASCAL LibMain (HINSTANCE hInstance,
                        WORD /* DataSeg */,
                        WORD /* HeapSize */,
                        LPSTR lpCmdLine)
{
    DLLModule = new TDLLModule ("DLLModule", hInstance,
        lpCmdLine);

    if (DLLModule->Status != 0)
    {
        delete DLLModule;
        DLLModule = NULL;
      MessageBeep (0);
      return 0;
    }
    else
    {
```

```
            // Start Paradox Engine
            ParadoxEngine = new WParadoxEngine ("ParadoxDLL");
            if (ParadoxEngine->Status != 0)
            {
                MessageBox (NULL, PXErrMsg (ParadoxEngine->Status),
                            "LibMain", MB_OK);
                return 0;
            }
        else return 1;   // Success
    }
}
```

The *WParadoxEngine* Class

The WParadoxEngine class code, shown in Listings 7.6 and 7.7, is very simple. It initializes the Engine in its constructor and shuts down the Engine in its destructor. A static variable called Status is used to let applications know the status of the Engine. Status is set to 0 when the Engine is initialized properly, to –1 when the Engine is not initialized, or to a positive error code when an error is encountered while the WParadoxEngine class tries to initialize the Engine. The Status data member is static so that it can be accessed by any object that needs to know the current state of the Engine. It is accurate even when no WParadoxEngine object has been created yet. Notice how the storage for the Status data member is allocated:

```
int WParadoxEngine::Status = -1;
```

LISTING 7.6. WPARADOXENGINE.H header file.

```
// WPARADOXENGINE.H - Header file for WParadoxEngine class

#ifndef WParadoxEngine_H
#     define WParadoxEngine_H

// Note that the following code is executed only
// if this file has not been previously included


// #include files for both PC and SUN
```

continues

LISTING 7.6. continued

```c
#include "pxengine.h"

#ifdef __BORLANDC__
    // PC-specific #includes
#    include    <owl.h>

#endif

#ifdef Unix
    // UNIX-specific #includes

#endif

//*****************************************************
// WParadoxEngine - Initialize and control Paradox
//                        Engine
//
//     Notes:
//         None
//
//     Copyright:
//             Copyright (c) 1993, William H. Roetzheim
//             All Rights Reserved
//
//*****************************************************

_CLASSDEF (WParadoxEngine)
class WParadoxEngine
{
    public:
            // Public data members ********************
        static int Status;


            // Public member functions ****************
            // Constructors and destructors
            WParadoxEngine (LPSTR szApplication);
            ~WParadoxEngine ();
};

#endif WParadoxEngine_H
```

LISTING 7.7. WPARADOXENGINE.CPP source code file.

```cpp
// WPARADOXENGINE.CPP - Source file for WParadoxEngine class

#include "WPdoxEngine.h"   // ALL other #include statements
                           // are in this file


// Initialize static data member
int WParadoxEngine::Status = -1;  // Anything but zero is invalid

//****************************************************
// Constructors and destructors for WParadoxEngine
//
//     Copyright:
//             Copyright (c) 1993, William H. Roetzheim
//             All Rights Reserved
//
//****************************************************

WParadoxEngine::WParadoxEngine (LPSTR szApplication)
{
    Status = PXWinInit (szApplication, PXSHARED);
    if (Status != 0)
    {
      MessageBox (NULL,
      PXErrMsg (Status),
      "WParadoxEngine",
      MB_OK);
      return;
    }
    PXTblCreateMode (PARADOX40);
}


WParadoxEngine::~WParadoxEngine ()
{
    Status = -1;  // Paradox Engine is deactivated
    PXExit ();
}
```

The *WParadoxTable* Class

Listings 7.8 and 7.9 show the code that implements the WParadoxTable class. The constructor checks the Paradox Engine status to ensure that it is loaded, then attempts to open the specified table. If the open attempt fails, and table specification data was included in the parameter list, the constructor attempts to create a new table. After a table is opened successfully, a record buffer (a WParadoxRecord object) is created and initialized to the first record in the database. For newly created databases, attempting to read the first record causes an error (because the record is nonexistent). The error is harmless, but it can be avoided either by adding code to test for this possibility or by initializing a dummy blank record in the newly created database. The rest of the member function code is straightforward. It often maps directly to two or three Paradox Engine function calls.

HINT: Be sure to test for a table's existence before you attempt to create a new table. If you create a new table, and a table with the same name already exists, the existing table is deleted without warning.

LISTING 7.8. WPARADOXTABLE.H header listing.

```
// WPARADOXTABLE.H - Header file for WParadoxTable class

#ifndef WParadoxTable_H
#    define WParadoxTable_H

// Note that the following code is executed only
// if this file has not been previously included


// #include files for both PC and SUN
#include   <DIR.H>
#include   "WStr.h"
#include   "pxengine.h"
#include   "WPdoxEngine.h"
#include   "WPdoxRecord.h"
```

```
#ifdef __BORLANDC__
     // PC-specific #includes
#     include   <owl.h>

#endif

#ifdef Unix
     // UNIX-specific #includes

#endif



//****************************************************
// WParadoxTable - Encapsulate a Paradox relational
//                      Table
//
//     Notes:
//         None
//
//     Copyright:
//            Copyright (c) 1993, William H. Roetzheim
//            All Rights Reserved
//
//****************************************************


_CLASSDEF (WParadoxTable)
class WParadoxTable
{
     public:
          // Public data members ********************
          int   Status;
        PWParadoxRecord   Record;
          TABLEHANDLE HTable;


          // Public member functions ****************
          // Constructors and destructors
          WParadoxTable (LPSTR TableName,
                              int IndexField = 0,
                              int nFields = 0,
                              char *Names[] = NULL,
                      char *Types[] = NULL);
          ~WParadoxTable ();

          // Member functions
          void DeleteAll ();
```

continues

LISTING 7.8. continued

```
            RECORDNUMBER TotalRecords ();
            RECORDNUMBER CurrentRecord ();

        void RecordUpdate ();
          void RecordDelete ();
          void RecordAdd ();

          void ReadFirst ();
          void ReadLast ();
          void ReadNext ();
          void ReadPrev ();
          void ReadRecord (RECORDNUMBER RecordNumber);

          void IndexDelete (char *Field);
        void IndexDelete (FIELDHANDLE FieldNumber);
          void IndexAdd (char *Field, int Mode = INCSECONDARY);
          void IndexAdd (FIELDHANDLE FieldNumber,
                         int Mode = INCSECONDARY);

          void Find (WStr Match, LPSTR FieldName,
                     int Mode = SEARCHFIRST);
          void Find (WStr Match, FIELDHANDLE FieldNumber,
                     int Mode = SEARCHFIRST);
};

#endif WParadoxTable_H
```

LISTING 7.9. WPARADOXTABLE.CPP source listing.

```
// WPARADOXTABLE.CPP - Source file for WParadoxTable class

#include "WPdoxTable.h"  // ALL other #include statements
                         // are in this file


//*******************************************************
// Constructors and destructors for WParadoxTable
//
//    Local error codes for Status variable:
//        -1   Paradox Engine not initialized
//
//    Copyright:
//            Copyright (c) 1993, William H. Roetzheim
```

```
//              All Rights Reserved
//
//*****************************************************
WParadoxTable::WParadoxTable (LPSTR TableName,
          int IndexField,
          int nFields,
          char *Names[],
        char *Types[])
{
    // Initialize Table and Record to default (invalid) values
    HTable = 0;
    Record = NULL;

    if (WParadoxEngine::Status != 0)  // Invalid Engine
    {
        MessageBox (NULL, "Paradox Engine not active!",
                          "WParadoxTable", MB_OK);
        exit (-1);
    }

    // Attempt to open the hopefully existing table
    Status = PXTblOpen (TableName, &HTable, IndexField, TRUE);
    if (Status != 0)
    {
        if (nFields != 0)
        {
            // Attempt to create a new table
            Status = PXTblCreate (TableName, nFields,
                                  Names, Types);
        }
        if (Status == 0)  // Table now exists
        {
            // Now try to open the newly created table
            Status = PXTblOpen (TableName, &HTable,
                                IndexField, TRUE);
        }
    }
    if (Status == 0)  // We were successful in opening
    {
        Record = new WParadoxRecord (this);
        ReadFirst ();

    }
}


WParadoxTable::~WParadoxTable ()
```

continues

LISTING 7.9. continued

```
{
    delete Record;
    PXTblClose (HTable);
}




//*****************************************************
// Member functions for class
//
//    Copyright:
//            Copyright (c) 1993, William H. Roetzheim
//            All Rights Reserved
//
//*****************************************************


//*****************************************************
// WParadoxTable::DeleteAll - Delete all records
//
//    Purpose:
//        Delete all records in the table, leaving
//        the basic table structure intact.
//
//    General Notes:
//        Obviously, be careful using this function!
//
//     Testing Notes:
//        Be sure that internal class variables still
//        are valid after the call. (For example, Record
//        should not be left with now invalid data in it.)
//
//    Copyright:
//            Copyright (c) 1993, William H. Roetzheim
//            All Rights Reserved
//
//*****************************************************

void WParadoxTable::DeleteAll ()
{
    char *Buffer = new char [MAXPATH];

    // Get table name
    PXTblName (HTable, MAXPATH, Buffer);
```

```
        // Empty the table
        Status = PXTblEmpty (Buffer);

        //Reset the Record
        if (Status == 0) ReadFirst ();

    delete[] Buffer;
}


//*****************************************************
// WParadoxTable::TotalRecords
//
//     Purpose:
//          Return the total number of records in the
//          database.
//
//     General Notes:
//          Because Paradox is a multi-user DBMS, the return
//          value will change as other users add and delete
//          records.
//
//        Testing Notes:
//         None
//
//     Copyright:
//             Copyright (c) 1993, William H. Roetzheim
//             All Rights Reserved
//
//*****************************************************

RECORDNUMBER WParadoxTable::TotalRecords ()
{
    RECORDNUMBER Total = -1;

    Status = PXTblNRecs (HTable, &Total);
    return Total;
}


//*****************************************************
// WParadoxTable::Current Record - Return current record
//
//     Purpose:
//          Return the current record number of the Paradox
//          internal pointer.
//
```

continues

LISTING 7.9. continued

```
//    General Notes:
//        This number may change as other users add records to
//        or delete records from the same table.
//
//    Testing Notes:
//        None
//
//    Copyright:
//        Copyright (c) 1993, William H. Roetzheim
//        All Rights Reserved
//
//*****************************************************

RECORDNUMBER WParadoxTable::CurrentRecord ()
{
    RECORDNUMBER Rec = -1;
    Status = PXRecNum (HTable, &Rec);
    return Rec;
}


//*****************************************************
// WParadoxTable - Record functions
//
//    Purpose:
//        Update, delete, and add records to the database.
//
//    General Notes:
//        1.    RecordUpdate modifies the current record using
//              the contents of the Record object in this
//              class.
//        2.    RecordDelete deletes the current record.
//        3.    RecordAdd adds the Record object to the
//              database. If an Index field was specified
//              when the Table object was created, the item
//              is added in the appropriate location.
//              Otherwise, the item is inserted in the
//              current location.
//        4.    The Paradox Engine also supports an append
//              function that can be added in the future.
//
//
//    Testing Notes:
//        None
//
```

```
//      Copyright:
//              Copyright (c) 1993, William H. Roetzheim
//              All Rights Reserved
//
//****************************************************

void WParadoxTable::RecordUpdate ()
{
    Status = Record->Update ();
}


void WParadoxTable::RecordDelete ()
{
    Status = PXRecDelete (HTable);
}


void WParadoxTable::RecordAdd ()
{
    Status = Record->Add ();
}




//****************************************************
// WParadoxTable - Record reading functions
//
//      Purpose:
//          These functions read data from the database
//          into the Record object stored in this object.
//
//      General Notes:
//          1.      ReadFirst reads the first record based on the
//                  logical order in the database (for example, using
//                  the index field if specified).
//          2.      ReadLast reads the last logical record.
//          3.      ReadNext reads the next logical record.
//          4.      ReadPrev reads the previous logical record.
//          5.      ReadRecord reads a specified logical record.
//                  This function should be used with care, because
//                  record numbers may change with time based on
//                  actions of other users working on the database.
//
//      Testing Notes:
//          None
//
```

continues

LISTING 7.9. continued

```
//    Copyright:
//            Copyright (c) 1993, William H. Roetzheim
//            All Rights Reserved
//
//*****************************************************

void WParadoxTable::ReadFirst ()
{
    Status = PXRecFirst (HTable);
    if (Status == 0) Status = Record->Read ();
}


void WParadoxTable::ReadLast ()
{
    Status = PXRecLast (HTable);
    if (Status == 0) Status = Record->Read ();
}


void WParadoxTable::ReadNext ()
{
    Status = PXRecNext (HTable);
    if (Status == 0) Status = Record->Read ();
}


void WParadoxTable::ReadPrev ()
{
    Status = PXRecPrev (HTable);
    if (Status == 0) Status = Record->Read ();
}


void WParadoxTable::ReadRecord (RECORDNUMBER RecordNumber)
{
    Status = PXRecGoto (HTable, RecordNumber);
    if (Status == 0) Status = Record->Read ();
}
```

```
//*******************************************************
// WParadoxTable - Index functions
//
//     Purpose:
//         Add indexes to and delete indexes from the table.
//
//     General Notes:
//         1.   Functions take either a field name
//              or a field number as an argument.
//         2.   Field numbers start with 1, not 0.
//         3.   Be careful when using field numbers,
//              because a user might want to add new
//              fields to your database using Paradox
//              itself, which would make your hard-coded
//              field numbers invalid!
//
//     Testing Notes:
//         None
//
//     Copyright:
//             Copyright (c) 1993, William H. Roetzheim
//             All Rights Reserved
//
//*******************************************************

void WParadoxTable::IndexDelete (char *Field)
{
    FIELDHANDLE FieldHandle;

    Status = PXFldHandle (HTable, Field, &FieldHandle);
    if (Status == 0)
    {
    IndexDelete (FieldHandle);
    }
}


void WParadoxTable::IndexDelete (FIELDHANDLE FieldNumber)
{
    char szBuffer [MAXPATH];
    PXTblName (HTable, MAXPATH, szBuffer);
    Status = PXKeyDrop (szBuffer, FieldNumber);
}


void WParadoxTable::IndexAdd (char *Field, int Mode)
{
    FIELDHANDLE FieldHandle;
```

continues

LISTING 7.9. continued

```
    Status = PXFldHandle (HTable, Field, &FieldHandle);
    if (Status == 0)
    {
    IndexAdd (FieldHandle, Mode);
    }
}



void WParadoxTable::IndexAdd (FIELDHANDLE FieldNumber, int Mode)
{
    char szBuffer [MAXPATH];
    PXTblName (HTable, MAXPATH, szBuffer);
    Status = PXKeyAdd (szBuffer, 1, &FieldNumber, Mode);
}



//****************************************************
// WParadoxTable - Search functions
//
//    Purpose:
//        Search for a match for the specified field.
//
//    General Notes:
//        Mode can be SEARCHFIRST, SEARCHNEXT, or
//        CLOSESTRECORD
//
//     Testing Notes:
//         None
//
//    Copyright:
//          Copyright (c) 1993, William H. Roetzheim
//          All Rights Reserved
//
//****************************************************

void WParadoxTable::Find (WStr Match, LPSTR FieldName, int Mode)
{
    FIELDHANDLE FieldHandle;

    Status = PXFldHandle (HTable, FieldName, &FieldHandle);
    if (Status == 0)
    {
    Find (Match, FieldHandle, Mode);
    }
```

```
}

void WParadoxTable::Find (WStr Match, FIELDHANDLE FieldNumber,
                          int Mode)
{
    WParadoxRecord SearchRec (this);

    SearchRec.PutField (FieldNumber, Match);
    Status = PXSrchFld (HTable, SearchRec.HRecord,
                         FieldNumber, Mode);
}
```

The *WParadoxRecord* Class

Listings 7.10 and 7.11 show the implementation of the WParadoxRecord class. The two key functions of this class are PutField and GetField. Both of these functions use a Paradox Engine function (PXFldType) to obtain the field type string. Then they parse this string to determine how to properly put data into the field or get data from the field. The rest of the functions are unimportant.

INT: Notice that the WPARADOXTABLE.H file is dependent on WPARADOXRECORD.H for some type definitions, and that WPARADOXRECORD.H is dependent on WPARADOXTABLE.H for some type definitions. This circular dependency between #include files is best handled by using forward declarations, as demonstrated just before the beginning of the WParadoxRecord class definition in WPDOXREC.H.

In Chapter 8, "Using Windows with SQL Databases in Client-Server Architecture," you have an opportunity to contrast this approach to integrating database capabilities into your application with an approach based on embedded SQL and Oracle.

LISTING 7.10. WPARADOXRECORD.H header file.

```
// WPARADOXRECORD.H - Header file for WParadoxRecord class

#ifndef WParadoxRecord_H
#    define WParadoxRecord_H

// Note that the following code is executed only
// if this file has not been previously included


// #include files for both PC and SUN
#include <ctype.h>
#include "PxEngine.h"
#include "WStr.h"

#ifdef __BORLANDC__
     // PC-specific #includes
#    include    <owl.h>

#endif

#ifdef Unix
     // UNIX-specific #includes

#endif

//****************************************************
// WParadoxRecord - Encapsulate Paradox record
//
//     Notes:
//          None
//
//     Copyright:
//             Copyright (c) 1993, William H. Roetzheim
//             All Rights Reserved
//
//****************************************************

// Forward declaration
_CLASSDEF (WParadoxTable);

_CLASSDEF (WParadoxRecord)
class WParadoxRecord
{
     private:
          // Private data members ********************
          PWParadoxTable ParentTable;
```

```
            // Private member functions ****************

    public:
            // Public data members *********************
            RECORDHANDLE HRecord;
        int     Status;

            // Public member functions *****************
            // Constructors and destructors
            WParadoxRecord (PWParadoxTable);
            ~WParadoxRecord ();

            // Member functions
            void RawGet (void *, int BufferSize);
            void RawPut (void *, int BufferSize);

            WStr GetField (FIELDHANDLE FieldNumber);
            WStr GetField (LPSTR FieldName);
            void PutField (FIELDHANDLE FieldNumber, WStr);
            void PutField (LPSTR FieldName, WStr);

            int Update ();
            int Add ();
        int Read ();
};

#include "WPdoxTable.h"

#endif WParadoxRecord_H
```

LISTING 7.11. WPARADOXRECORD.CPP source file.

```
// WPARADOXRECORD.CPP - Source file for WParadoxRecord class

#include "WPdoxRecord.h"  // ALL other #include statements
                          // are in this file

//*****************************************************
// Constructors and destructors for WParadoxRecord
//
//      Copyright:
//              Copyright (c) 1993, William H. Roetzheim
//              All Rights Reserved
```

continues

LISTING 7.11. continued

```
//
//*****************************************************

WParadoxRecord::WParadoxRecord (PWParadoxTable Table)
{
    ParentTable = Table;
    Status = PXRecBufOpen (Table->HTable, &HRecord);
    if (Status == 0) PXRecBufEmpty (HRecord);
}


WParadoxRecord::~WParadoxRecord ()
{
    PXRecBufClose (HRecord);
}



//*****************************************************
// Member functions for class
//
//     Copyright:
//             Copyright (c) 1993, William H. Roetzheim
//             All Rights Reserved
//
//*****************************************************


//*****************************************************
// WParadoxRecord::RawGet and RawPut
//
//     Purpose:
//         Read or write a record buffer in raw format.
//
//     General Notes:
//         These functions are very fast, but YOU are
//         responsible for all data integrity tests.
//         You must also be aware that using these
//         functions implies that you anticipate that
//         the structure of the record data will not
//         change. This restricts users of your
//         application from modifying your database
//         to add fields that they may need.
//
//      Testing Notes:
//         None
//
```

```
//     Copyright:
//              Copyright (c) 1993, William H. Roetzheim
//              All Rights Reserved
//
//*****************************************************

void WParadoxRecord::RawGet (void *Buffer, int BufferSize)
{
     Status = PXRawGet (HRecord, Buffer, BufferSize);
}


void WParadoxRecord::RawPut (void *Buffer, int BufferSize)
{
     Status = PXRawPut (HRecord, Buffer, BufferSize);
}




//*****************************************************
// WParadoxRecord - Functions to get and put fields
//
//     Purpose:
//         These functions get and put data into
//         Record fields while taking advantage of
//         the Paradox checks. All values are
//         Str types as far as the outside world
//         is concerned.
//
//     General Notes:
//         None
//
//      Testing Notes:
//         None
//
//     Copyright:
//              Copyright (c) 1993, William H. Roetzheim
//              All Rights Reserved
//
//*****************************************************

WStr WParadoxRecord::GetField (LPSTR FieldName)
{
     FIELDHANDLE FieldHandle;

     Status = PXFldHandle (ParentTable->HTable, FieldName,
                           &FieldHandle);
     if (Status == 0)
```

continues

209

LISTING 7.11. continued

```
    {
    return GetField (FieldHandle);
    }
    else return "";
}


// Note 1:  This code does not handle BLOBs.

// Note 2:  Passing back an entire object (Str)
//          on the stack is not a good idea if you
//          are dealing with very large fields or
//          BLOBs. Modify the code if necessary.

WStr WParadoxRecord::GetField (FIELDHANDLE FieldNumber)
{
    char *Buffer = NULL;
    double Value;

    // Test for blank field
    int IsBlank;
    PXFldBlank (HRecord, FieldNumber, &IsBlank);
    if (IsBlank) return "";

    // Determine field type
    char Type [16];
    PXFldType (ParentTable->HTable, FieldNumber, 16, Type);

    Type [0] = toupper (Type[0]);
    switch (Type[0])
    {
        case 'A':  // Alphanumeric
        int FieldSize = atoi (&Type[1]);
            Buffer = new char [FieldSize];
            Status = PXGetAlpha (HRecord, FieldNumber,
                        FieldSize, Buffer);
        break;

        case 'D':  // Date
            long Date;
            int Month, Day, Year;
          Buffer = new char [15];
            Status = PXGetDate (HRecord, FieldNumber, &Date);
            if (Status == 0)
        {
```

```
                    PXDateDecode (Date, &Month, &Day, &Year);
                    sprintf (Buffer, "%d/%d/%d", Month, Day, Year);
            }
        break;

        case 'N':  // Numeric
          Buffer = new char [15];
              Status = PXGetDoub (HRecord, FieldNumber, &Value);
          if (Status == 0) sprintf (Buffer, "%5.0lf", Value);
        break;

        case '$':  // Currency
              Buffer = new char [15];
              Status = PXGetDoub (HRecord, FieldNumber, &Value);
          if (Status == 0) sprintf (Buffer, "%4.2lf", Value);
        break;

        case 'S':  // Short
              short sValue;
          Buffer = new char [15];
              Status = PXGetShort (HRecord, FieldNumber, &sValue);
              if (Status == 0) sprintf (Buffer, "%d", sValue);
              break;

    }
    WStr Temp = Buffer;
    delete[] Buffer;
   return Temp;
}

void WParadoxRecord::PutField (LPSTR FieldName, WStr NewValue)
{
    FIELDHANDLE FieldHandle;

    Status = PXFldHandle (ParentTable->HTable, FieldName,
                          &FieldHandle);
    if (Status == 0)
    {
    PutField (FieldHandle, NewValue);
    }
}


void WParadoxRecord::PutField (FIELDHANDLE FieldNumber, WStr
Buffer)
{
    // Test for blank field
    if (strcmp (Buffer, "") == 0)
```

continues

211

LISTING 7.11. continued

```
    {
        PXPutBlank (HRecord, FieldNumber);
        return;
    }

  // Determine field type
  char Type [16];
  PXFldType (ParentTable->HTable, FieldNumber, 16, Type);

  Type [0] = toupper (Type[0]);
  switch (Type[0])
  {
      case 'A':  // Alphanumeric
      Status = PXPutAlpha (HRecord, FieldNumber, Buffer);
      break;

      case 'D':  // Date
          long Date;
          int Month, Day, Year;
          sscanf (Buffer, "%d/%d/%d", &Month, &Day, &Year);
          PXDateEncode (Month, Day, Year, &Date);
          Status = PXPutDate (HRecord, FieldNumber, Date);
      break;

      case 'N':  // Numeric
    case '$':  // Currency
          double Value;
          sscanf (Buffer, "%lf", &Value);
        PXPutDoub (HRecord, FieldNumber, Value);
      break;

      case 'S':  // Short
          short sValue;
          sscanf (Buffer, "%d", &sValue);
        PXPutShort (HRecord, FieldNumber, sValue);
          break;

  }

}
```

```
//*****************************************************
//   WParadoxRecord - Functions to read and write records
//
//   Purpose:
//       Functions to update, add, and read the
//       Paradox record found in the parent table
//       object.
//
//   General Notes:
//       None
//
//     Testing Notes:
//       None
//
//   Copyright:
//           Copyright (c) 1993, William H. Roetzheim
//           All Rights Reserved
//
//*****************************************************
int WParadoxRecord::Update ()
{
    Status = PXRecUpdate (ParentTable->HTable, HRecord);
    return Status;
}

int WParadoxRecord::Add ()
{
    Status = PXRecAppend (ParentTable->HTable, HRecord);
    return Status;
}

int WParadoxRecord::Read ()
{
    Status = PXRecGet (ParentTable->HTable, HRecord);
    return Status;
}
```

The Paradox Engine in Depth

Table 7.7 summarizes the functions, constants, and macros provided with the Paradox Engine. They are broken down by category.

TABLE 7.7. Paradox Engine functions.

Function	Description
BLANKDATE	Constant that tests for blank value of type date
BLANKDOUBLE	Constant that tests for blank value of type double
BLANKLONG	Constant that tests for blank value of type long
BLANKSHORT	Constant that tests for blank value of type short
ISBLANKALPHA	A macro that tests for blank value of type alphanumeric
ISBLANKDATE	Macro that tests for blank value of type date
ISBLANKDOUBLE	Macro that tests for blank value of type double
ISBLANKLONG	Macro that tests for blank value of type long
ISBLANKSHORT	Macro that tests for blank value of type short
PXBlobClone	Copies a BLOB and makes it private
PXBlobClose	Closes the BLOB
PXBlobDrop	Deletes a BLOB field from the record
PXBlobGet	Reads a portion of a BLOB field
PXBlobGetSize	Returns the size of the BLOB field
PXBlobOpenRead	Opens the BLOB for reading
PXBlobOpenWrite	Opens the BLOB for writing
PXBlobPut	Writes a portion of a BLOB field

Function	Description
PXBlobQuickGet	Reads the BLOB header in the record
PXDateDecode	Returns the year, month, and day from a date value
PXDateEncode	Returns a date value from the year, month, and day
PXErrMsg	Returns an error message string associated with an error code
PXExit	Shuts down the Engine
PXFldBlank	Tests whether a field has a blank value in the record buffer
PXFldHandle	Returns a field handle from a field name
PXFldName	Returns a field name from a field handle
PXFldType	Returns the field type from a field handle
PXGetAlpha	Gets a string from a record buffer
PXGetDate	Gets a date value from a record buffer
PXGetDefaults	Gets the current default settings
PXGetDoub	Gets a double-precision floating-point number from a record buffer
PXGetLong	Gets a 32-bit integer from a record buffer
PXGetShort	Gets a 16-bit integer from a record buffer
PXInit	Initializes the DOS version of the Engine in single-user mode
PXKeyAdd	Creates an index for a table
PXKeyDrop	Destroys an index for a table

continues

215

TABLE 7.7. continued

Function	Description
PXKeyMap	Registers a composite or case-insensitive single-field index for subsequent creation by PXKeyAdd
PXKeyNFlds	Returns the number of fields in the primary key
PXKeyQuery	Returns the index fields of a composite or case-insensitive single-field index
PXNetErrUser	Indicates the owner of the lock on locking conflict
PXNetFileLock	Puts a lock on a file
PXNetFileUnlock	Removes a lock from a file
PXNetInit	Initializes the DOS version of the Engine in shared mode
PXNetRecGotoLock	Makes a previously locked record the current record
PXNetRecLock	Locks the current record
PXNetRecLocked	Determines whether the current record is locked
PXNetRecUnlock	Unlocks the current record
PXNetTblChanged	Tests whether a table has been changed by other users
PXNetTblLock	Puts a lock on a table
PXNetTblRefresh	Synchronizes the image of a table with what other users see
PXNetTblUnlock	Removes a lock from a table
PXNetUserName	Returns the name of the current user
PXPswAdd	Registers a user-specified password with the Engine

Function	Description
PXPswDel	Unregisters a user-specified password
PXPutAlpha	Puts a string into a record buffer
PXPutBlank	Puts a blank value into a record buffer for a specified field
PXPutDate	Puts a date value into a record buffer
PXPutDoub	Puts a double-precision floating-point number into a record buffer
PXPutLong	Puts a 32-bit integer into a record buffer
PXPutShort	Puts a 16-bit integer into a record buffer
PXRawGet	Copies a record buffer into the user's buffer without translation
PXRawPut	Copies the user's buffer into a record buffer without translation
PXRecAppend	Adds a new record to a table at the end (if there is no index)
PXRecBufClose	Closes a record buffer
PXRecBufCopy	Copies a record buffer to another
PXRecBufEmpty	Empties a record buffer
PXRecBufOpen	Opens a record buffer
PXRecDelete	Deletes a record from a table
PXRecFirst	Positions the internal DB pointer on the first record in a table
PXRecGet	Reads a record from a table into memory
PXRecGoto	Goes to the record given by a record number
PXRecInsert	Inserts a new record into a table

continues

217

TABLE 7.7. continued

Function	Description
PXRecLast	Positions the internal DB pointer on the last record in a table
PXRecNext	Positions the internal DB pointer on the next record in a table
PXRecNFlds	Returns the number of fields for a table
PXRecNum	Returns the record number of the current record in a table
PXRecPrev	Positions the internal DB pointer on the previous record in a table
PXRecUpdate	Posts a modified record back to a table
PXSetDefaults	Sets defaults for the DOS version of the Engine (Windows defaults are set in WIN.INI)
PXSetHWHandler	Sets up a handler for critical errors
PXSrchFld	Searches a table on a secondary index
PXSrchKey	Searches a table on the primary index
PXTblAdd	Appends the contents of one table to another
PXTblClose	Closes an open table
PXTblCopy	Copies an open table
PXTblCreate	Creates an empty table
PXTblCreateMode	Controls the Paradox version for new tables
PXTblDecrypt	Decrypts a table
PXTblEncrypt	Encrypts a table
PXTblExist	Determines whether a certain table exists

Function	Description
PXTblMaxSize	Controls the maximum size of tables
PXTblName	Returns the name of an open table
PXTblNRecs	Returns the number of records currently in a table
PXTblOpen	Opens an existing table with a specified index
PXTblProtected	Tests whether a certain table has been encrypted
PXTblRename	Renames a table
PXTblUpgrade	Upgrades an older table format to the latest table format
PXWinInit	Initializes the Windows version of the Engine

Status Data Member Error Codes

Table 7.8 summarizes the possible error codes that the WParadoxEngine, WParadoxTable, and WParadoxRecord Status data member can take.

TABLE 7.8. Status **data member error codes.**

Number	Error Message
1	Drive not ready
2	Directory not found
3	File is busy
4	File is locked

continues

TABLE 7.8. continued

Number	Error Message
5	Could not find file
6	Table is corrupted
7	Primary index is corrupted
8	Primary index is out-of-date
9	Record is locked
10	Sharing violation
11	Sharing violation
12	No access to directory
13	Sort for index different from table
14	Single user but directory is shared
15	Multiple Paradox net files found
16	Directory is in use by Paradox 3.5
17-20	[reserved]
21	Insufficient password rights
22	Table is write-protected
23-29	[reserved]
30	Data type mismatch
31	Argument is out of range
32	[reserved]
33	Invalid argument
34-39	[reserved]
40	Not enough memory to complete operation
41	Not enough disk space to complete operation
42-49	[reserved]

Number	Error Message
50	Another user deleted the record
51	Operation not applicable for BLOB open mode
52	BLOB already open
53	Invalid offset into BLOB
54	Invalid size for BLOB
55	Another user modified the BLOB
56	BLOB file corrupted
57	Cannot index on a BLOB
58	[reserved]
59	Invalid BLOB handle
60	Cannot search on a BLOB field
61-69	[reserved]
70	No more file handles available
71	[reserved]
72	No more table handles available
73	Invalid date given
74	Invalid field name
75	Invalid field handle
76	Invalid table handle
77	[reserved]
78	Engine not initialized
79	Previous fatal error; cannot proceed
80	[reserved]
81	Table structures are different
82	Engine already initialized

continues

TABLE 7.8. continued

Number	Error Message
83	Unable to perform operation on open table
84-85	[reserved]
86	No more temporary names available
87-88	[reserved]
89	Record was not found
90-91	[reserved]
92	Table cannot be upgraded
93	Feature not available for tables older than Paradox 4.0
94	Table is indexed
95	Table is not indexed
96	Secondary index is out of date
97	Key violation
98	Could not log in on network
99	Table name is invalid
100	[reserved]
101	End of table
102	Start of table
103	No more record handles available
104	Invalid record handle
105	Operation on empty table
106	Invalid lock code
107	Engine not initialized with PXNetInit
108	Invalid filename

Number	Error Message
109	Invalid unlock
110	Invalid lock handle
111	Too many locks on table
112	Invalid sort order table
113	Invalid net type
114	Invalid directory name
115	Too many passwords specified
116	Invalid password
117	Buffer is too small for result
118	Table is busy
119	Table is locked
120	Table was not found
121	Secondary index was not found
122	Secondary index is corrupted
123	[reserved]
124	Disk is write-protected
125	Record too big
126	General system error
127	Not enough stack space to complete operation
128	Table is full
129	Not enough swap buffer space to complete operation
130	Table is SQL replica
131	Too many clients for the Engine DLL

continues

TABLE 7.8. continued

Number	Error Message
132	Exceeds limits specified in WIN.INI
133	No more slots for file handle remapping
134	Can't share Paradox net file. Is SHARE.EXE loaded?
135	Can't run Engine in Windows real mode
136	Can't modify table opened on nonmaintained secondary index
137	Timed out trying to achieve a lock

CHAPTER

8

Using Windows with SQL Databases in Client-Server Architecture

Problem

One of the hottest topics in the computer world is client-server architecture. If you program PCs for a corporation, at some point you will implement an application using client-server architecture. Unfortunately, it's also very likely that the people asking you to perform this task will have only a sketchy understanding of exactly what is meant by client-server architecture. They will have little advice to offer on how you should develop the software.

Solution

As with many problems in computer science, the best solution is to take the bull by the horns and become the expert. You need to understand what is meant by client-server architecture. Because most corporate client-server architectures incorporate a Structured Query Language (SQL) database as the database server, you need to understand how to work with a SQL database from within your C++ Windows code.

This chapter provides an overview of client-server architectures and SQL. It also provides specific advice, with examples, on integrating SQL code into your application. Although much of the discussion applies to any SQL database product, I use Oracle for the sample problems and explanations. Oracle enjoys widespread popularity and is available for a wide range of PC and minicomputer platforms. For the sample client-server application, I use the videotape library program I used in Chapter 7, "Interfacing with Paradox," to demonstrate the Paradox Engine.

INT: Don't skip this chapter just because you don't have a copy of Oracle to experiment with. The discussion and examples in this chapter are educational even if you can't compile and run the sample application yourself. When it runs, the application looks the same as the sample Paradox application presented earlier, anyway! Almost all of what I discuss in this chapter applies to *any* major SQL database you can purchase.

The Many Faces of Client-Server

In the simplest sense, a client-server system is any computer architecture in which an application server provides services to various client applications. Consider, for example, a file server on a network. The file server (both the hardware and the file server network's software) provides a service (shared data access) to various client applications (PCs on the network). In this sense, you can view a network-based application that uses a Paradox database engine with a single file server-based database as a client-server application. In fact, this architecture embodies most of the characteristics of true client-server architecture. Data is shared among applications in real time by means of the central database. Application processing is performed in a distributed fashion on multiple PCs interconnected by means of a network.

Some purists restrict the definition of client-server architecture to that in which the database management system itself is the server and the PC applications are the clients. Under this definition, the Paradox architecture would *not* be a client-server architecture because the database management software is resident and executing at *each* PC; only the data is shared. To have a true client-server architecture under this definition, you must have a database management system that resides on the file server and processes queries *on the server* from the clients on the network. The server can be a PC, a minicomputer, or a mainframe. Local application-specific processing (totaling columns, performing user interface functions, displaying data graphically, validating data, and so on) can and should be performed on the PC-based clients.

HINT: Servers typically are either a PC running a true multitasking operating system, such as OS/2 or Windows NT (when it becomes available), or a minicomputer running UNIX. As a rule of thumb, if I think the server might ever be required to process more than 25 to 50 database transactions per second (TPS), I recommend a UNIX server. It is much easier to upgrade UNIX to more powerful computers as the need arises, and UNIX is far superior to OS/2 in input/output efficiency. A mainframe rarely operates as a server. More commonly, a mainframe is required to use a three-tiered

architecture in which the mainframe acts as a centralized data repository, UNIX-based minicomputers act as distributed servers, and PCs act as clients to the UNIX servers.

Most database servers have adopted SQL as the language used to define the database transactions. Applications using straight SQL for all database applications are easily ported from one SQL database server to another. Examples of SQL-based database servers are Oracle, Informix, Sybase, and SQLBase. In addition, many of the more popular PC databases are beginning to offer at least limited SQL support.

The *chpt8* Sample Application

Figure 8.1 shows the sample application for this chapter in operation. If you refer to Chapter 7, "Interfacing with Paradox," you will notice that Figure 8.1 looks identical to the Paradox Engine sample application. I intentionally used the identical application—a maintenance application for a videotape library—and dialog box to make it easy for you to compare a Paradox Engine implementation with a SQL implementation. Because this implementation is based on SQL, it can use any SQL database server. For example, the application code (described later) operates largely without change whether the database server is Oracle on a PC, Oracle on a UNIX-based minicomputer, Sybase on a VAX computer, or DB2 on an IBM mainframe.

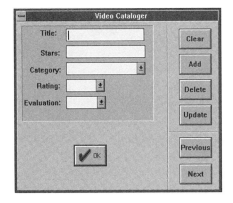

Figure 8.1. The chpt8 *sample application.*

Oracle-Based Client-Server Architecture

Oracle offers a tool product set (see Table 8.1) and a database product set (see Table 8.2). The tool product set is available separately from the database product set. The server portion of the client-server architecture requires the Oracle database management system. Normally, it also requires utilities such as SQL*DBA, EXP, IMP, and TKPROF. The client portion of the architecture can be implemented in native C code by using the Oracle precompilers and libraries. Then, you can distribute the client portion without paying any royalties.

TABLE 8.1. The Oracle tool product set.

Oracle Tool Product	Description
SQL*Plus	Interactive SQL interpreter
SQL*ReportWriter	Menu-driven program for generating reports
SQL*Forms	Program for designing and using data entry and display forms
SQL*Menu	Program for generating menus
ClientManager (for DOS only)	Menu-based application development environment that supports access to other Oracle tools

TABLE 8.2. The Oracle database product set.

Oracle Database Product	Description
Oracle RDBMS	Oracle relational database management system
SQL*DBA	Oracle database administration tool

continues

TABLE 8.2. continued

Oracle Database Product	Description
EXP	Tool used to export data from the database to a file
IMP	Tool used to import data exported with EXP
TKPROF	Tool used to tune the database performance
SQL*Loader	Tool used to load an Oracle database with files in a variety of formats, including ASCII, dBASE III PLUS, and Lotus 1-2-3
PRO*C	Tool that enables you to embed SQL statements in your C programs

If your client process and the Oracle database itself reside on the same physical machine, you do not need to purchase any additional products. More often, though, you want multiple clients connected to Oracle over a local area network. Oracle provides a mechanism to accomplish this automatically without changing your source code in any way. The appropriate components from the SQL*Net set of products (see Table 8.3) can be purchased—one for the server and one for each of the clients. These products enable you to execute commands transparently on the server.

TABLE 8.3. The Oracle SQL*Net product line.

SQL*Net Product	Description
SQL*Net DECnet	Provides SQL*Net capability for servers with DECnet and PCs with DEC's DECnet DOS
SQL*Net TCP/IP	Provides SQL*Net capability for TCP/IP-based LANs, typically running on top of EtherNet

SQL*Net *Product*	*Description*
SQL*Net 3270	Provides SQL*Net capability to IBM mainframes by using 3270 protocol
SQL*Net APPC/LU6.2	Provides SQL*Net support to IBM mainframes that use IBM's newer Advanced Program to Program Communications (APPC) protocol, normally over SDLC or Token Ring
SQL*Net Vines	Provides a SQL*Net connection to a PC-based server using Banyan's Vines LAN operating system, normally over EtherNet, Token Ring, or ARCnet
SQL*Net Asynch	Provides SQL*Net connectivity over a standard serial port. SQL*Net Asynch is used by clients communicating with a server over a modem.
SQL*Connect	Provides transparent connectivity between an Oracle server's database and an IBM mainframe's DB2 database

The connection to the server is established automatically when you open the desired database, and all requests directed to that database are then automatically redirected to the server. You can open multiple databases on different database servers simultaneously, then execute queries against an individual database or a combination of databases by using a SQL join command. The SQL*Net products in use redirect all queries to the proper databases. This provides true distributed database processing.

INT: It is not as difficult as you might think to implement your own SQL*Net-type protocol to connect a client with a server. This is especially true if your application enables you to establish the initial connection between the client and the Oracle Server

manually (for example, from the command line), to execute the application that interacts with Oracle, and to manually close the connection with Oracle. In this context, the word *manually* includes either commands physically entered by the end-user or a spawned COMMAND.COM process with the appropriate parameter list within your application.

In addition, I consider this option only when I must connect to only one Oracle database server at a time, and when I know ahead of time exactly what the physical connection will be. There are two major advantages to implementing your own SQL*Net-type protocol. You can potentially save a lot of money if you're dealing with a large number of clients (because you must purchase SQL*Net for each client), and you can build in additional security or prioritization algorithms.

To install Oracle on a PC, you need 3MB or more of RAM and approximately 11MB of hard disk space. Table 8.4 shows the *additional* hard disk space required to install each of the optional Oracle tools.

TABLE 8.4. Hard disk space required by Oracle tools.

Tool	Hard Disk Space Required
Tools Utilities	1,960K
SQL*Plus	875K
SQL*ReportWriter	8,240K
SQL*Forms	7,240K
SQL*Menu	6,325K
Client Manager	90K

If you use Oracle's automatic installation feature, Oracle creates an \ORACLE6 directory with the seven subdirectories shown in Table 8.5. In addition, other Oracle tools that are installed might create their own subdirectories in the \ORACLE6 directory.

TABLE 8.5. \ORACLE6 subdirectories.

Subdirectory Under \ORACLE6	Description
\BIN	Executable programs and batch files for the Oracle database and tools
\PBIN	Protected-mode executables for the Oracle database and tools
\DBS	Files containing database definitions, associated data files, and parameter files
\PRO	Library and object files necessary for user exits
\MENU	Files used by SQL*Menu
\SRW	Files used by SQL*ReportWriter
\LOADER	Files used by SQL*Loader

HINT: Version 6 of Oracle has only half-hearted support for Windows. Far from running as a true Windows application, Oracle doesn't even run in a DOS window. The program runs in only full-screen mode under Windows, not in a text window. The database itself, SQL*Forms, SQL*Menu, and SQL*ReportWriter run only in protected mode. This means that they can work only if you run Windows in standard mode (use the /s switch when you start Windows). Also, you must be sure to run the protected-mode

versions of Oracle executables if they are available. Simply make sure that the \PBIN subdirectory precedes the \BIN subdirectory in your PATH statement.

To run Oracle under Windows, you must modify the CONFIG.ORA file used by Oracle to configure itself during start-up. Change the ORACLE_TIO parameter to the value VIDEO and set the DYNAMIC_MEMORY parameter to the amount of protected-mode memory that you want Oracle to use. Remember that this memory will not be available to Windows for its own use. A minimum value of 2,500 should be specified. In addition, you should modify the .PIF file for all the Oracle tools you will use. I suggest the following modifications:

1. Ensure that the protected-mode version of the file is specified. Normally these have a .COM extension. Real-mode versions use an .EXE extension.

2. Use the Optional Parameters box to specify the required parameters, or use ? to allow parameters to be entered at runtime.

3. In the XMS Memory box, set KB Required to 0 and KB Limit to 0.

4. Initially, leave the Close Window on Exit box unchecked. Run the tool. Ensure that it operates properly and does not display an error message and exit. When you are satisfied, check the Close Window on Exit box.

HINT: To start Oracle, use the ORACLE.BAT file. You must either enter the password as a parameter to the batch file (for example, Oracle Password) or have the password stored in your CONFIG.ORA file in a line that reads DBA_AUTHORIZATION=Password. To terminate Oracle, use the following commands in the order shown:

1. SQLDBA DISCONNECT (terminates the connection to the database)

2. SQLDBA SHUTDOWN (shuts down the database)

3. REMORA ALL (removes all Oracle drivers from protected memory)

4. REMPME (returns the reserved protected memory to Windows)

An Overview of SQL

Structured Query Language was developed by IBM from 1974 to 1975 at its San Jose research center. SQL was made available to the industry in 1979 and quickly became a standard supported by more than 100 database vendors. SQL is now an ANSI standard (ANSI X3.135-1986). It shows every indication of maintaining its dominant position in the world of relational databases.

As summarized in Table 8.6, SQL defines a wide range of database operations. I touch on a few of the more significant operations in this section. One database operation is the command to create a new table. The general syntax for creating a table is as follows (SQL is not case-sensitive, but I use uppercase for SQL keywords):

```
CREATE TABLE TableName
(
    ColumnName      ColumnType      [NOT NULL],
    ColumnName      ColumnType      [NOT NULL],
    . . .
);
```

The optional NOT NULL makes the field a required field. A valid value must be entered for the record to be accepted. Valid column types are shown in Table 8.7. A sample SQL statement to create a table is as follows:

```
CREATE TABLE Video
(
    Title        CHAR(35),
    Stars        CHAR(76),
    Category     CHAR(21),
    Rating       CHAR(6),
    Evaluation   CHAR(6)
);
```

TABLE 8.6. Summary of Oracle SQL statements.

Oracle SQL Statement	Modifiers Allowed	Statement Type	Description
BEGIN DECLARE SECTION		Declarative	Start of data declaration area. This is the area where you tell Oracle which C++ variables you will be using in embedded SQL commands. The data declaration area must precede any other embedded SQL commands.
END DECLARE SECTION		Declarative	End of the data declaration area
DECLARE		Declarative	Defines a database cursor. A cursor is a pointer to the database, the associated data, and error/status codes that are associated with

Oracle SQL Statement	Modifiers Allowed	Statement Type	Description
			that pointer. More than one cursor may be declared simultaneously for a single table.
INCLUDE		Declarative	Includes a file that contains other embedded SQL or C commands
WHENEVER		Declarative	Defines what Oracle should do if errors or unexpected conditions are encountered. The WHENEVER statement defines an error event handler.
ALTER	CLUSTER, DATABASE, INDEX, ROLLBACK SEGMENT, SEQUENCE, SESSION, TABLE, TABLESPACE, USER	Data definition	Modifies a specified aspect of a database
CREATE	CLUSTER, DATABASE, DATABASE	Data definition	Creates a specified aspect of a database

continues

TABLE 8.6. continued

Oracle SQL Statement	Modifiers Allowed	Statement Type	Description
	LINK INDEX, ROLLBACK SEGMENT, SEQUENCE, SYNONYM, TABLE, TABLESPACE, VIEW		
DROP	CLUSTER, DATABASE LINK INDEX, ROLLBACK SEGMENT, SEQUENCE, SYNONYM, TABLE, TABLESPACE, VIEW	Data definition	Drops a specified item from a database
RENAME		Data definition	Renames a table, view, or synonym
CONNECT		Access control	Provides direct access to the Oracle RDBMS
GRANT		Access control	Provides access to a database
LOCK TABLE		Access control	Manually overrides automatic locking to lock one or more tables

Oracle SQL Statement	Modifiers Allowed	Statement Type	Description
REVOKE		Access control	Revokes access to a database
DELETE		Data manipulation	Removes rows from a table
INSERT		Data manipulation	Inserts rows into a table
UPDATE		Data manipulation	Changes data in a specified table
CLOSE		Data retrieval	Closes a cursor
FETCH		Data retrieval	Retrieves the next selected row from a database for a specified cursor
OPEN		Data retrieval	Opens a cursor
SELECT		Data retrieval	Retrieves one or more rows from a specified table
COMMIT		Transaction processing	Makes permanent any changes that were made in the current transaction
ROLLBACK		Transaction processing	Undoes all work already done in the current transaction

continues

239

TABLE 8.6. continued

Oracle SQL Statement	Modifiers Allowed	Statement Type	Description
SAVEPOINT		Transaction processing	Identifies a place in a transaction that you can roll back to with the ROLLBACK TO SAVEPOINT statement
SET TRANSACTION		Transaction processing	Establishes the current transaction as read-only
DESCRIBE		Dynamic SQL	Allocates and initializes a descriptor to hold the host variable descriptions from a SQL statement previously prepared in a PREPARE statement
EXECUTE		Dynamic SQL	Executes an INSERT, DELETE, or UPDATE statement previously prepared in a PREPARE statement, or prepares and executes a SQL statement that contains no host variables
PREPARE		Dynamic SQL	Parses a SQL statement from a host variable character string

TABLE 8.7. Valid Oracle column types.

Type	Description	Notes
CHAR	Variable-length character strings up to 255 characters in length	An embedded SQL does not recognize the C convention of NULL-terminated strings, so a VARCHAR structure that includes the string length is defined. Oracle uses storage space internally for only the actual characters stored, not the maximum field length.
NUMBER	Fixed or floating-point number	You can specify desired *precision* (number of digits) and *scale* (digit at which rounding occurs). Precision can be 1 through 38. Scale can be –84 (84 digits left of the decimal) through 127 (127 digits right of the decimal).
DATE	Date, including century	
LONG	Variable-length character strings up to 65,535 characters in length	LONG columns can't be used in WHERE, GROUP BY, and CONNECT BY SQL statements, and only one LONG column is allowed per table. LONG columns cannot be indexed.
RAW	Same as CHAR, except that Oracle doesn't attempt to perform conversions when transferring data to a different machine (for example, ASCII to EBCDIC)	
RAW LONG	Same as LONG, except as described for RAW	

To add a record into a table, you can use the INSERT command:

```
INSERT INTO Video
VALUES
(
    'Dirty Dancing',
    'Patrick Swayze',
    'Drama',
    'PG-13',
    '***'
);
```

You can display the title and rating of all movies with a three-star rating by using the SELECT command:

```
SELECT Title, Rating FROM Video
WHERE Evaluation = '***';
```

Finally, using the DELETE command, you can delete the movie that was just entered:

```
DELETE FROM Video
WHERE Title = 'Dirty Dancing';
```

Embedding SQL into Your Application

Embedded SQL is pretty much like, well, SQL. The Oracle PRO*C precompiler takes a source file that consists of a mixture of C or C++ code and embedded SQL statements, and outputs a pure C or C++ source file that can be compiled with the Borland C++ compiler. Each embedded SQL statement follows the syntax of ordinary SQL, with the addition of the keywords EXEC SQL before the beginning of each SQL statement.

In SQL*Plus, input values are specified at runtime by the user, and outputs are directed to the terminal. Unlike SQL*Plus, embedded SQL often must take its inputs from, and return the query results in, variables in your application program. You accomplish this by telling the Oracle preprocessor which program variables you will be using for this purpose in the DECLARE SECTION, as follows:

```
EXEC SQL BEGIN DECLARE SECTION;
    VARCHAR    TitleOracle[35];
    VARCHAR    StarsOracle[76];
```

```
       VARCHAR    CategoryOracle[21];
       VARCHAR    RatingOracle[6];
       VARCHAR    EvaluationOracle[6];
EXEC SQL END DECLARE SECTION;
```

VARCHAR is defined by Oracle as a `struct` that represents a Fortran-style string with the length stored in front of the string itself. For example, the precompiler will expand the `Title` VARCHAR declaration as follows:

```
struct
{
    unsigned short len;
    unsigned char arr[35];
} TitleOracle;
```

In addition to VARCHAR, Oracle supports the following data types: `char`, `char[n]`, `int`, `short`, `long`, `float`, `double`, and `VARCHAR[n]`. Oracle supports one-dimensional arrays of simple C types. Two-dimensional arrays are permitted for only `char` and VARCHAR. Oracle supports pointers to simple C types but not pointers to arrays. Oracle does not support references.

You need the VARCHAR structure when you work with Oracle because Oracle neither returns NULL-terminated strings nor recognizes the NULL as having any special significance in a string passed to it. Oracle does, however, use the `len` member of the VARCHAR-defined `struct` on both input and output. For example, to search for a specific title and to obtain the rating, I use the following code:

```
strcpy (TitleOracle.arr, "Dirty Dancing");  /* Or you could get */
                                   /* input from dialog box */
TitleOracle.len = strlen (TitleOracle.arr);
EXEC SQL SELECT Rating
    INTO :RatingOracle
    WHERE Title = :TitleOracle;
```

Notice that when I refer to a variable from my program in an embedded SQL statement, I must prepend a colon (:) to the variable name. The Oracle parser requires this. When it encounters a colon, the Oracle parser attempts to match the name that follows with the list of variables declared in the declaration section. If no match is found, an error message is displayed.

In the following section, I describe in detail the embedded SQL code used to implement the sample application for this chapter.

The *chpt8* Code

Table 8.8 summarizes the files applicable to the sample application for this chapter. Notice that some of the files mentioned in Table 8.8 are the same files used in the Paradox application. I chose to implement this application so that it would duplicate the functionality found in the Paradox sample application as closely as possible. This approach enables you to compare the Oracle implementation side-by-side with the equivalent Paradox implementation.

TABLE 8.8. The `chpt8` files.

File	Description
CHPT8.CPP	Source code for the `chpt8` main program
WORACLEV.H	Header file for the `WOracleVideoDialog` class
WORACLEV.PC	`PRO*C`-compatible source file that consists of a mixture of embedded SQL and C++
WORACLEV.CPP	C++ file that is output by the `PRO*C` preprocessor. Because the output file ends in .CPP rather than .C, you must specify the output filename as a parameter to the precompiler (as in `ONAME=WOracleV.cpp`).
CHPT7.RC	Resource file from the `chpt7` application that contains the dialog box definition
DVIDEO.H	`#defines` used to identify dialog box fields and controls. This file is the same file used in the `chpt7` application.
CHPT8.EXE	Executable version of the sample application for `chpt8`
SQLPROTO.H	Modified prototypes for Oracle calls
CHPT8.DEF	Linker definition file for the `chpt8` sample application

244

To run the chpt8 sample application, you must have Oracle installed. Configure Oracle so that the user "System" can log on to Oracle with the identifier "Manager" (this is the default on installation); otherwise, modify the source code. You also need to create a table called Video that contains the required fields. The SQL*Plus command that creates the required table is as follows:

```
CREATE TABLE Video
(
     Title          CHAR(35),
     Stars          CHAR(76),
     Category       CHAR(21),
     Rating         CHAR(6),
     Evaluation     CHAR(6)
);
```

HINT: Of course, you can create tables by using embedded SQL within your own application. The sample application doesn't include this code, because doing so would have required a discussion of database views stored by Oracle—a topic that would cloud the introductory discussion in this book. You can use these database views when you want to check whether a table already exists. The Oracle SQL reference manual contains a complete description of them.

Although it is possible to encapsulate Oracle completely in a C++ object-oriented wrapper—as I did with the Paradox Engine—the conceptual architecture of the database is sufficiently different from that used by Paradox that the design of this wrapper would be completely different. Because Oracle is very complex, even a relatively high-level discussion of this topic would quickly expand to fill a complete book. To keep this chapter at a manageable level, I've chosen simply to embed the appropriate SQL code directly in my C++ class where it is appropriate. Although this method doesn't take full advantage of an object-oriented view of the world, I think the resultant code is easy to understand as an introduction to embedded SQL.

The CHPT8.CPP Source Code Listing

The CHPT8.CPP file, shown in Listing 8.1, is virtually identical to the CHPT7.CPP file found in Chapter 7, "Interfacing with Paradox." Only two statements required modification. This one:

```
#include "WVideoDialog.h"
```

became

```
#include "WOracleVideoDialog.h"
```

and the statement in the `InitMainWindow` member function:

```
MainWindow = new WVideoDialog (NULL, "VideoDialog", this);
```

became

```
MainWindow = new WOracleVideoDialog (NULL, "VideoDialog", this);
```

LISTING 8.1. CHPT8.CPP source code listing.

```
#define        _CLASSDLL
#define     WIN31
#define     STRICT
#include    <owl.h>
#include    "DVideo.h"
#include    "WOracleVideoDialog.h"


//****************************************************
// chpt8 - chpt8 application class
//
//      Purpose:
//          This class is the overall application
//          executive for chpt8.
//
//      Notes:
//          None
//
//      Copyright:
//              Copyright (c) 1993, William H. Roetzheim
//              All Rights Reserved
//
//****************************************************
```

```
_CLASSDEF (chpt8)
class chpt8 : public TApplication
{
    public:
            // Public member functions *****************
            // Constructors and destructors
            chpt8 (LPSTR szName, HINSTANCE hInstance,
                    HINSTANCE hPrevInstance, LPSTR lpCmdLine,
                    int nCmdShow);

            // Member functions
            virtual void InitMainWindow ();
};


//*******************************************************
// Constructors and destructors for chpt8
//
//     Copyright:
//             Copyright (c) 1993, William H. Roetzheim
//             All Rights Reserved
//
//*******************************************************

#pragma argsused  // Turn off arguments not used warning
chpt8::chpt8(LPSTR szName, HINSTANCE hInstance,
            HINSTANCE hPrevInstance, LPSTR lpCmdLine,
            int nCmdShow)
            : TApplication (szName, hInstance,
            hPrevInstance, lpCmdLine, nCmdShow)
{
    return;
}




//*******************************************************
// Member functions for class chpt8
//
//     Copyright:
//             Copyright (c) 1993, William H. Roetzheim
//             All Rights Reserved
//
//*******************************************************

void chpt8::InitMainWindow ()
```

continues

LISTING 8.1. continued

```
{
    MainWindow = new WOracleVideoDialog(NULL, "VideoDialog", this);
}



// Here is the main () for the program
int PASCAL WinMain (HINSTANCE hInstance,
    HINSTANCE hPrevInstance, LPSTR lpCmdLine,
    int)
{
    // Force DLL to be loaded
    HINSTANCE BWCCDll = LoadLibrary ("bwcc.dll");

    // Create chpt8 application from class
    chpt8 ochpt8 ("chpt8", hInstance,
                    hPrevInstance, lpCmdLine, SW_NORMAL);

    // Start created application running
    ochpt8.Run ();  // Run till window closed

    if (BWCCDll) FreeLibrary (BWCCDll);

    // Return termination status when window closed
    return ochpt8.Status;
}
```

The *WOracleVideoDialog* Header File

Listing 8.2 shows the WOracleVideoDialog header file. This file is similar to the equivalent Paradox file, WVIDEODIALOG.H. The RecordToDialog and DialogToRecord functions have been replaced with the DialogToOracle and OracleToDialog functions. OracleToDialog transfers data from variables recognized by Oracle to the dialog fields. DialogToOracle transfers data from the dialog fields to variables recognized by Oracle. No other changes to the WVideoDialog header are required for it to function as the WOracleVideoDialog header. If only the other changes were as simple to make as the changes to these first two files!

HINT: Although the PRO*C preprocessor enables you to put embedded SQL statements in your header file, generally it is not a good idea to do so. The problem is that people who want to use your class normally want to include your header file in their application, and the compiler they are using obviously will take strong exception to the presence of embedded SQL. If you do decide to put embedded SQL in your header file, you must preprocess it explicitly. (Files referred to in an #include in the main file are not preprocessed automatically.) You probably also will want to use a .PH extension for the original source file instead of an .H extension.

LISTING 8.2. WORACLEVIDEODIALOG.H header file.

```
// WORACLEVIDEODIALOG.H - Header file for WOracleVideoDialog class

#ifndef WOracleVideoDialog_H
#    define WOracleVideoDialog_H

// Note that the following code is executed only
// if this file has not been previously included


// #include files for both PC and SUN
#include  "WStr.h"
#include  "DVideo.h"
#include  <string.h>

#ifdef __BORLANDC__
    // PC-specific #includes
#    include   <owl.h>
#    include <edit.h>
#    include <combobox.h>

#endif

#ifdef Unix
```

continues

LISTING 8.2. continued

```
        // UNIX-specific #includes

#endif

#define   MAX_TITLE 36
#define MAX_STARS    77
#define MAX_CATEGORY 22
#define MAX_RATING 7
#define MAX_EVALUATION 7

// NOTE: Do NOT put EXEC SQL statements in your header file


//*****************************************************
// WOracleVideoDialog - Handler for Video dialog box
//
//      Purpose:
//          Demonstrate the use of Paradox from a dialog
//          handling class.
//
//      Notes:
//
//      Copyright:
//              Copyright (c) 1993, William H. Roetzheim
//              All Rights Reserved
//
//*****************************************************

_CLASSDEF (WOracleVideoDialog)
class WOracleVideoDialog : public TDialog
{
    private:
            // Private data members ********************

          // Pointers to dialog box controls
            PTEdit Title;
            PTEdit Stars;
            PTComboBox Category;
            PTComboBox Rating;
            PTComboBox Evaluation;

            // Private member functions
            void InitVariables ();

    public:
            // Public data members ********************
```

```
// Public member functions ******************
// Constructors and destructors
WOracleVideoDialog (PTWindowsObject, LPSTR, PTModule);
~WOracleVideoDialog ();

// Member functions
void DialogToOracle ();
void OracleToDialog ();
virtual void SetupWindow ();
virtual void Reset () =
    [ID_FIRST + IDD_Clear];
virtual void Add () =
    [ID_FIRST + IDD_Add];
virtual void Delete () =
    [ID_FIRST + IDD_Delete];
virtual void Update() =
    [ID_FIRST + IDD_Update];
virtual void Next () =
    [ID_FIRST + IDD_Next];
virtual void Previous () =
    [ID_FIRST + IDD_Previous];
};

#endif WOracleVideoDialog_H
```

The *WOracleVideoDialog* Source Code File

The source code for the WOracleVideoDialog class contains the embedded
SQL commands to manipulate the Oracle database directly from the dialog handler. I step through the key portions of the file, focusing on the
embedded SQL and the code that is changed from the WVideoDialog class.
The C++ file produced by the Oracle PRO*C preprocessor is included at the
end of this chapter.

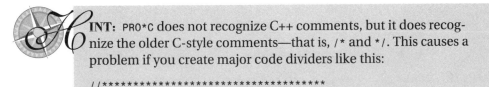

INT: PRO*C does not recognize C++ comments, but it does recognize the older C-style comments—that is, /* and */. This causes a
problem if you create major code dividers like this:

```
//************************************
```

PRO*C interprets the preceding line as an extraneous character (/) followed by a C comment (/*) with no end-of-comment mark. You must either avoid using this type of code divider or put a slash at the end so that PRO*C sees both a C beginning comment and a C ending comment. The following comment line is correct for both C++ and PRO*C:

```
//*************************************/
```

INT: Borland C++ displays and highlights syntax errors in the .CPP file generated by PRO*C, not in the original source .PC file. If you're not careful, you might quickly fix a problem in the .CPP file only to later discover that the next time you run PRO*C on your original .PC file, your changes have been overwritten. Remember to always make changes to the .PC file and to let the PRO*C preprocessor regenerate the .CPP file.

INT: The code generated by the Oracle preprocessor requires a stack larger than the one provided by the default OWL.DEF file. I didn't experiment to find the minimum size that works, but 32K compiles and runs well.

INT: PRO*C doesn't accept lines longer than 80 characters—even in your C++ code. Break your longer lines into shorter pieces.

DECLARE Blocks

Communication between the class and the Oracle database is accomplished by using variables recognized by both the C++ code and the Oracle preprocessor. These variables must be defined in a DECLARE block. You can have multiple DECLARE blocks in your program, but at least one must be defined in the global area of your file—even if it is empty. Otherwise, the precompiler gives you an error message.

Variables that are used with Oracle within only a single function body normally should be declared in a DECLARE block within that function. These variables then have local scope. You should declare variables that are shared by multiple functions outside the body of any member function so that they will be globally accessible to all the functions in this file. It would be nice to give the variables global scope within the class by declaring them as class data elements, but doing so would require that you put embedded SQL in the class header file. The DECLARE block for the WOracleVideoDialog class is

```
EXEC SQL BEGIN DECLARE SECTION;
     VARCHAR TitleOracle [35];
     VARCHAR StarsOracle [76];
     VARCHAR CategoryOracle [21];
     VARCHAR RatingOracle [6];
     VARCHAR EvaluationOracle [6];
EXEC SQL END DECLARE SECTION;
```

INT: Remember that because the Oracle preprocessor runs ahead of the C++ preprocessor, you cannot use #defines in your embedded SQL code.

Using *sqlca*

Oracle uses a structure called sqlca (SQL Communications Area) to communicate status information to your application at runtime. Each embedded SQL command updates this structure. To make sqlca available to yourself and to the Oracle functions, use this statement:

```
EXEC SQL INCLUDE sqlca;
```

The sqlca structure definition is as follows:

```
struct sqlca
{
    char        sqlcaid[8];    // Character string "SQLCA"
    long        sqlabc;        // Length of SQLCA structure in bytes
    long        sqlcode;       // Oracle return code from function
    struct
    {
        unsigned short sqlerrml;  // Length of error message
        char sqlerrmc[70];        // Text of error message
    } sqlerrm;
    char        sqlerrp[8];        // Reserved
    long        sqlerrd[6];        // [0..1] reserved
                                   // [2] total rows processed for a
                                   // cursor
                                   // [3..5] reserved
    char            sqlwarn[8];    // [0] another warning flag set
                                   // [1] character string truncated
                                   // [2] reserved
                                   // [3] SELECT list not equal to
                                   // INTO list
                                   // [4] DELETE or UPDATE without
                                   // WHERE clause
                                   // [5..7] reserved
    char            sqlext[8]      // Reserved
};
```

Opening and Closing a Connection to the Database

Before you perform any database operations, you must establish a connection between your application and the database. This is accomplished by using the CONNECT statement, as in the following example:

```
EXEC SQL BEGIN DECLARE SECTION;
    VARCHAR UserName [20];
    VARCHAR Password [20];
EXEC SQL END DECLARE SECTION;

strcpy ((char *)UserName.arr, "SYSTEM");
strcpy ((char *)Password.arr, "MANAGER");
UserName.len = strlen ((char *)UserName.arr);
Password.len = strlen ((char *)Password.arr);

EXEC SQL CONNECT :UserName IDENTIFIED BY :Password;
```

You should always check the sqlca structure for an error, because errors during CONNECT are quite common. The following code demonstrates the proper way to do this:

```
if (sqlca.sqlcode < 0)
{
    MessageBeep (0);
    sqlca.sqlerrm.sqlerrmc[sqlca.sqlerrm.sqlerrml] = 0;
    MessageBox (NULL, sqlca.sqlerrm.sqlerrmc,
                        "WOracleVideoDialog", MB_OK);
    exit (-1);
}
```

If an error is detected (if sqlcode < 0), this code NULL-terminates the sqlca error message (which is stored in sqlca.sqlerrm.sqlerrmc), displays it in a message box, then terminates the program.

HINT: During CONNECT, if you receive an error numbered over 9000, don't bother trying to look it up. Errors above 9000 are undocumented, and the people at Oracle Corporation tell me that even *they* don't have any written list of these errors! The only time I ran into this error was when I ran Windows in enhanced mode by mistake. If you receive a 9000 series error, make sure you are running Windows in standard mode.

HINT: If your program crashes during testing, the connection to Oracle is left open, and you can't reconnect as long as Oracle is running. You also will experience this problem if you are running your application with the debugger and you terminate the application without closing the connection. If this happens, you will have a 3000 series error during CONNECT the next time you try to open a connection. The only way I know of to terminate the connection—other than rebooting and restarting Oracle—is to use the commands REMORA ALL and REMPME to remove the Oracle drivers, then restart Oracle. There might be a better way to do this from within SQL*DBA, but I can't find it.

Oracle Cursors

Oracle uses the term *cursor* to refer to a record pointer. Whenever you want to step through the database sequentially, you need a cursor to keep track of your current record position. To create a cursor, use the DECLARE CURSOR command:

```
EXEC SQL DECLARE VideoCursor CURSOR FOR
    SELECT Title, Stars, Category, Rating, Evaluation
    FROM Video;
```

Notice that the cursor includes the SELECT clause. It would also include the SORT clause, if it were used. The cursor does not include an INTO clause, however. The INTO clause is used only when you want to retrieve the actual data that the cursor points to. This is accomplished by using the FETCH statement:

```
EXEC SQL FETCH VideoCursor INTO
    :TitleOracle,
    :StarsOracle,
    :CategoryOracle,
    :RatingOracle,
    :EvaluationOracle;
```

To reset a cursor to the first record, you can reopen it, as in the following:

```
EXEC SQL OPEN VideoCursor;
```

All SQL statements that take a WHERE clause can operate on the record that a cursor currently points to. For example, to delete the record pointed to by VideoCursor, use the following code:

```
EXEC SQL DELETE FROM Video WHERE CURRENT OF VideoCursor;
```

WORACLEVIDEO.PC Source Code Listing

Listing 8.3 is the WOracleVideo source file.

LISTING 8.3. WORACLEVIDEO.PC source file listing.

```
// WORACLEVIDEODIALOG.CPP - Source file for WOracleVideoDialog class

#include "WOracleVideoDialog.h"   // ALL other #include statements
                                  // are in this file
```

```
// Must use C protoypes for Oracle functions with CPP

extern "C"
{
#include "sqlproto.h"
}


// Must have a global Oracle declare area, even if empty


EXEC SQL BEGIN DECLARE SECTION;
     VARCHAR TitleOracle [36];
     VARCHAR StarsOracle [77];
     VARCHAR CategoryOracle [22];
     VARCHAR RatingOracle [7];
     VARCHAR EvaluationOracle [7];
EXEC SQL END DECLARE SECTION;


// Declare status variable

EXEC SQL INCLUDE sqlca;


// Create a cursor for database queries

EXEC SQL DECLARE VideoCursor CURSOR FOR
     SELECT Title, Stars, Category, Rating, Evaluation
     FROM Video;


// NOTE:       This code assumes that the database and Video
//             table are already created outside of this
//             application (using ordinary Oracle tools).


//--------------------------------------------------*
// Constructors and destructors for WOracleVideoDialog
//
//     Copyright:
//             Copyright (c) 1993, William H. Roetzheim
//             All Rights Reserved
//
//--------------------------------------------------*

WOracleVideoDialog::WOracleVideoDialog (PTWindowsObject Parent,
            LPSTR Name, PTModule Module)
```

continues

LISTING 8.3. continued

```
               : TDialog (Parent, Name, Module)
{

     Title = new TEdit (this, IDD_Title,
          MAX_TITLE, Module);
     Stars = new TEdit (this, IDD_Stars,
          MAX_STARS, Module);
     Category = new TComboBox (this, IDD_Category,
          MAX_CATEGORY, Module);
     Rating = new TComboBox (this, IDD_Rating,
          MAX_RATING, Module);
     Evaluation = new TComboBox (this, IDD_Evaluation,
          MAX_EVALUATION, Module);

     // Connect to the database


     EXEC SQL BEGIN DECLARE SECTION;
          VARCHAR UserName [20];
          VARCHAR Password [20];
     EXEC SQL END DECLARE SECTION;

     strcpy ((char *)UserName.arr, "SYSTEM");
     strcpy ((char *)Password.arr, "MANAGER");
     UserName.len = strlen ((char *)UserName.arr);
     Password.len = strlen ((char *)Password.arr);


     EXEC SQL CONNECT :UserName IDENTIFIED BY :Password;

     if (sqlca.sqlcode < 0)
     {
          MessageBeep (0);
          sqlca.sqlerrm.sqlerrmc[sqlca.sqlerrm.sqlerrml] = 0;
          MessageBox (NULL, sqlca.sqlerrm.sqlerrmc,
                              "WOracleVideoDialog", MB_OK);
          exit (-1);
     }
}


WOracleVideoDialog::~WOracleVideoDialog ()
{

     EXEC SQL CLOSE VideoCursor;
```

```
      EXEC SQL COMMIT RELEASE;

}


//--------------------------------------------------
// Member functions for class
//
//    Copyright:
//            Copyright (c) 1993, William H. Roetzheim
//            All Rights Reserved
//
//--------------------------------------------------*

void WOracleVideoDialog::SetupWindow ()
{
    TDialog::SetupWindow ();

    Category->AddString ("Action/Adventure");
    Category->AddString ("Childrens");
    Category->AddString ("Comedy");
    Category->AddString ("Drama");
    Category->AddString ("Home Movie");
    Category->AddString ("Horror");
    Category->AddString ("Musical");
    Category->AddString ("Science Fiction");
    Category->AddString ("Western");

    Rating->AddString ("G");
    Rating->AddString ("PG");
    Rating->AddString ("PG 13");
    Rating->AddString ("R");
    Rating->AddString ("X");

    Evaluation->AddString ("*");
    Evaluation->AddString ("**");
    Evaluation->AddString ("***");
    Evaluation->AddString ("****");
    Evaluation->AddString ("*****");

    Reset ();
}


void WOracleVideoDialog::Reset ()
{

    Title->Clear();
```

continues

LISTING 8.3. continued

```
        Stars->Clear();
        Category->SetSelIndex (-1);
        Rating->SetSelIndex (-1);
        Evaluation->SetSelIndex (-1);


        // Reset the Video database cursor

        EXEC SQL OPEN VideoCursor;

}


void WOracleVideoDialog::Add ()
{
        DialogToOracle ();



        EXEC SQL INSERT INTO Video
            (Title, Stars, Category, Rating, Evaluation)
            VALUES (:TitleOracle, :StarsOracle, :CategoryOracle,
                        :RatingOracle, :EvaluationOracle);
        EXEC SQL COMMIT;

        Reset ();
}


void WOracleVideoDialog::Delete ()
{
        DialogToOracle ();


        EXEC SQL DELETE FROM Video WHERE CURRENT OF VideoCursor;

        if (sqlca.sqlcode < 0)
        {
            sqlca.sqlerrm.sqlerrmc[sqlca.sqlerrm.sqlerrml] = 0;
            MessageBox (NULL, sqlca.sqlerrm.sqlerrmc,
                "WOracleVideoDialog::Delete", MB_OK);
        }
```

```
        else Reset ();

Reset ();

}


void WOracleVideoDialog::Update ()
{
    DialogToOracle ();


    EXEC SQL UPDATE Video
        SET Title = :TitleOracle,
            Stars = :StarsOracle,
            Category = :CategoryOracle,
            Rating = :RatingOracle,
            Evaluation = :EvaluationOracle
        WHERE CURRENT OF VideoCursor;

    Reset ();
}


void WOracleVideoDialog::Next ()
{
    // Initialize the Oracle variables
    InitVariables ();


    EXEC SQL FETCH VideoCursor INTO
        :TitleOracle,
        :StarsOracle,
        :CategoryOracle,
        :RatingOracle,
        :EvaluationOracle;

    if (sqlca.sqlcode == 0)
    {
        OracleToDialog ();
    }
}
```

continues

LISTING 8.3. continued

```cpp
void WOracleVideoDialog::Previous ()
{
    long Row = sqlca.sqlerrd[2] -1;
    if (Row < 0) Row = 0;

    // Reset the Video cursor

    EXEC SQL OPEN VideoCursor;

    // Reposition just prior to what we want
    // Note: Oracle indexes starting at 1, not 0
    for (int i = 1; i < Row; i++)
    {
        // Initialize the Oracle variables
        InitVariables ();


        EXEC SQL FETCH VideoCursor INTO
            :TitleOracle,
            :StarsOracle,
            :CategoryOracle,
            :RatingOracle,
            :EvaluationOracle;

    }

    Next ();
}

void WOracleVideoDialog::InitVariables ()
{
    TitleOracle.arr[0] = 0;
    StarsOracle.arr[0] = 0;
    CategoryOracle.arr[0] = 0;
    RatingOracle.arr[0] = 0;
    EvaluationOracle.arr[0] = 0;

    TitleOracle.len = 0;
    StarsOracle.len = 0;
    CategoryOracle.len = 0;
    RatingOracle.len = 0;
    EvaluationOracle.len = 0;
}
```

```
void WOracleVideoDialog::DialogToOracle ()
{
    char Buffer [MAX_STARS];

    Title->GetText (Buffer, MAX_TITLE);
    strcpy ((char *)TitleOracle.arr, Buffer);

    Stars->GetText (Buffer, MAX_STARS);
    strcpy ((char *)StarsOracle.arr, Buffer);

    if (Category->GetSelString (Buffer, MAX_CATEGORY) < 0)
    {
        strcpy ((char *) CategoryOracle.arr, "");
    }
    else strcpy ((char *) CategoryOracle.arr, Buffer);

    if (Rating->GetSelString (Buffer, MAX_RATING) < 0)
    {
        strcpy ((char *) RatingOracle.arr, "");
    }
    else strcpy ((char *) RatingOracle.arr, Buffer);

    if (Evaluation->GetSelString (Buffer, MAX_EVALUATION) < 0)
    {
        strcpy ((char *) EvaluationOracle.arr, "");
    }
    else strcpy ((char *) EvaluationOracle.arr, Buffer);


    TitleOracle.len = strlen ((char *)TitleOracle.arr);
    StarsOracle.len = strlen ((char *)StarsOracle.arr);
    CategoryOracle.len = strlen ((char *)CategoryOracle.arr);
    RatingOracle.len = strlen ((char *)RatingOracle.arr);
    EvaluationOracle.len = strlen ((char *)EvaluationOracle.arr);
}

void WOracleVideoDialog::OracleToDialog ()
{
    // NULL-terminate the Oracle fields
    TitleOracle.arr [TitleOracle.len] = 0;
    StarsOracle.arr [StarsOracle.len] = 0;
    CategoryOracle.arr [CategoryOracle.len] = 0;
    RatingOracle.arr [RatingOracle.len] = 0;
    EvaluationOracle.arr [EvaluationOracle.len] = 0;
```

continues

LISTING 8.3. continued

```
        // Now copy
        Title->SetText ((char *) TitleOracle.arr);
        Stars->SetText ((char *) StarsOracle.arr);
        Category->SetSelString (CategoryOracle.arr, -1);
        Rating->SetSelString (RatingOracle.arr, -1);
        Evaluation->SetSelString (EvaluationOracle.arr, -1);
}
```

SQLPROTO.H Header File

Oracle provides a header file with prototypes for all of the functions used
by the PRO*C preprocessor and the Oracle Call Interface (OCI). Unfortunately, this file is not compatible with the newer versions of ANSI C, including Borland C++. To make the file work properly with Borland C++, I
changed char *s to unsigned char *s and changed several shorts to unsigned
shorts. The modified file, SQLPROTO.H, shown in Listing 8.4, is included
on the source disk.

LISTING 8.4. SQLPROTO.H header listing.

```
#ifndef SQLPROTO
#  define SQLPROTO

extern void sqlab2(  int *, unsigned char *[], unsigned long[],
                     unsigned short[], unsigned short*[]  );
                     extern void sqlad2(  int*, unsigned char*[],
                     unsigned long[], unsigned short[],
                     unsigned short*[]  );
extern void sqlbcc(  int*, int*  );
extern void sqlbs2(  int*, unsigned char*[], unsigned long[],
                     unsigned short[], unsigned short*[], int*,
                     int*  );
extern void sqlcls(  int*  );
extern void sqlcom(  int*  );
extern void sqlexe(  int*  );
extern void sqlfcc(  void  );
extern void sqlfch(  int*, int*  );
```

```
extern void sqlgb2(  unsigned int*, unsigned int*,
                     unsigned char *[], unsigned short[],
                     unsigned short[], unsigned char *[],
                     unsigned short[], unsigned short[],
                     unsigned short[]  );
extern void sqlgd2(  unsigned int*, int*, unsigned char *[],
                     unsigned short[], unsigned short[],
                     unsigned long[], unsigned short[]  );
extern void sqlgf2(  int*, unsigned char**, unsigned long*,
                     unsigned short*, int*, unsigned char**,
                     unsigned long*, unsigned short*  );
extern void sqlgri(  int*, unsigned char *[]);
extern void sqliem(  unsigned char *, int*  );
extern void sqllo2(  int*, unsigned char*[], unsigned long[],
                     unsigned short[], unsigned long*, int*, int*,
                     unsigned long*  );
extern void sqloca(  struct oraca *, unsigned char *, int*, int*
);
extern void sqlopn(  int*, int*, unsigned long*  );
extern void sqlos2(  int*, unsigned char*[], unsigned long[],
                     unsigned short[], unsigned short*[]  );
                     extern void sqlosq(  unsigned char *, int*  );
extern void sqlpf2(  int*, unsigned char**, unsigned long*,
                     unsigned short*, int*, unsigned char **,
                     unsigned long*, unsigned short*  );
extern void sqlrol(  int*  );
extern void sqlsc2(  struct sqlca *  );
extern void sqlsca(  struct sqlca *  );
extern void sqlscc(  int*  );
extern void sqlsch(  int*  );
extern void sqlsqs(  unsigned char *, unsigned int *  );
extern void sqltfl(  int*, int*  );
extern void sqltoc(  int*, int*, unsigned long*  );
extern void sqlwnr(  void  );

#endif
```

The Oracle Call Interface

Embedded SQL offers portability to other SQL database management systems that provide an embedded SQL preprocessor similar to PRO*C in Oracle. Your source code with its embedded SQL statements can be run

through the appropriate preprocessor for conversion to manufacturer-specific C function calls. There might be cases, however, where you need to use, or prefer to use, C function libraries yourself instead of relying on the preprocessor. These C libraries are provided by the manufacturer in .LIB form and can be called like any other C function.

If the preprocessor generates code that doesn't compile properly with your C or C++ compiler, you need to use the C library directly. If you're absolutely sure that your application will never need to operate with a different manufacturer's SQL database management system, you can use the C library directly and avoid the extra step in compilation.

In Oracle, the C library that provides access to the database management system is called the Oracle Call Interface. The OCI consists of the C functions shown in Table 8.9. The term *cursor* refers to a data structure that Oracle uses to maintain the current record number and to pass data to and from the OCI functions. Multiple cursors can be active simultaneously for a single Oracle database.

TABLE 8.9. Oracle Call Interface functions.

Function	Description
obndrn	Associates the address of a program variable with a specified placeholder by number
obndrv	Associates the address of a program variable with a specified placeholder by name
obreak	Performs an immediate (asynchronous) abort of any currently executing OCI function
ocan	Cancels a query
oclose	Disconnects a cursor from the Oracle context area
ocof	Disables the automatic COMMIT of every SQL data manipulation statement
ocom	Commits the current transaction
ocon	Enables the automatic COMMIT of every SQL data manipulation statement

Function	Description
odefin	Defines an output variable for a specified select-list item of a SQL query
odsc	Describes select-list items for dynamic SQL queries
oerhms	Returns the text of an Oracle error message
oermsg	Returns the Oracle message text that corresponds to the return code
oexec	Executes the SQL statement associated with a cursor
oexn	Executes a SQL statement with array variables used for input data
ofen	Fetches multiple rows into arrays of variables
ofetch	Returns rows of a query to the program one row at a time
ologof	Disconnects from an Oracle database
olon	Connects to an Oracle database
oname	Retrieves the names of select-list items in a SQL query statement. Provided for backward compatibility. You should always use odsc instead of oname.
oopen	Opens a cursor
oopt	Sets rollback options for a nonfatal Oracle error
orlon	Logs on to an Oracle database with support for multiple simultaneous logons by the same user
orol	Rolls back the current transaction
osql3	Parses a SQL statement or a PL/SQL block and associates it with a cursor
osqlda	Provided for programs that mix precompiler code and OCI calls

INT: The version of Oracle I work with—6.0—was not designed with C++ in mind, so the function names in the library are not mangled. To make the Borland C++ compiler use the proper, unmangled names when you make the calls, you must specify that the functions are C functions when the prototypes are declared. This can be accomplished by including the OCI header file as follows:

```
extern "C"
{
  #include "sqlproto.h"
}
```

Listing 8.5 shows a sample of OCI code. In this case, the code is generated by the PRO*C preprocessor.

LISTING 8.5. WVIDEODIALOG.CPP: OCI code generated by the PRO*C preprocessor.

```
// WORACLEVIDEODIALOG.CPP - Source file for WOracleVideoDialog class

#include "WOracleVideoDialog.h"  // ALL other #include statements
                                 // are in this file


// Must use C prototypes for Oracle functions with CPP

extern "C"
{
#include "sqlproto.h"
}


// Must have a global Oracle declare area, even if empty


/* SQL stmt #1
EXEC SQL BEGIN DECLARE SECTION;
        VARCHAR TitleOracle [36];
*/
```

```
struct {
  unsigned short len;
  unsigned char arr[36];
  } TitleOracle;
/*
        VARCHAR StarsOracle [77];
*/
struct {
  unsigned short len;
  unsigned char arr[77];
  } StarsOracle;
/*
        VARCHAR CategoryOracle [22];
*/
struct {
  unsigned short len;
  unsigned char arr[22];
  } CategoryOracle;
/*
        VARCHAR RatingOracle [7];
*/
struct {
  unsigned short len;
  unsigned char arr[7];
  } RatingOracle;
/*
        VARCHAR EvaluationOracle [7];
*/
struct {
  unsigned short len;
  unsigned char arr[7];
  } EvaluationOracle;
/* SQL stmt #2
EXEC SQL END DECLARE SECTION;
*/
static struct {
int            sq001N;
unsigned char  *sq001V[4];
unsigned long   sq001L[4];
unsigned short  sq001T[4];
unsigned short *sq001I[4];
} sq001 = {4};
static struct {
int            sq002N;
unsigned char  *sq002V[1];
unsigned long   sq002L[1];
unsigned short  sq002T[1];
unsigned short *sq002I[1];
```

continues

LISTING 8.5. continued

```
} sq002 = {1};
static struct {
int          sq003N;
unsigned char  *sq003V[1];
unsigned long   sq003L[1];
unsigned short  sq003T[1];
unsigned short *sq003I[1];
} sq003 = {1};
static struct {
int          sq004N;
unsigned char  *sq004V[1];
unsigned long   sq004L[1];
unsigned short  sq004T[1];
unsigned short *sq004I[1];
} sq004 = {1};
static char sq005[57] =
"SELECT TITLE,STARS,CATEGORY,RATING,EVALUATION FROM VIDEO"
;
static struct {
int          sq006N;
unsigned char  *sq006V[1];
unsigned long   sq006L[1];
unsigned short  sq006T[1];
unsigned short *sq006I[1];
} sq006 = {1};
static char sq007[85] =
"INSERT INTO VIDEO(TITLE,STARS,CATEGORY,RATING,EVALUATION)\
                  VALUES(:b1,:b2,:b3,:b4,:b5)"
;
static struct {
int          sq008N;
unsigned char  *sq008V[5];
unsigned long   sq008L[5];
unsigned short  sq008T[5];
unsigned short *sq008I[5];
} sq008 = {5};
static struct {
int          sq009N;
unsigned char  *sq009V[1];
unsigned long   sq009L[1];
unsigned short  sq009T[1];
unsigned short *sq009I[1];
} sq009 = {1};
static struct {
int          sq010N;
unsigned char  *sq010V[1];
```

```
unsigned long    sq010L[1];
unsigned short  sq010T[1];
unsigned short *sq010I[1];
} sq010 = {1};
static char sq011[34] =
"DELETE FROM VIDEO WHERE ROWID=:b1"
;
static struct {
int             sq012N;
unsigned char  *sq012V[1];
unsigned long    sq012L[1];
unsigned short   sq012T[1];
unsigned short *sq012I[1];
} sq012 = {1};
static struct {
int             sq013N;
unsigned char  *sq013V[1];
unsigned long    sq013L[1];
unsigned short   sq013T[1];
unsigned short *sq013I[1];
} sq013 = {1};
static char sq014[92] =
"UPDATE VIDEO SET TITLE=:b1,STARS=:b2,CATEGORY=:b3,RATING=:b4,\
EVALUATION=:b5 WHERE ROWID=:b6"
;
static struct {
int             sq015N;
unsigned char  *sq015V[6];
unsigned long    sq015L[6];
unsigned short   sq015T[6];
unsigned short *sq015I[6];
} sq015 = {6};
static struct {
int             sq016N;
unsigned char  *sq016V[1];
unsigned long    sq016L[1];
unsigned short   sq016T[1];
unsigned short *sq016I[1];
} sq016 = {1};
static struct {
int             sq017N;
unsigned char  *sq017V[5];
unsigned long    sq017L[5];
unsigned short   sq017T[5];
unsigned short *sq017I[5];
} sq017 = {5};
static struct {
int             sq018N;
```

continues

LISTING 8.5. continued

```
unsigned char   *sq018V[1];
unsigned long    sq018L[1];
unsigned short   sq018T[1];
unsigned short  *sq018I[1];
} sq018 = {1};
static char sq019[57] =
"SELECT TITLE,STARS,CATEGORY,RATING,EVALUATION FROM VIDEO"
;
static struct {
int              sq020N;
unsigned char   *sq020V[1];
unsigned long    sq020L[1];
unsigned short   sq020T[1];
unsigned short  *sq020I[1];
} sq020 = {1};
static struct {
int              sq021N;
unsigned char   *sq021V[5];
unsigned long    sq021L[5];
unsigned short   sq021T[5];
unsigned short  *sq021I[5];
} sq021 = {5};
static int SQLTM[8];
static int sqlcun[4] = {
0,0,0,0};
static int sqlusi[1] = {
0};
static unsigned long sqlami = 0;
static int SQLBT0 = 1;
static int SQLBT1 = 2;
static int SQLBT2 = 4;
static int SQLBT3 = 9;
static unsigned long sqlvsn = 10317;
static int IAPSUCC = 0;
static int IAPFAIL = 1403;
static int IAPFTL  = 535;
#ifndef SQLPROTO
extern    sqlab2();
extern    sqlad2();
extern    sqlbs2();
extern    sqlcls();
extern    sqlcom();
extern    sqlexe();
extern    sqlfch();
extern    sqliem();
```

```
extern     sqllo2();
extern     sqlopn();
extern     sqlosq();
extern     sqlsca();
extern     sqlscc();
extern     sqlsch();
extern     sqltfl();
extern     sqlwnr();
extern     sqlgri();
extern     sqltoc();
#endif /* SQLPROTO */


// Declare status variable

/* SQL stmt #3
EXEC SQL INCLUDE sqlca;
*/
/* Copyright (c) 1985, 1986 by Oracle Corporation */

/*
NAME
  SQLCA : SQL Communications Area
FUNCTION
  Contains no code. Oracle fills in SQLCA with status info
  during the execution of a SQL stmt.
NOTES
  If the symbol SQLCA_STORAGE_CLASS is defined, SQLCA
  will be defined to have this storage class. For example,

    #define SQLCA_STORAGE_CLASS extern

  will define SQLCA as an extern.

  If the symbol SQLCA_INIT is defined, SQLCA will be
  statically initialized. Although this isn't necessary in order
  to use SQLCA, it's good programming practice not to have
  uninitialized variables. However, some C compilers/OS's don't
  allow automatic variables to be initialized in this manner.
  Therefore, if you are INCLUDEing SQLCA in a place where it
  would be an automatic, AND your C compiler/OS doesn't allow this
  style of initialization, then SQLCA_INIT should be left
  undefined. All others can define SQLCA_INIT if they wish.

  New rules for defining SQLCA_INIT, SQLCA_STORAGE_CLASS, and DLL
  in OS/2:
  Users should not define SQLCA_STORAGE_CLASS if defining
```

continues

LISTING 8.5. continued

```
a DLL. SQLCA_STORAGE_CLASS is used primarily for single-threaded
programs and for internal development.

MODIFIED
  Okamura     08/15/89 - OS/2: users must define SQLMT for multi-
                                threaded case
  Okamura     06/23/89 - OS/2: modify for multi-threaded case
  Clare       12/06/84 - Ch SQLCA to not be an extern
  Clare       10/21/85 - Add initialization
  Bradbury    01/05/86 - Initialize only when SQLCA_INIT set
  Clare       06/12/86 - Add SQLCA_STORAGE_CLASS option
*/

#ifndef SQLCA
#define SQLCA 1

struct    sqlca
          {
          /* ub1 */ char     sqlcaid[8];
          /* b4  */ long     sqlabc;
          /* b4  */ long     sqlcode;
          struct
            {
            /* ub2 */ unsigned short sqlerrml;
            /* ub1 */ char           sqlerrmc[70];
            } sqlerrm;
          /* ub1 */ char     sqlerrp[8];
          /* b4  */ long     sqlerrd[6];
          /* ub1 */ char     sqlwarn[8];
          /* ub1 */ char     sqlext[8];
          };

#ifdef SQLMT
   extern struct sqlca *sqlcamt(); /* For multi-threaded version */
#  define sqlca (*sqlcamt())
#else /* SQLMT */

#ifdef SQLCA_STORAGE_CLASS
  SQLCA_STORAGE_CLASS struct sqlca sqlca
#  ifdef   SQLCA_INIT
          = {
          {'S', 'Q', 'L', 'C', 'A', ' ', ' ', ' '},
          sizeof(struct sqlca),
          0,
          { 0, {0}},
          {'N', 'O', 'T', ' ', 'S', 'E', 'T', ' '},
```

```
          {0, 0, 0, 0, 0, 0},
          {0, 0, 0, 0, 0, 0, 0, 0},
          {0, 0, 0, 0, 0, 0, 0, 0}
          }
# endif /* SQLCA_INIT */
          ;

#else /* SQLCA_STORAGE_CLASS */
   struct sqlca sqlca  /* For single-threaded version */

#  ifdef  SQLCA_INIT
          = {
          {'S', 'Q', 'L', 'C', 'A', ' ', ' ', ' '},
          sizeof(struct sqlca),
          0,
          { 0, {0}},
          {'N', 'O', 'T', ' ', 'S', 'E', 'T', ' '},
          {0, 0, 0, 0, 0, 0},
          {0, 0, 0, 0, 0, 0, 0, 0},
          {0, 0, 0, 0, 0, 0, 0, 0}
          }
#  endif /* SQLCA_INIT */
          ;
#endif /* SQLCA_STORAGE_CLASS */

#endif /* SQLMT */

/* End SQLCA */
#endif /* SQLCA */


// Create a cursor for database queries

/* SQL stmt #4
EXEC SQL DECLARE VideoCursor CURSOR FOR
       SELECT Title, Stars, Category, Rating, Evaluation
       FROM Video;
*/


// NOTE:      This code assumes that the database and Video
//            table are already created outside of this
//            application (using ordinary Oracle tools).


//------------------------------------------------*
// Constructors and destructors for WOracleVideoDialog
```

continues

LISTING 8.5. continued

```
//
//      Copyright:
//            Copyright (c) 1993, William H. Roetzheim
//            All Rights Reserved
//
//-----------------------------------------------*

WOracleVideoDialog::WOracleVideoDialog (PTWindowsObject Parent,
                      LPSTR Name, PTModule Module)
          : TDialog (Parent, Name, Module)
{

        Title = new TEdit (this, IDD_Title,
               MAX_TITLE, Module);
        Stars = new TEdit (this, IDD_Stars,
               MAX_STARS, Module);
        Category = new TComboBox (this, IDD_Category,
               MAX_CATEGORY, Module);
        Rating = new TComboBox (this, IDD_Rating,
               MAX_RATING, Module);
        Evaluation = new TComboBox (this, IDD_Evaluation,
               MAX_EVALUATION, Module);

        // Connect to the database


/* SQL stmt #5
        EXEC SQL BEGIN DECLARE SECTION;
                VARCHAR UserName [20];
*/
struct {
  unsigned short len;
  unsigned char arr[20];
  } UserName;
/*
                VARCHAR Password [20];
*/
struct {
  unsigned short len;
  unsigned char arr[20];
  } Password;
/* SQL stmt #6
    EXEC SQL END DECLARE SECTION;
*/

        strcpy ((char *)UserName.arr, "SYSTEM");
```

```
                strcpy ((char *)Password.arr, "MANAGER");
                UserName.len = strlen ((char *)UserName.arr);
            Password.len = strlen ((char *)Password.arr);


/* SQL stmt #7
        EXEC SQL CONNECT :UserName IDENTIFIED BY :Password;
*/
{       /* Beginning of SQL code gen stmt */
sqlsca(&sqlca);
sq001.sq001V[0] = (unsigned char *)&UserName.len;
sq001.sq001L[0] = (unsigned long)22;
sq001.sq001T[0] = (unsigned short)9;
sq001.sq001I[0] = (unsigned short *)0;
sq001.sq001V[1] = (unsigned char *)&Password.len;
sq001.sq001L[1] = (unsigned long)22;
sq001.sq001T[1] = (unsigned short)9;
sq001.sq001I[1] = (unsigned short *)0;
sq001.sq001T[2] = (unsigned short)10;
sq001.sq001T[3] = (unsigned short)10;
SQLTM[0] = (int)0;
SQLTM[1] = (int)10;
sqllo2(
  &sq001.sq001N,sq001.sq001V,sq001.sq001L,sq001.sq001T,
  &sqlami, &SQLTM[0], &SQLTM[1], &sqlvsn);
}    /* End of SQL code gen stmt */

        if (sqlca.sqlcode < 0)
        {
                MessageBeep (0);
                sqlca.sqlerrm.sqlerrmc[sqlca.sqlerrm.sqlerrml] = 0;
                MessageBox (NULL, sqlca.sqlerrm.sqlerrmc,
                                    "WOracleVideoDialog", MB_OK);
                exit (-1);
        }
}



WOracleVideoDialog::~WOracleVideoDialog ()
{

/* SQL stmt #8
        EXEC SQL CLOSE VideoCursor;
*/
{       /* Beginning of SQL code gen stmt */
sqlsca(&sqlca);
```

continues

LISTING 8.5. continued

```c
if ( !sqlusi[0] )
  {  /* OPEN SCOPE */
sq002.sq002T[0] = (unsigned short)10;
SQLTM[0] = (int)4;
sqlbs2(&sq002.sq002N, sq002.sq002V,
  sq002.sq002L, sq002.sq002T, sq002.sq002I,
  &SQLTM[0], &sqlusi[0]);
  }  /* CLOSE SCOPE */
sqlsch(&sqlusi[0]);
sqlscc(&sqlcun[0]);
SQLTM[0] = (int)0;
sqlcls(&SQLTM[0]);
}   /* End of SQL code gen stmt */
/* SQL stmt #9
        EXEC SQL COMMIT RELEASE;
*/
{      /* Beginning of SQL code gen stmt */
sqlsca(&sqlca);
if ( !sqlusi[0] )
  {  /* OPEN SCOPE */
sq003.sq003T[0] = (unsigned short)10;
SQLTM[0] = (int)4;
sqlbs2(&sq003.sq003N, sq003.sq003V,
  sq003.sq003L, sq003.sq003T, sq003.sq003I,
  &SQLTM[0], &sqlusi[0]);
  }  /* CLOSE SCOPE */
sqlsch(&sqlusi[0]);
SQLTM[0] = (int)1;
sqlcom(&SQLTM[0]);
}   /* End of SQL code gen stmt */

}


//-------------------------------------------------------
// Member functions for class
//
//     Copyright:
//             Copyright (c) 1993, William H. Roetzheim
//             All Rights Reserved
//
//----------------------------------------------------*

void WOracleVideoDialog::SetupWindow ()
{
```

```
        TDialog::SetupWindow ();

        Category->AddString ("Action/Adventure");
        Category->AddString ("Childrens");
        Category->AddString ("Comedy");
        Category->AddString ("Drama");
        Category->AddString ("Home Movie");
        Category->AddString ("Horror");
        Category->AddString ("Musical");
        Category->AddString ("Science Fiction");
        Category->AddString ("Western");

        Rating->AddString ("G");
        Rating->AddString ("PG");
        Rating->AddString ("PG 13");
        Rating->AddString ("R");
        Rating->AddString ("X");

        Evaluation->AddString ("*");
        Evaluation->AddString ("**");
        Evaluation->AddString ("***");
        Evaluation->AddString ("****");
        Evaluation->AddString ("*****");

        Reset ();
}


void WOracleVideoDialog::Reset ()
{

        Title->Clear();
        Stars->Clear();
        Category->SetSelIndex (-1);
        Rating->SetSelIndex (-1);
        Evaluation->SetSelIndex (-1);


        // Reset the Video database cursor

/* SQL stmt #10
        EXEC SQL OPEN VideoCursor;
*/
{      /* Beginning of SQL code gen stmt */
sqlsca(&sqlca);
if ( !sqlusi[0] )
  {  /* OPEN SCOPE */
```

continues

LISTING 8.5. continued

```
sq004.sq004T[0] = (unsigned short)10;
SQLTM[0] = (int)4;
sqlbs2(&sq004.sq004N, sq004.sq004V,
  sq004.sq004L, sq004.sq004T, sq004.sq004I,
  &SQLTM[0], &sqlusi[0]);
  }  /* CLOSE SCOPE */
sqlsch(&sqlusi[0]);
sqlscc(&sqlcun[0]);
SQLTM[1] = (int)16384;
sqltoc(&SQLTM[0],&SQLTM[1],&sqlvsn);
 if ( !SQLTM[0] )
   {  /* OPEN SCOPE */
SQLTM[0] = (int)56;
sqlosq(sq005, &SQLTM[0]);
  }  /* CLOSE SCOPE */
SQLTM[0] = (int)1;
sqlexe(&SQLTM[0]);
}   /* End of SQL code gen stmt */


}


void WOracleVideoDialog::Add ()
{
        DialogToOracle ();



/* SQL stmt #11
        EXEC SQL INSERT INTO Video
                (Title, Stars, Category, Rating, Evaluation)
                VALUES (:TitleOracle, :StarsOracle, :CategoryOracle,
                                :RatingOracle, :EvaluationOracle);
*/
{      /* Beginning of SQL code gen stmt */
sqlsca(&sqlca);
if ( !sqlusi[0] )
  {  /* OPEN SCOPE */
sq006.sq006T[0] = (unsigned short)10;
SQLTM[0] = (int)4;
sqlbs2(&sq006.sq006N, sq006.sq006V,
  sq006.sq006L, sq006.sq006T, sq006.sq006I,
  &SQLTM[0], &sqlusi[0]);
  }  /* CLOSE SCOPE */
sqlsch(&sqlusi[0]);
```

```
sqlscc(&sqlcun[1]);
sqltfl(&SQLTM[0], &SQLBT0);
if ( !SQLTM[0] )
  {  /* OPEN SCOPE */
SQLTM[0] = (int)16384;
sqlopn(&SQLTM[0], &SQLBT3, &sqlvsn);
SQLTM[0] = (int)84;
sqlosq(sq007, &SQLTM[0]);
  }  /* CLOSE SCOPE */
sq008.sq008V[0] = (unsigned char *)&TitleOracle.len;
sq008.sq008L[0] = (unsigned long)38;
sq008.sq008T[0] = (unsigned short)9;
sq008.sq008I[0] = (unsigned short *)0;
sq008.sq008V[1] = (unsigned char *)&StarsOracle.len;
sq008.sq008L[1] = (unsigned long)79;
sq008.sq008T[1] = (unsigned short)9;
sq008.sq008I[1] = (unsigned short *)0;
sq008.sq008V[2] = (unsigned char *)&CategoryOracle.len;
sq008.sq008L[2] = (unsigned long)24;
sq008.sq008T[2] = (unsigned short)9;
sq008.sq008I[2] = (unsigned short *)0;
sq008.sq008V[3] = (unsigned char *)&RatingOracle.len;
sq008.sq008L[3] = (unsigned long)9;
sq008.sq008T[3] = (unsigned short)9;
sq008.sq008I[3] = (unsigned short *)0;
sq008.sq008V[4] = (unsigned char *)&EvaluationOracle.len;
sq008.sq008L[4] = (unsigned long)9;
sq008.sq008T[4] = (unsigned short)9;
sq008.sq008I[4] = (unsigned short *)0;
sqlab2(&sq008.sq008N, sq008.sq008V,
  sq008.sq008L, sq008.sq008T, sq008.sq008I);
SQLTM[0] = (int)1;
sqlexe(&SQLTM[0]);
}    /* End of SQL code gen stmt */
/* SQL stmt #12
        EXEC SQL COMMIT;
*/
{      /* Beginning of SQL code gen stmt */
sqlsca(&sqlca);
if ( !sqlusi[0] )
  {  /* OPEN SCOPE */
sq009.sq009T[0] = (unsigned short)10;
SQLTM[0] = (int)4;
sqlbs2(&sq009.sq009N, sq009.sq009V,
  sq009.sq009L, sq009.sq009T, sq009.sq009I,
  &SQLTM[0], &sqlusi[0]);
  }  /* CLOSE SCOPE */
sqlsch(&sqlusi[0]);
```

continues

LISTING 8.5. continued

```
SQLTM[0] = (int)0;
sqlcom(&SQLTM[0]);
}   /* End of SQL code gen stmt */

        Reset ();
}


void WOracleVideoDialog::Delete ()
{
        DialogToOracle ();


/* SQL stmt #13
        EXEC SQL DELETE FROM Video WHERE CURRENT OF VideoCursor;
*/
{      /* Beginning of SQL code gen stmt */
sqlsca(&sqlca);
if ( !sqlusi[0] )
  {  /* OPEN SCOPE */
sq010.sq010T[0] = (unsigned short)10;
SQLTM[0] = (int)4;
sqlbs2(&sq010.sq010N, sq010.sq010V,
  sq010.sq010L, sq010.sq010T, sq010.sq010I,
  &SQLTM[0], &sqlusi[0]);
  }  /* CLOSE SCOPE */
sqlsch(&sqlusi[0]);
sqlscc(&sqlcun[2]);
sqltfl(&SQLTM[0], &SQLBT0);
if ( !SQLTM[0] )
  {  /* OPEN SCOPE */
SQLTM[0] = (int)16384;
sqlopn(&SQLTM[0], &SQLBT3, &sqlvsn);
SQLTM[0] = (int)33;
sqlosq(sq011, &SQLTM[0]);
  }  /* CLOSE SCOPE */
sqlgri(&sqlcun[0],&sq012.sq012V[0]);
sq012.sq012L[0] = 14;
sq012.sq012T[0] = (unsigned short)11;
sq012.sq012I[0] = (unsigned short *)0;
sqlab2(&sq012.sq012N, sq012.sq012V,
  sq012.sq012L, sq012.sq012T, sq012.sq012I);
SQLTM[0] = (int)1;
sqlexe(&SQLTM[0]);
sqlwnr();
```

```
}    /* End of SQL code gen stmt */

        if (sqlca.sqlcode < 0)
        {
                sqlca.sqlerrm.sqlerrmc[sqlca.sqlerrm.sqlerrml] = 0;
                MessageBox (NULL, sqlca.sqlerrm.sqlerrmc,
                        "WOracleVideoDialog::Delete", MB_OK);
        }
        else Reset ();

Reset ();

}


void WOracleVideoDialog::Update ()
{
        DialogToOracle ();



/* SQL stmt #14
        EXEC SQL UPDATE Video
                SET Title = :TitleOracle,
                        Stars = :StarsOracle,
                        Category = :CategoryOracle,
                        Rating = :RatingOracle,
                        Evaluation = :EvaluationOracle
                WHERE CURRENT OF VideoCursor;
*/
{    /* Beginning of SQL code gen stmt */
sqlsca(&sqlca);
if ( !sqlusi[0] )
  { /* OPEN SCOPE */
sq013.sq013T[0] = (unsigned short)10;
SQLTM[0] = (int)4;
sqlbs2(&sq013.sq013N, sq013.sq013V,
  sq013.sq013L, sq013.sq013T, sq013.sq013I,
  &SQLTM[0], &sqlusi[0]);
  } /* CLOSE SCOPE */
sqlsch(&sqlusi[0]);
sqlscc(&sqlcun[3]);
sqltfl(&SQLTM[0], &SQLBT0);
if ( !SQLTM[0] )
  { /* OPEN SCOPE */
SQLTM[0] = (int)16384;
```

continues

LISTING 8.5. continued

```
sqlopn(&SQLTM[0], &SQLBT3, &sqlvsn);
SQLTM[0] = (int)91;
sqlosq(sq014, &SQLTM[0]);
    }   /* CLOSE SCOPE */
sq015.sq015V[0] = (unsigned char *)&TitleOracle.len;
sq015.sq015L[0] = (unsigned long)38;
sq015.sq015T[0] = (unsigned short)9;
sq015.sq015I[0] = (unsigned short *)0;
sq015.sq015V[1] = (unsigned char *)&StarsOracle.len;
sq015.sq015L[1] = (unsigned long)79;
sq015.sq015T[1] = (unsigned short)9;
sq015.sq015I[1] = (unsigned short *)0;
sq015.sq015V[2] = (unsigned char *)&CategoryOracle.len;
sq015.sq015L[2] = (unsigned long)24;
sq015.sq015T[2] = (unsigned short)9;
sq015.sq015I[2] = (unsigned short *)0;
sq015.sq015V[3] = (unsigned char *)&RatingOracle.len;
sq015.sq015L[3] = (unsigned long)9;
sq015.sq015T[3] = (unsigned short)9;
sq015.sq015I[3] = (unsigned short *)0;
sq015.sq015V[4] = (unsigned char *)&EvaluationOracle.len;
sq015.sq015L[4] = (unsigned long)9;
sq015.sq015T[4] = (unsigned short)9;
sq015.sq015I[4] = (unsigned short *)0;
sqlgri(&sqlcun[0],&sq015.sq015V[5]);
sq015.sq015L[5] = 14;
sq015.sq015T[5] = (unsigned short)11;
sq015.sq015I[5] = (unsigned short *)0;
sqlab2(&sq015.sq015N, sq015.sq015V,
  sq015.sq015L, sq015.sq015T, sq015.sq015I);
SQLTM[0] = (int)1;
sqlexe(&SQLTM[0]);
sqlwnr();
}   /* End of SQL code gen stmt */

        Reset ();
}


void WOracleVideoDialog::Next ()
{
        // Initialize the Oracle variables
        InitVariables ();


/* SQL stmt #15
```

```
        EXEC SQL FETCH VideoCursor INTO
                :TitleOracle,
                :StarsOracle,
                :CategoryOracle,
                :RatingOracle,
                :EvaluationOracle;
*/
{      /* Beginning of SQL code gen stmt */
sqlsca(&sqlca);
if ( !sqlusi[0] )
  {  /* OPEN SCOPE */
sq016.sq016T[0] = (unsigned short)10;
SQLTM[0] = (int)4;
sqlbs2(&sq016.sq016N, sq016.sq016V,
  sq016.sq016L, sq016.sq016T, sq016.sq016I,
  &SQLTM[0], &sqlusi[0]);
  }   /* CLOSE SCOPE */
sqlsch(&sqlusi[0]);
sqlscc(&sqlcun[0]);
sq017.sq017V[0] = (unsigned char *)&TitleOracle.len;
sq017.sq017L[0] = (unsigned long)38;
sq017.sq017T[0] = (unsigned short)9;
sq017.sq017I[0] = (unsigned short *)0;
sq017.sq017V[1] = (unsigned char *)&StarsOracle.len;
sq017.sq017L[1] = (unsigned long)79;
sq017.sq017T[1] = (unsigned short)9;
sq017.sq017I[1] = (unsigned short *)0;
sq017.sq017V[2] = (unsigned char *)&CategoryOracle.len;
sq017.sq017L[2] = (unsigned long)24;
sq017.sq017T[2] = (unsigned short)9;
sq017.sq017I[2] = (unsigned short *)0;
sq017.sq017V[3] = (unsigned char *)&RatingOracle.len;
sq017.sq017L[3] = (unsigned long)9;
sq017.sq017T[3] = (unsigned short)9;
sq017.sq017I[3] = (unsigned short *)0;
sq017.sq017V[4] = (unsigned char *)&EvaluationOracle.len;
sq017.sq017L[4] = (unsigned long)9;
sq017.sq017T[4] = (unsigned short)9;
sq017.sq017I[4] = (unsigned short *)0;
sqlad2(&sq017.sq017N, sq017.sq017V,
  sq017.sq017L, sq017.sq017T, sq017.sq017I);
SQLTM[0] = (int)1;
SQLTM[1] = (int)0;
sqlfch(&SQLTM[0], &SQLTM[1]);
}    /* End of SQL code gen stmt */

        if (sqlca.sqlcode == 0)
        {
```

continues

LISTING 8.5. continued

```
                    OracleToDialog ();
        }
}


void WOracleVideoDialog::Previous ()
{

        long Row = sqlca.sqlerrd[2] -1;
        if (Row < 0) Row = 0;

        // Reset the Video cursor

/* SQL stmt #16
        EXEC SQL OPEN VideoCursor;
*/
{     /* Beginning of SQL code gen stmt */
sqlsca(&sqlca);
if ( !sqlusi[0] )
  {  /* OPEN SCOPE */
sq018.sq018T[0] = (unsigned short)10;
SQLTM[0] = (int)4;
sqlbs2(&sq018.sq018N, sq018.sq018V,
  sq018.sq018L, sq018.sq018T, sq018.sq018I,
  &SQLTM[0], &sqlusi[0]);
  }  /* CLOSE SCOPE */
sqlsch(&sqlusi[0]);
sqlscc(&sqlcun[0]);
SQLTM[1] = (int)16384;
sqltoc(&SQLTM[0],&SQLTM[1],&sqlvsn);
 if ( !SQLTM[0] )
   {  /* OPEN SCOPE */
SQLTM[0] = (int)56;
sqlosq(sq019, &SQLTM[0]);
  }  /* CLOSE SCOPE */
SQLTM[0] = (int)1;
sqlexe(&SQLTM[0]);
}   /* End of SQL code gen stmt */

        // Reposition just prior to what we want
        // Note: Oracle indexes starting at 1, not 0
        for (int i = 1; i < Row; i++)
        {
                // Initialize the Oracle variables
                InitVariables ();

/* SQL stmt #17
```

```
                EXEC SQL FETCH VideoCursor INTO
                        :TitleOracle,
                        :StarsOracle,
                        :CategoryOracle,
                        :RatingOracle,
                        :EvaluationOracle;
*/
{      /* Beginning of SQL code gen stmt */
sqlsca(&sqlca);
if ( !sqlusi[0] )
  { /* OPEN SCOPE */
sq020.sq020T[0] = (unsigned short)10;
SQLTM[0] = (int)4;
sqlbs2(&sq020.sq020N, sq020.sq020V,
  sq020.sq020L, sq020.sq020T, sq020.sq020I,
  &SQLTM[0], &sqlusi[0]);
  }  /* CLOSE SCOPE */
sqlsch(&sqlusi[0]);
sqlscc(&sqlcun[0]);
sq021.sq021V[0] = (unsigned char *)&TitleOracle.len;
sq021.sq021L[0] = (unsigned long)38;
sq021.sq021T[0] = (unsigned short)9;
sq021.sq021I[0] = (unsigned short *)0;
sq021.sq021V[1] = (unsigned char *)&StarsOracle.len;
sq021.sq021L[1] = (unsigned long)79;
sq021.sq021T[1] = (unsigned short)9;
sq021.sq021I[1] = (unsigned short *)0;
sq021.sq021V[2] = (unsigned char *)&CategoryOracle.len;
sq021.sq021L[2] = (unsigned long)24;
sq021.sq021T[2] = (unsigned short)9;
sq021.sq021I[2] = (unsigned short *)0;
sq021.sq021V[3] = (unsigned char *)&RatingOracle.len;
sq021.sq021L[3] = (unsigned long)9;
sq021.sq021T[3] = (unsigned short)9;
sq021.sq021I[3] = (unsigned short *)0;
sq021.sq021V[4] = (unsigned char *)&EvaluationOracle.len;
sq021.sq021L[4] = (unsigned long)9;
sq021.sq021T[4] = (unsigned short)9;
sq021.sq021I[4] = (unsigned short *)0;
sqlad2(&sq021.sq021N, sq021.sq021V,
  sq021.sq021L, sq021.sq021T, sq021.sq021I);
SQLTM[0] = (int)1;
SQLTM[1] = (int)0;
sqlfch(&SQLTM[0], &SQLTM[1]);
}   /* End of SQL code gen stmt */

        }

        Next ();
```

continues

LISTING 8.5. continued

```
}

void WOracleVideoDialog::InitVariables ()
{
        TitleOracle.arr[0] = 0;
        StarsOracle.arr[0] = 0;
        CategoryOracle.arr[0] = 0;
        RatingOracle.arr[0] = 0;
        EvaluationOracle.arr[0] = 0;

        TitleOracle.len = 0;
        StarsOracle.len = 0;
        CategoryOracle.len = 0;
        RatingOracle.len = 0;
        EvaluationOracle.len = 0;
}


void WOracleVideoDialog::DialogToOracle ()
{
        char Buffer [MAX_STARS];

        Title->GetText (Buffer, MAX_TITLE);
        strcpy ((char *)TitleOracle.arr, Buffer);

        Stars->GetText (Buffer, MAX_STARS);
        strcpy ((char *)StarsOracle.arr, Buffer);

        if (Category->GetSelString (Buffer, MAX_CATEGORY) < 0)
        {
                strcpy ((char *) CategoryOracle.arr, "");
        }
        else strcpy ((char *) CategoryOracle.arr, Buffer);

        if (Rating->GetSelString (Buffer, MAX_RATING) < 0)
        {
                strcpy ((char *) RatingOracle.arr, "");
        }
        else strcpy ((char *) RatingOracle.arr, Buffer);

        if (Evaluation->GetSelString (Buffer, MAX_EVALUATION) < 0)
        {
                strcpy ((char *) EvaluationOracle.arr, "");
        }
```

```
            else strcpy ((char *) EvaluationOracle.arr, Buffer);


        TitleOracle.len = strlen ((char *)TitleOracle.arr);
        StarsOracle.len = strlen ((char *)StarsOracle.arr);
        CategoryOracle.len = strlen ((char *)CategoryOracle.arr);
        RatingOracle.len = strlen ((char *)RatingOracle.arr);
    EvaluationOracle.len = strlen ((char *)EvaluationOracle.arr);
}

void WOracleVideoDialog::OracleToDialog ()
{
        // NULL-terminate the Oracle fields
        TitleOracle.arr [TitleOracle.len] = 0;
        StarsOracle.arr [StarsOracle.len] = 0;
        CategoryOracle.arr [CategoryOracle.len] = 0;
        RatingOracle.arr [RatingOracle.len] = 0;
        EvaluationOracle.arr [EvaluationOracle.len] = 0;

        // Now copy
        Title->SetText ((char *) TitleOracle.arr);
        Stars->SetText ((char *) StarsOracle.arr);
        Category->SetSelString (CategoryOracle.arr, -1);
        Rating->SetSelString (RatingOracle.arr, -1);
        Evaluation->SetSelString (EvaluationOracle.arr, -1);

}
```

Implementing a
Screen Saver

Problem

Screen savers are fun. They give programmers the opportunity to demonstrate their creativity in a fun, highly visible manner. Unfortunately, screen savers are difficult to implement, and they require a good understanding of assembly language. Or do they? In any case, implementing a screen saver under Windows requires only a little knowledge of Windows—which you could get from the Device Driver Development Kit (DDK). Or does it? Let's find out!

Solution

Good news! Screen savers under Windows 3.1 and later versions are easy to implement. Furthermore, they are simple to design so that users can install and configure them directly from the Windows Control Panel. In this chapter, I dissect the guts of a screen saver to show you how to implement one of your own.

I use a class that displays metafiles in a slide show format. The WSlideShow class supports the transitions shown in Table 9.1.

TABLE 9.1. Special effects supported by WSlideShow.

Effect	Description
REPLACE	The new slide replaces the old slide almost instantly
FADE	The new slide fades over the old slide
TILE	The new slide replaces the old slide one square at a time in a tile pattern
SPIRAL	The new slide replaces the old slide in a spiral pattern
WIPE_LEFT	The old slide is dragged from the screen to the right, and the new slide is exposed gradually from the left

Effect	Description
WIPE_RIGHT	Same as WIPE_LEFT but from the right
WIPE_TOP	Same as WIPE_LEFT but from the top
WIPE_BOTTOM	Same as WIPE_LEFT but from the bottom
TUNNEL	The new slide is exposed in concentric circles outward from the center
FROM_LEFT	The new slide is dragged onto the screen from the left
FROM_RIGHT	Same as FROM_LEFT but from the right
FROM_TOP	Same as FROM_LEFT but from the top
FROM_BOTTOM	Same as FROM_LEFT but from the bottom
RANDOM	The transition is selected randomly from those that are available and enabled

Figure 9.1 shows the screen saver Chpt 9 Demo in action. This screen saver is simple. It terminates only between slides, which sometimes results in a two- to three-second delay in regaining control of your computer. As written, this screen saver demonstrates a concept instead of functioning as a production-quality screen saver.

To install and run this program, copy the files shown in Table 9.2 into your Windows directory (C:\WINDOWS).

TABLE 9.2. Screen saver installation files.

File	Description
CHPT9.SCR	The executable for the Chpt 9 Demo screen saver
SCREEN1.MF through SCREEN10.MF	Metafiles displayed by CHPT9.SCR

Figure 9.1. The Chpt 9 Demo screen saver in action.

Next, go to the Windows Desktop configuration screen and select the Windows Main icon, then the Control Panel icon, and finally the Desktop icon. If your Windows directory isn't \WINDOWS, modify the `chpt8Window` constructor to reflect the correct directory name. From Control Panel, select the Chpt 9 Demo screen saver and set the time to one minute, then press the OK pushbutton (see Figure 9.2). Wait about one minute to see the screen saver in action.

Figure 9.2. Selecting and configuring a new screen saver.

Screen Saver Code

Screen savers are executable applications with just a few special characteristics. In fact, normally the first step in writing a screen saver is to write the application as an ordinary executable that works as you expect. To convert the application to a screen saver, do the following:

1. Modify your .DEF file to include the name of the screen saver in a format that Windows recognizes.

2. Overload the WMSysCommand function of the main window class to watch for 0xF140, the screen save request message, and to respond TRUE if it is detected.

3. Overload the DefWndProc function of the main window class to watch for key presses and mouse events. Close the application if any are detected.

4. Modify your drawing code to update the screen a little at a time, then tie this code to the IdleAction member function of the TApplication class.

5. Add a configuration dialog box that enables users to configure the screen saver from the Windows Control Panel.

6. Rename your .EXE file with an .SCR extension so that it can be installed under Windows 3.1.

I cover each of these steps in more detail. At the end of this section, you'll find the chpt9 header and source file listings, which show a complete example.

Modify Your .DEF File

When the linker links a Windows application, it looks for a .DEF file to obtain link-related information. This file can be used to control code and data segments, heap size, stack size, and many other characteristics of your final application. Until now, I've been able to use the Borland standard OWL.DEF or OWLDLL.DEF definition files because I could control all the parameters that interested me directly through options in the IDE menu. Unfortunately, the Windows Control Panel looks in the description area

of the executable file for a specific string when it attempts to add a screen saver to its dialog box. The easiest way to add this string is to modify the .DEF file.

Listing 9.1 shows the CHPT9.DEF file. The key line is

```
DESCRIPTION 'SCRNSAVE :Chpt 9 Demo'
```

For your screen saver, include this line, but replace everything between the colon and the trailing apostrophe with the name of your own screen saver. You must include `'SCRNSAVE :[screen saver name]'` exactly as shown.

> **HINT:** If you don't want to bother understanding the complete syntax of a .DEF file, the simplest way to modify a .DEF file is to copy OWL.DEF or OWLDLL.DEF to your directory, rename it to a name of your choice (ending with .DEF), then modify the copy.

LISTING 9.1. CHPT9.DEF listing.

```
NAME        chpt9
DESCRIPTION 'SCRNSAVE :Chpt 9 Demo'
EXETYPE WINDOWS
CODE PRELOAD MOVEABLE DISCARDABLE
DATA PRELOAD MOVEABLE MULTIPLE
HEAPSIZE 4096
STACKSIZE 5120
```

Overload the *WMSysCommand* Function

When Windows tries to load your screen saver application, it sends your application's main window a message asking whether it wants to work as a screen saver. An application that responds TRUE to this message (0xF140) is treated as a screen saver. An application that responds FALSE is not loaded as a screen saver. The code that properly handles this within an object derived from TWindows is as follows:

```
#define SC_SCREENSAVE 0xF140
void chpt9Window::WMSysCommand (RTMessage Msg)
{
    if ((Msg.WParam & 0xFFF0) == SC_SCREENSAVE)
    {
        Msg.Result = TRUE;
    }
    else DefWndProc (Msg);
}
```

Overload the *DefWndProc* Function

Your screen saver application needs to watch for events that cause it to terminate and return the screen to its normal mode. So that the program can look for appropriate events, you must modify DefWndProc, as shown in the following code:

```
void chpt9Window::DefWndProc (RTMessage Msg)
{
    switch (Msg.Message)
    {
        case WM_ACTIVATE:
        case WM_ACTIVATEAPP:
            if (Msg.WParam != 0) break;
            else PostMessage (HWindow, WM_CLOSE, 0, 0L);
            break;

        case WM_MOUSEMOVE:
        case WM_KEYDOWN:
        case WM_SYSKEYDOWN:
        case WM_LBUTTONDOWN:
        case WM_MBUTTONDOWN:
        case WM_RBUTTONDOWN:
        PostMessage (HWindow, WM_CLOSE, 0, 0L);
            break;
    }
    TWindow::DefWndProc (Msg);
}
```

INT: If you want to build password protection into your screen saver, this is the place to do it. A password-protected screen saver prompts the user for a password before it closes and displays the

normal screen. Password protection offers a basic form of security for your personal computer. Because your screen saver application receives all messages before they are routed to other applications, you can prevent a user without a valid password from taking any action except rebooting the computer.

Modify Your Drawing Code to Use *IdleAction*

If your drawing program draws forever without releasing control of the CPU, it can prevent a user's action (for example, a key press) from ever causing your screen saver application to terminate. If you avoid this problem, but the program draws under your complete control (for example, you add a PeekMessage loop to your drawing code), you prevent background tasks from functioning. This is a particularly serious blunder for screen savers. The reason that the computer is idle for a long time is often because a background task is printing a document, recalculating a spreadsheet, updating a database, and so on.

The solution is to break your drawing task into small pieces that can be accomplished in response to a function call. For example, the Chpt 9 Demo screen saver draws one of its slides in response to a function call. To make this code into a production-quality screen saver, I need to break it down further so that it draws only part of a slide in response to a function call. These small pieces are then drawn when your application's IdleAction function is called. This function is called by Windows whenever it doesn't have anything to do. Windows expects you to do a small amount of processing and then to return control of the CPU to Windows. The chpt9 code that performs this is as follows:

```
void chpt9::IdleAction ()
{
    // This application may be created just to display a
    // configuration dialog box. In that case, the ConfigureFlag
    // Boolean is set to TRUE.

    if (ConfigureFlag == FALSE)
    {
        ((Pchpt9Window) MainWindow)->NextSlide ();
    }
}
```

ConfigureFlag is necessary because the Windows Control Panel could create the screen saver simply to display its configuration dialog box, update the configuration, then terminate. (I cover this in the next section.) While the user works on the configuration dialog box, there probably will be idle moments during which Windows will call the IdleAction function. Because the MainWindow in this case is the dialog box itself, which is not a chpt9Window object, a call to NextSlide would certainly crash the system.

Add a Configuration Dialog Box

The Windows control panel includes a Setup button that the user can press for each screen saver. Pressing this button causes Windows to create your application with the configure option ('/c'). The Chpt 9 Demo uses the simplest possible version of a configuration dialog box: one that does nothing. The dialog box, shown in Figure 9.3, was created in the Resource Workshop and named CONFIGUREDIALOG. For a production-quality version of this screen saver, the configuration dialog box should at least enable the user, using wildcards, to specify the filenames that contain the metafiles to be displayed. The application's InitMainWindow code, which handles a configuration request, follows.

Figure 9.3. The Chpt 9 Demo configuration dialog box.

```
void chpt9::InitMainWindow ()
{
    // Being called to display just a configuration dialog
    // box?
    if ( *((WORD FAR *) lpCmdLine) == '/c' ||
         *((WORD FAR *) lpCmdLine) == '-c' )
    {
        ConfigureFlag = TRUE;
        MainWindow = new TDialog (NULL, "CONFIGUREDIALOG");
```

```
    }
    // Actually being called to begin real work
    else
    {
        ConfigureFlag = FALSE;
        MainWindow = new chpt9Window (NULL, NULL, NULL);
    }
}
```

As I discussed earlier, `ConfigureFlag` is used only to tell the `IdleAction` member function whether the main window is a dialog box or the real application. If your application needs a configuration dialog box, simply implement it like any other dialog box as a class derived from `TDialog`.

INT: The information for the screen saver configuration must be stored somewhere so that it remains properly set each time the screen saver is created. Normally you accomplish this either by creating an .INI file in the Windows directory specifically for your application (the preferred approach) or by adding your configuration information to the WIN.INI file. Then, the screen saver application must retrieve this information when it is started. The screen saver application uses the information as the initial values in the configuration dialog box (that is, in configuration mode) or as parameters to the screen saver's main window (that is, in running mode).

CHPT9.CPP Listing

Listing 9.2 shows the complete code for the Chapter 9 program.

LISTING 9.2. The complete listing of `chpt9`.

```
#define WIN31
#define STRICT
#define _CLASSDLL

// #include files for both PC and SUN
```

```
#include  "WSlideShow.h"

#ifdef __BORLANDC__
      // PC-specific #includes
#    include    <owl.h>

#endif

#ifdef Unix
      // UNIX-specific #includes

#endif


//****************************************************
// chpt9Window - chpt9 main window
//
//     Purpose:
//         This class is the main window for the
//         chpt9 application.
//
//     Notes:
//
//     Copyright:
//             Copyright (c) 1993, William H. Roetzheim
//             All Rights Reserved
//
//****************************************************
_CLASSDEF (chpt9Window)
class chpt9Window : public TWindow
{
    private:
        PWSlideShow SlideShow;

    public:
        chpt9Window (PTWindowsObject Parent, LPSTR Title,
                            PTModule Module = NULL);
        ~chpt9Window ();
        virtual void DefWndProc (RTMessage);
        virtual void WMSysCommand (RTMessage) =
            [WM_FIRST + WM_SYSCOMMAND];
        virtual void NextSlide ();
};
```

continues

301

LISTING 9.2. continued

```
//****************************************************
// chpt9 - chpt9 application class
//
//     Purpose:
//         This class is the overall application
//         executive for chpt9.
//
//     Notes:
//         Application names should contain seven characters
//         or fewer for this to work optimally in terms of
//         automatic code using global search-and-replace.
//
//     Copyright:
//             Copyright (c) 1993, William H. Roetzheim
//             All Rights Reserved
//
//****************************************************

_CLASSDEF (chpt9)
class chpt9 : public TApplication
{
    private:
        // Private data members *******************
        //   None


        // Private member functions ****************
        //   None

    public:
        // Public data members ********************
        BOOL ConfigureFlag;

        // Public member functions *****************
        // Constructors and destructors
        chpt9 (char *szName, HINSTANCE hInstance,
                HINSTANCE hPrevInstance, LPSTR lpCmdLine,
                int nCmdShow);

        // Member functions
        virtual void InitMainWindow ();
      virtual void IdleAction ();
};
```

```
//*****************************************************
// Constructors and destructors for chpt9Window
//
//    Copyright:
//            Copyright (c) 1993, William H. Roetzheim
//            All Rights Reserved
//
//*****************************************************

chpt9Window::chpt9Window (PTWindowsObject Parent,
    LPSTR Title, PTModule Module)
    : TWindow (Parent, Title, Module)
{
    ShowCursor (FALSE);
    Attr.Style = WS_POPUP;
    SlideShow = new WSlideShow ("\\Windows\\Screen*.mf");
}


chpt9Window::~chpt9Window ()
{
    ShowCursor (TRUE);
    delete SlideShow;

    // Refresh the entire display
    InvalidateRect (NULL, NULL, TRUE);
    UpdateWindow (NULL);
}


//*****************************************************
// Member functions for class
//
//    Copyright:
//            Copyright (c) 1993, William H. Roetzheim
//            All Rights Reserved
//
//*****************************************************


//*****************************************************
// chpt9Window::DefWndProc - Replacement default
//                window procedure
//
//    Purpose:
//        This function looks for a keystroke or a mouse
//        action, then terminates the screen saver (this
//        application) if one is detected. Because the
```

continues

303

LISTING 9.2. continued

```
//          screen saver normally runs as a spawned application
//          of the Windows Program Manager, it receives all
//          messages. (Other applications receive messages
//          destined only for those applications.)
//
//     General Notes:
//          This is a good place to add logic for password
//          protection to prevent someone without the needed
//          password from turning off your screen saver.
//
//       Testing Notes:
//
//     Copyright:
//          Copyright (c) 1993, William H. Roetzheim
//          All Rights Reserved
//
//******************************************************

void chpt9Window::DefWndProc (RTMessage Msg)
{
     switch (Msg.Message)
     {
          case WM_ACTIVATE:
          case WM_ACTIVATEAPP:
               if (Msg.WParam != 0) break;
               else PostMessage (HWindow, WM_CLOSE, 0, 0L);
               break;

          case WM_KEYDOWN:
          case WM_SYSKEYDOWN:
          case WM_LBUTTONDOWN:
          case WM_MBUTTONDOWN:
          case WM_RBUTTONDOWN:
          PostMessage (HWindow, WM_CLOSE, 0, 0L);
               break;
     }
     TWindow::DefWndProc (Msg);
}


//******************************************************
// chpt9Window::WMSysCommand - Handle system messages
//
//     Purpose:
//          This function is necessary to tell Windows that
```

```
//          the application is willing to operate as a
//          screen saver.
//
//     General Notes:
//
//      Testing Notes:
//
//     Copyright:
//             Copyright (c) 1993, William H. Roetzheim
//             All Rights Reserved
//
//****************************************************

#define SC_SCREENSAVE 0xF140
void chpt9Window::WMSysCommand (RTMessage Msg)
{
    if ((Msg.WParam & 0xFFF0) == SC_SCREENSAVE)
    {
        Msg.Result = TRUE;
    }
    else DefWndProc (Msg);
}




// Display next slide. This code will be specific
// to your particular screen saver.
void chpt9Window::NextSlide ()
{
    SlideShow->NextSlide ();
}




//****************************************************
// Constructors and destructors for chpt9
//
//     Copyright:
//             Copyright (c) 1993, William H. Roetzheim
//             All Rights Reserved
//
//****************************************************

#pragma argsused  // Turn off arguments not used warning
```

continues

LISTING 9.2. continued

```
chpt9::chpt9(char *szName, HINSTANCE hInstance,
             HINSTANCE hPrevInstance, LPSTR lpCmdLine,
             int nCmdShow)
             : TApplication (szName, hInstance,
             hPrevInstance, lpCmdLine, nCmdShow)
{
    return;
}



//*****************************************************
// Member functions for class
//
//    Copyright:
//            Copyright (c) 1993, William H. Roetzheim
//            All Rights Reserved
//
//*****************************************************

//*****************************************************
// chpt9::IdleAction - Perform background processing
//
//    Purpose:
//        This function enables you to perform a small hunk
//        of processing when Windows has nothing else to do.
//        In this case, a slide is displayed. It is even
//        better to break the slide display into smaller
//        pieces. (A single slide can take up to a couple
//        of seconds to display.)
//
//    General Notes:
//        Screen savers should always perform processing
//        in response to IdleAction to allow Windows to
//        continue with functions such as printing, which
//        often are the reason the computer is not in
//        use in the first place! Also, remember that
//        CPU time spent drawing your screen saver graphics
//        is time spent not doing other background tasks.
//
//        Testing Notes:
//
//    Copyright:
//            Copyright (c) 1993, William H. Roetzheim
//            All Rights Reserved
```

```
//
//*******************************************************

void chpt9::IdleAction ()
{
    // This application may be created to display just a
    // configuration dialog box. In that case, the ConfigureFlag
    // Boolean is set to TRUE.

    if (ConfigureFlag == FALSE)
    {
        ((Pchpt9Window) MainWindow)->NextSlide ();
    }
}


void chpt9::InitMainWindow ()
{
    // Being called to display just a configuration dialog
    // box?
    if ( *((WORD FAR *) lpCmdLine) == '/c' ||
         *((WORD FAR *) lpCmdLine) == '-c' )
    {
        ConfigureFlag = TRUE;
        MainWindow = new TDialog (NULL, "CONFIGUREDIALOG");
    }
    // Actually being called to begin real work
    else
    {
        ConfigureFlag = FALSE;
        MainWindow = new chpt9Window (NULL, NULL, NULL);
    }
}



// Here is the main () for the program
int PASCAL WinMain (HINSTANCE hInstance,
    HINSTANCE hPrevInstance, LPSTR lpCmdLine,
    int)
{

    // Create chpt9 application from class
    chpt9 ochpt9 ("chpt9", hInstance,
                  hPrevInstance, lpCmdLine, SW_NORMAL);

    // Start created application running
```

continues

LISTING 9.2. continued

```
ochpt9.Run ();   // Runs till window closed

// Return termination status when window closed
return ochpt9.Status;
}
```

The *WSlideShow* Class

The WSlideShow class is fun. It enables you to display a series of metafiles stored so that they match a filename with wildcards. For example, the chpt9 sample application displays all files matching SCREEN*.MF. It contains four public functions.

WSlideShow Public Functions

The ResetAll function is used to initialize variables to default values. It is a convenient function:

```
void  WSlideShow::ResetAll (void)
{
    // Reset all variables to defaults
    EscapePressed = FALSE;
    SlideNumber = 0;
    for (int i = 0; i < TOTAL_TRANSITIONS; i++)
    {
        EnableTransition ((Transition) i);
    }
}
```

The Start function is used to start the slide show. By default, the slides are displayed one-by-one until no more slides remain. After that, the Start function returns. When TRUE is passed as a parameter, the slide show loops continuously. Passing FALSE displays the slide show only once. For either form, pressing the Escape key terminates the slide show after the current slide is displayed. The Start function uses the Go() class private function to determine whether it can proceed with the show. Go() simply tests whether the user presses the Escape key. Before the slides are displayed, the random number generator is seeded to ensure that random transitions do not repeat every time the application runs. When the slide show is over, the screen is cleaned with `InvalidateRect`.

```
void WSlideShow::Start(BOOL LoopBack)
{
    time_t Dummy;
    srand ((unsigned) time (&Dummy));

    while (Go ())
    {
        // NextSlide displays the current slide and returns
        // the number of the slide that will be displayed next

        if ((NextSlide() == 0) && (LoopBack != TRUE))
        {
            break;
        }
    }

    // Refresh the display
     InvalidateRect  (NULL, NULL, TRUE);
    UpdateWindow (NULL);
}
```

This version of the class uses random transitions among all slides. You can use `EnableTransition` and `DisableTransition` (which are discussed later) to specify which transitions are available. If you disable all the transitions except one, that transition is used for all the slides.

HINT: A production-quality version of this code should enable the transition between slides to be specified independently and should include an individually specified pause between each slide. One way to accomplish this is to store a filename, a transition number, and a pause value for each slide in a file read by this class. This enables end-users to configure easily an application built using this class.

`NextSlide` displays the current slide and returns the slide number of the next slide. This return value is important. When it is 0, the calling application knows that `NextSlide` is about to `LoopBack`, which it does automatically.

Unfortunately, the only way that NextSlide can know when it has reached the last slide in a series is to try to read the next value. (An error condition indicates that there are no more files.) When it is called again, NextSlide must use findfirst and findnext to reposition itself to the proper file number. You can avoid this logic either by storing the filenames in an internal array or by counting the matching files one time (perhaps when the class is constructed). NextSlide assumes that the slides are displayed on the entire screen. (The WMetafile class, however, displays slides on a device context, which could just as well be a window client area.) The code for NextSlide is as follows:

```cpp
int WSlideShow::NextSlide ()
{
    struct ffblk ffBlock;
    int Flag;
    PWMetafile Metafile;

    HDC hDC;
    int ScreenWidth, ScreenHeight;

    hDC = CreateDC ("DISPLAY", NULL, NULL, NULL);
    ScreenWidth = GetSystemMetrics (SM_CXSCREEN);
    ScreenHeight = GetSystemMetrics (SM_CYSCREEN);


    // Read the slide at SlideNumber
    Flag = findfirst (FileName, &ffBlock, 0);
    for (int i = 0; i < SlideNumber; i++)
        Flag = findnext (&ffBlock);

    if (Flag == 0)
    {
        // Display the file ffBlock.ff_name
        Metafile = new WMetafile (ffBlock.ff_name);
        for (int i = 0; i < TOTAL_TRANSITIONS; i++)
        {
            if (ValidTransitions [i] == TRUE)
            {
                Metafile->EnableTransition ((Transition) i);
            }
            else Metafile->DisableTransition ((Transition) i);
        }
        Metafile->InitBitmap (ScreenWidth, ScreenHeight);
        Metafile->DisplayBitmap (hDC, 0, 0, RANDOM);

        delete Metafile;
```

```
    }
    DeleteDC (hDC);

    // See what the next slide number is
    Flag = findnext (&ffBlock);
    if (Flag != 0) SlideNumber = 0;
  else SlideNumber++;
    return SlideNumber;
}
```

> **HINT:** At some point, you might be tempted to write code that creates many WMetafile class objects simultaneously. This is fine, but be careful of the InitBitmap function. This function creates *and stores* a bitmap of the specified size in the WMetafile object. For a full screen, this means that a full-color bitmap of the entire screen is stored (in other words, $640 \times 480 \times 4$, or 1.2 million, bits). You don't want to have many of those!

The EnableTransition and DisableTransition functions simply enable you to turn transitions on or off for a selection if a random transition is requested. Transitions are stored in a Boolean array called ValidTransitions. The #defines for each available transition are found in WMETAFILE.H. Only one point is somewhat tricky: To avoid an infinite search for an available random transition, DisableTransition checks to ensure that at least one transition is still valid.

Listings 9.3 and 9.4 show the complete listing for WSLIDESHOW.H and WSLIDESHOW.CPP.

LISTING 9.3. WSLIDESHOW.H header file listing.

```
// WSLIDESHOW.H - Header file for WSlideShow class

#ifndef WSlideShow_H
#    define WSlideShow_H

// Note that the following code is executed only
// if this file has not been previously included
```

continues

LISTING 9.3. continued

```
// #include files for both PC and SUN
#include <dir.h>
#include "WStr.h"
#include "WMetafile.h"


#ifdef __BORLANDC__
     // PC-specific #includes
#    include    <owl.h>

#endif

#ifdef Unix
     // UNIX-specific #includes

#endif

//****************************************************
// WSlideShow - Slide show class
//
//     Purpose:
//         Display a series of metafiles with
//         special effects
//
//     Notes:
//
//     Copyright:
//            Copyright (c) 1993, William H. Roetzheim
//            All Rights Reserved
//
//****************************************************

_CLASSDEF (WSlideShow)
class WSlideShow
{
    private:
        // Private data members ********************
        WStr FileName;  // Allows wildcards
        // ValidTransitions is used when drawing random
        // transitions
        BOOL ValidTransitions [TOTAL_TRANSITIONS];

        BOOL EscapePressed;  // Has user pressed the Esc key?
```

```
        int   SlideNumber;    // Next slide number to be drawn


        // Private member functions ****************
        BOOL Go ();   // Was Esc pressed?

    public:
        // Public data members *********************


        // Public member functions ****************
        // Constructors and destructors
        WSlideShow (WStr FileName);

        // Standard functions
        virtual void ResetAll(void);

        // Member functions
        void Start(BOOL LoopBack = FALSE);
      int NextSlide ();
        void EnableTransition (Transition);
      void DisableTransition (Transition);
};

#endif WSlideShow_H
```

LISTING 9.4. WSLIDESHOW.CPP source file listing.

```
//  WSLIDESHOW.CPP - Source file for WSlideShow class

#include "WSlideShow.h"   // ALL other #include statements
                          // are in this file


//****************************************************
// Constructors and destructors for WSlideShow
//
//      Copyright:
//              Copyright (c) 1993, William H. Roetzheim
//              All Rights Reserved
//
//****************************************************

WSlideShow::WSlideShow (WStr File)
```

continues

LISTING 9.4. continued

```
{
    FileName = File;
    ResetAll ();
}



//****************************************************
// Standard functions
//
//    Copyright:
//             Copyright (c) 1993, William H. Roetzheim
//             All Rights Reserved
//
//****************************************************

void  WSlideShow::ResetAll (void)
{
    // Reset all variables to defaults
    EscapePressed = FALSE;
    SlideNumber = 0;
    for (int i = 0; i < TOTAL_TRANSITIONS; i++)
    {
        EnableTransition ((Transition) i);
    }
}



//****************************************************
// Member functions for class
//
//    Copyright:
//             Copyright (c) 1993, William H. Roetzheim
//             All Rights Reserved
//
//****************************************************

//****************************************************
// WSlideShow::Start - Start a complete slide show
//
//    Purpose:
//        Display all slides matching FileName (including
//        wildcards). If LoopBack is TRUE, the slide show
//        continues until Esc is pressed.
//
```

```
//    General Notes:
//        For real-world slide shows, you will want to
//        modify this class (or derive a class from it)
//        so that the delay between slides and the
//        transition from one slide to the next can be
//        set on a slide-by-slide basis. For example, you
//        might want a slide with lots of text displayed
//        longer than a simple slide.
//
//     Testing Notes:
//
//    Copyright:
//            Copyright (c) 1993, William H. Roetzheim
//            All Rights Reserved
//
//****************************************************

void WSlideShow::Start(BOOL LoopBack)
{
    time_t Dummy;
    srand ((unsigned) time (&Dummy));

    while (Go ())
    {
        // NextSlide displays the current slide and returns
        // the number of the slide that will be displayed next

        if ((NextSlide() == 0) && (LoopBack != TRUE))
        {
            break;
        }
    }

    // Refresh the display
     InvalidateRect   (NULL, NULL, TRUE);
    UpdateWindow (NULL);
}


//****************************************************
// WSlideShow::NextSlide - Display the current slide
//
//     Purpose:
//         Display the current slide, then return the
//         number of the next slide to be displayed
//
//     General Notes:
//         NextSlide requires some pretty weird logic to be
```

continues

LISTING 9.4. continued

```
//         able to properly return the next slide to be
//         displayed. When the last slide is displayed, the
//         next slide to be displayed is zero! If it returns
//         just the number of the slide just displayed, the
//         logic here is simple. A calling application,
//         however, won't know about a loop-back to the
//         beginning of the show until AFTER the first slide
//         is redisplayed, by which time it is too late. An
//         alternative is for the class to count all the
//         slides in its constructor; this simplifies the
//         logic in NextSlide.
//
//         Testing Notes:
//
//    Copyright:
//            Copyright (c) 1993, William H. Roetzheim
//            All Rights Reserved
//
//****************************************************

int WSlideShow::NextSlide ()
{
    struct ffblk ffBlock;
    int Flag;
    PWMetafile Metafile;

    HDC hDC;
    int ScreenWidth, ScreenHeight;

    hDC = CreateDC ("DISPLAY", NULL, NULL, NULL);
    ScreenWidth = GetSystemMetrics (SM_CXSCREEN);
    ScreenHeight = GetSystemMetrics (SM_CYSCREEN);


    // Read the slide at SlideNumber
    Flag = findfirst (FileName, &ffBlock, 0);
    for (int i = 0; i < SlideNumber; i++)
        Flag = findnext (&ffBlock);

    if (Flag == 0)
    {
        // Display the file ffBlock.ff_name
        Metafile = new WMetafile (ffBlock.ff_name);
        for (int i = 0; i < TOTAL_TRANSITIONS; i++)
        {
            if (ValidTransitions [i] == TRUE)
```

```
                {
                        Metafile->EnableTransition ((Transition) i);
                }
                else Metafile->DisableTransition ((Transition) i);
        }
        Metafile->InitBitmap (ScreenWidth, ScreenHeight);
        Metafile->DisplayBitmap (hDC, 0, 0, RANDOM);

        delete Metafile;
    }
    DeleteDC (hDC);

    // See what the next slide number is
    Flag = findnext (&ffBlock);
    if (Flag != 0) SlideNumber = 0;
  else SlideNumber++;
    return SlideNumber;
}


//*****************************************************
// WSlideShow::Go - Test for OK to proceed
//
//      Purpose:
//            Return TRUE if OK to proceed, FALSE if not
//            OK.
//
//      General Notes:
//          This version simply looks for whether the Esc key
//          is pressed.
//
//       Testing Notes:
//
//      Copyright:
//            Copyright (c) 1993, William H. Roetzheim
//            All Rights Reserved
//
//*****************************************************

BOOL WSlideShow::Go ()
{
    MSG Msg;

    // As soon as Esc is pressed, we return FALSE until
    // the EscapePressed flag is cleared by someone
    if (EscapePressed == TRUE) return FALSE;

    // PeekMessage is non-blocking version of GetMessage
    // PM_NOREMOVE allows the message to remain in the queue
```

continues

317

LISTING 9.4. continued

```
    // for normal processing by someone else
    if (PeekMessage (&Msg, NULL, 0, 0, PM_NOREMOVE) != 0)
    {
        if ((Msg.message == WM_KEYDOWN) &&
            (Msg.wParam == VK_ESCAPE))
        {
            EscapePressed = TRUE;
            return FALSE;
        }
    }
    return TRUE;
}


// Enable specified transition; applies to random
// transition drawing mode only
void WSlideShow::EnableTransition (Transition T)
{
    if ((T < TOTAL_TRANSITIONS) && (T >= 0))
    {
        ValidTransitions [T] = TRUE;
    }
}


// Disable specified transition; applies to random
// transition drawing mode only
void WSlideShow::DisableTransition (Transition T)
{
    if ((T < TOTAL_TRANSITIONS) && (T >= 0))
    {
        ValidTransitions [T] = TRUE;
    }

    // Ensure that at least one transition is valid
    for (int i = 0; i < TOTAL_TRANSITIONS; i++)
    {
        if (ValidTransitions [T] == TRUE) return;
    }
    // If you got to here, no transitions are valid!
    MessageBox (NULL,
        "No valid transitions.  Setting REPLACE true.",
        "DisableTransition error", MB_OK);
    ValidTransitions [REPLACE] = TRUE;
}
```

The *WMetafile* Class

The last piece of the puzzle is the WMetafile class. This class encapsulates all the important aspects of a Windows metafile and its associated bitmap. Because the class is extremely useful for a wide range of applications, I have included several member functions not used by the sample application in this chapter but that are useful in other applications. Because even many advanced Windows programmers have had only limited exposure to Windows metafiles, I'll start with some introductory information.

An Introduction to Metafiles

Graphics images can be stored either as bitmaps or as graphics primitives, which can be used to redraw the image. An example of a popular bitmap storage format is *tagged image file format*. TIFF is used both in the computer industry and also by all facsimile machines. An example of a popular graphics primitive format is *encapsulated postscript*. EPS is used to store and to directly drive many devices, such as printers.

Metafiles store images as a series of Windows graphics primitives called *Graphic Device Interface (GDI)* calls. Bitmaps tend to require significantly more space, and they are very dependent on the display in terms of color capabilities and resolution. Metafiles require less space, and they are relatively display-independent, but they are slower to display than bitmaps.

Where do metafiles come from? Well, many commercial graphics programs, such as Arts & Letters and CorelDRAW!, support Windows Metafile as a valid export format. You also can roll your own, as follows:

```
HDC hMetaDC;
HMETAFILE hMF;

hMetaDC = CreateMetaFile ("Sample.MF");
. . . Code to draw on the specified device context
hMF = CloseMetaFile (hMetaDC);
```

To play back the GDI calls stored in the metafile, use PlayMetaFile():

```
PlayMetaFile (hDC, hMF);
```

If you want to keep the metafile on disk and open it later, use the
GetMetaFile function:

```
HMETAFILE hMF;
hMF = GetMetaFile ("Sample.MF");
PlayMetaFile (hDC, hMF);
```

HINT: If GetMetaFile() can't find a specified file, it displays the
infamous message box that asks the user to insert the Sample.MF
disk in drive A. Programmers who don't want their users to smash
monitors in frustration test for the file's existence with a DOS file
command (fopen, for example) before they call GetMetaFile().

HINT: In general, metafiles produced by these programs can be
incorporated legally into your application as long as the image
cannot be modified by the end-user. Check with the manufacturer
if you have any doubts. The specific rules about incorporating
metafiles are manufacturer-dependent and might be covered in
your license agreement.

HINT: I've oversimplified things a bit. There are actually three
metafile formats. One format, not covered in this book, is used
only by the clipboard. The second format is a standard metafile as
just described. The third format is a placeable metafile that includes additional header information at the beginning of the file,
describing the original image aspect ratio and so on. PlayMetaFile
recognizes only standard metafiles and doesn't work with
placeable metafiles—at least not yet.

Many graphics programs that export metafile images use the
placeable metafile format. To convert one of these files to a standard metafile, remove the first 22 bytes from the file (the header
information), and voila—you have a standard metafile.

HINT: Many applications need to use bitmaps for reasons of performance, yet it would be nice to preserve the device-independence of metafiles. One popular solution currently in use is to create and store different bitmaps for each support display mode in the resource file and then load the appropriate ones. However, this solution limits your application to supporting display modes that you anticipate now. What will you do when a user buys a nifty 1024-by-1024 256-color board you aren't familiar with?

A better solution is to store your images as metafiles, create the bitmaps after the application is running, and use the newly created bitmaps from then on. The bitmaps can be tailored to the exact display in use at runtime. The WMetafile class supports this approach with the InitBitmap function.

An Overview of the *WMetafile* Class

Because it is a relatively complex general-purpose class, the WMetafile code is rather lengthy. The functions supported are shown in Table 9.3. Some interesting code is required to support special-effect transitions when the file is displayed. I discuss only the more interesting or non-obvious code in detail. I leave the complete study of the class code as an exercise for the interested.

TABLE 9.3. WMetafile **functions.**

Function	Parameters	Access	Description
WMetafile()	char *FileName	Public	Opens a specified metafile from disk
WMetafile	char *ResourceName HINSTANCE	Public	Reads specified metafile data from the application's resource file

continues

TABLE 9.3. continued

Function	Parameters	Access	Description
ResetAll	Void	Public	Resets an object to default status by deleting all internal structures (bitmap and metafile) and by initializing all variables
SetROPCode	DWORD RopCode	Public	Defines the new raster operation (ROP) code. The ROP code is used when displaying bitmaps.
DeleteMF	Void	Public	Frees a metafile resource. The file itself is not affected.
DeleteBitmap	Void	Public	Frees a bitmap resource
LoadFile	char *FileName	Public	Initializes an object with a new metafile
LoadFile	char *ResourceName HINSTANCE	Public	Initializes an object with a new metafile from the application's resource area
SetBackground	HBRUSH	Public	Sets the brush used when painting a bitmap background
InitBitmap	int XSize = 32 int YSize = 32 HBRUSH Background = NULL	Public	Uses the metafile to draw an internal bitmap for later use. XSize and YSize are

Function	Parameters	Access	Description
			in pixels. The default background color (see SetBackground) is used if a background brush is not specified here.
DrawMetafile	HDC RECT	Public	Draws a metafile into a specified rectangle on the device context
EnableTransition	Transition	Public	Enables a specified transition during random transitions
DisableTransition	Transition	Public	Disables a specified transition during random transitions
DisplayBitmap	HDC int XOrg = 0 int YOrg = 0 Transition = REPLACE	Public	Displays a previously created bitmap (see InitBitmap) at the XOrg, YOrg offset by using the specified transition
InitMemoryDC	HDC int &Width int &Height HDC &hMemDC	Private	Initializes a memory device context
ReplaceBitmap FadeBitmap TileBitmap SpiralBitmap WipeLeftBitmap WipeRightBitmap WipeTopBitmap	HDC int XOrg int YOrg InitBitmap)	Private	Displays the previously initialized bitmap (see InitBitmap) on the specified device context at the XOrg, YOrg offset. Each

continues

323

TABLE 9.3. continued

Function	Parameters	Access	Description
WipeBottomBitmap			function displays the
TunnelBitmap			bitmap with a
FromLeftBitmap			different transition,
FromRightBitmap			as specified by the
FromTopBitmap			function name.
FromBottomBitmap			

Transition is an enum type defined as follows:

```
enum Transition
    {
        RANDOM,
        REPLACE,
        FADE,
        TILE,
        SPIRAL,
        WIPE_LEFT,
        WIPE_RIGHT,
        WIPE_TOP,
        WIPE_BOTTOM,
        TUNNEL,
        FROM_LEFT,
        FROM_RIGHT,
        FROM_TOP,
        FROM_BOTTOM
    };
```

A #define is used to describe the total number of transitions, not count-ing RANDOM (which isn't really a transition but rather a specification of no predefined transition). The #define looks like this:

```
#define TOTAL_TRANSITIONS 13   // Don't count RANDOM
```

HINT: The Resource Workshop enables you to add user-defined resources to your application's resource file (see Figure 9.4). These often are used to include user-formatted files, such as tutorial files

and text files, in your application's resource area. Simply define a user-specified resource name of METAFILE, and use this identifier for all your metafiles.

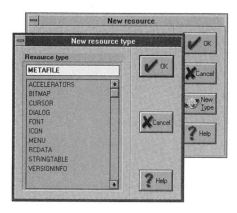

Figure 9.4. Adding a new resource type.

Some *WMetafile* Member Functions

Although I don't discuss every function in the WMetafile class, I do discuss a few selected functions.

SetROPCode

This function specifies the ROP code used during bitmap operations. The default is SRCCOPY, which simply replaces the existing bits with the bits in the bitmap. Table 9.4 shows other common ROP codes. In the table, S stands for source bitmap, D stands for destination bitmap, and P stands for the currently selected pattern (brush) bitmap.

TABLE 9.4. Common ROP codes.

ROP Code	Boolean Operation
BLACKNESS	0
DSTINVERT	~D
MERGECOPY	P&S
MERGEPAINT	~S¦D
NOTSRCCOPY	~S
NOTSRCERASE	~(S¦D)
PATCOPY	P
PATINVERT	P^D
PATPAINT	P¦~S¦D
SRCAND	S&D
SRCCOPY	S
SRCERASE	S&~D
SRCINVERT	S^D
SRCPAINT	S¦D
WHITENESS	1

HINT: SRCINVERT is an exclusive OR copy. This ROP code often is used during animation because the original image can be easily recovered by exclusive ORing the pattern again. For example, the first time I exclusive OR a 10-by-10 bitmap onto an existing image, the new bitmap appears. The second time I exclusive OR the same 10-by-10 bitmap onto the same place, the original image reappears. To animate a ball around the screen, exclusively OR the ball onto one location. Then, exclusively OR it onto the same location to erase it, and exclusively OR it onto a new location to draw it. Notice that you don't need to store, or even read, the original bitmap under the ball.

This process works for multiple bitmaps as long as you exclusive OR each image in LIFO (last in, first out) order when you recover the original image. The only drawback is that your bitmap changes color based on the color of the bitmap beneath it.

LoadFile

This function is overloaded to support loading a metafile from disk and from your application's resource area. Notice that when it loads a file from disk, LoadFile checks whether the file exists by using fopen before it calls GetMetaFile. This keeps Windows from displaying a message box that asks the user to insert the Sample.MF disk in drive A.

When you load the metafile from the resource area, use LoadResource to find the resource and make it available. Next, use LockResource to do the actual loading. (Microsoft chose the names, not I.) Use SetMetaFileBits to create a memory metafile from the data loaded by LockResource. Then, use UnlockResource to allow Windows to reclaim the memory used when it loaded the metafile from the resource area.

DrawMetafile

DrawMetafile is used to play the metafile into a rectangular region of the specified device context. To avoid changing the drawing characteristics of the device context, DrawMetafile uses SaveDC to save the device context state before it makes any changes; then, it uses RestoreDC just before it returns from the function. SetViewportExt and SetViewportOrg are used to control where the metafile is drawn within the specified rectangle. The mapping mode is set to MM_ANISOTROPIC, which causes the bitmap to stretch horizontally and vertically to fill the entire rectangle.

INT: Changing the mapping mode to MM_ISOTROPIC rather than to MM_ANISOTROPIC forces the bitmap to retain its original proportions when it is drawn into the rectangle. Normally, the result is that the bitmap only partially fills the rectangle in one dimension, but MM_ISOTROPIC ensures that the image retains its proper appearance.

WMETAFILE.CPP and WMETAFILE.H Listings

The code that implements the WMetafile class is found in Listings 9.5 and 9.6.

LISTING 9.5. WMETAFILE.H header file listing.

```
#define WIN31
#define STRICT
#define _CLASSDLL

// WMETAFILE.H - Header file for WMetafile class

#ifndef WMetafile_H
#    define WMetafile_H

// Note that the following code is executed only
// if this file has not been previously included


// #include files for both PC and SUN
#include <stdio.h>
#include <time.h>
#include <bios.h>
#include <math.h>

#ifdef __BORLANDC__
    // PC-specific #includes
#    include   <owl.h>

#endif

#ifdef Unix
```

```
        // UNIX-specific #includes

#endif

enum Transition
        {
            RANDOM,
            REPLACE,
            FADE,
            TILE,
            SPIRAL,
            WIPE_LEFT,
            WIPE_RIGHT,
            WIPE_TOP,
            WIPE_BOTTOM,
            TUNNEL,
            FROM_LEFT,
            FROM_RIGHT,
            FROM_TOP,
            FROM_BOTTOM
        };
#define TOTAL_TRANSITIONS 13  // Don't count RANDOM



//******************************************************
// WMetafile - Class to model WMetafiles
//
//      Purpose:
//          This class stores a metafile and has
//          member functions to load and display
//          the metafile as a metafile or a bitmap.
//          Fancy transitions also are supported.
//
//      Copyright:
//              Copyright (c) 1993, William H. Roetzheim
//              All Rights Reserved
//
//******************************************************

_CLASSDEF (WMetafile)
class WMetafile
{
    private:
            // Private data members *******************
            DWORD ROPCode;          // Drawing ROP code
```

continues

LISTING 9.5. continued

```
        HBITMAP hBitmap;     // Handle to this bitmap
        HMETAFILE hMF;       // Handle to this metafile
        BOOL bDisk;          // Disk file or resource?
        HBRUSH Background;   // Bitmap background brush
        BOOL ValidTransitions [TOTAL_TRANSITIONS];


        // Private member functions ****************
        void InitMemoryDC (HDC hDC, int &Width,
                     int &Height, HDC &hMemDC);
        void ReplaceBitmap (HDC, int XOrg, int YOrg);
        void FadeBitmap (HDC, int XOrg, int YOrg);
        void TileBitmap (HDC, int XOrg, int YOrg);
        void SpiralBitmap (HDC, int XOrg, int YOrg);
        void WipeLeftBitmap (HDC, int XOrg, int YOrg);
        void WipeRightBitmap (HDC, int XOrg, int YOrg);
        void WipeTopBitmap (HDC, int XOrg, int YOrg);
        void WipeBottomBitmap (HDC, int XOrg, int YOrg);
        void TunnelBitmap (HDC, int XOrg, int YOrg);
        void FromLeftBitmap (HDC, int XOrg, int YOrg);
        void FromRightBitmap (HDC, int XOrg, int YOrg);
        void FromTopBitmap (HDC, int XOrg, int YOrg);
        void FromBottomBitmap (HDC, int XOrg, int YOrg);

public:
        // Public data members *********************


        // Public member functions *****************
        // Constructors and destructors
        WMetafile (char *FileName);
        WMetafile (char *ResourceName, HINSTANCE);
        ~WMetafile ();

        // Standard functions
        virtual void ResetAll(void);

        // Member functions
        void SetROPCode (DWORD RopCode);
        void DeleteMF ();
      void DeleteBitmap ();
        void LoadFile (char *FileName);
        void LoadFile (char *ResourceName, HINSTANCE);
      void SetBackground (HBRUSH);
        void InitBitmap (int XSize = 32, int YSize = 32,
            HBRUSH hBackground = NULL);
```

```
            void DrawMetafile (HDC, RECT);
            void EnableTransition (Transition);
        void DisableTransition (Transition);
            void DisplayBitmap (HDC, int XOrg = 0, int YOrg = 0,
                                Transition = REPLACE);
};


#endif WMetafile_H
```

LISTING 9.6. WMETAFILE.CPP source file listing.

```cpp
// WMETAFILE.CPP - Source file for WMetafile class

#include "WMetafile.h"  // ALL other #include statements
                        // are in this file

//*****************************************************
// Constructors and destructors for WMetafile
//
//     Copyright:
//             Copyright (c) 1993, William H. Roetzheim
//             All Rights Reserved
//
//*****************************************************

// FileName must be a valid metafile. This
// version doesn't allow placeable metafiles.

WMetafile::WMetafile (char *FileName)
{
    LoadFile (FileName);
}


WMetafile::WMetafile (char *ResourceName, HINSTANCE hInstance)
{
    LoadFile (ResourceName, hInstance);
}


WMetafile::~WMetafile ()
{
```

continues

331

LISTING 9.6. continued

```
    ResetAll();
}



//****************************************************
// Standard functions
//
//    Copyright:
//            Copyright (c) 1993, William H. Roetzheim
//            All Rights Reserved
//
//****************************************************

void WMetafile::ResetAll (void)
{
    // Reset all variables to defaults
    DeleteBitmap ();
    DeleteMF ();
    for (int i = 0; i < TOTAL_TRANSITIONS; i++)
    {
        EnableTransition ((Transition) i);
    }
    ROPCode = SRCCOPY;
    bDisk = FALSE;
    Background = (HBRUSH) GetStockObject (BLACK_BRUSH);
}



//****************************************************
// Member functions for class
//
//    Copyright:
//            Copyright (c) 1993, William H. Roetzheim
//            All Rights Reserved
//
//****************************************************

// Public functions

// Set ROP code
void WMetafile::SetROPCode (DWORD Rop)
{
```

```
        ROPCode = Rop;
}


// Delete an internal metafile
void WMetafile::DeleteMF ()
{
    if ((bDisk == TRUE) && (hMF != 0))
    {
        // Never try to use DeleteMetaFile with a
        // resource in a resource file (UAE)!
        DeleteMetaFile (hMF);
        hMF = 0;
    }
}


// Delete an internal bitmap
void WMetafile::DeleteBitmap ()
{
    if (hBitmap != 0) DeleteObject (hBitmap);
    hBitmap = 0;
}


// Load a metafile from disk
void WMetafile::LoadFile (char *FileName)
{
    FILE *fp;

    ResetAll ();

    // Check to see whether file exists
    fp = fopen (FileName, "r");
    if (fp == NULL)
    {
        char *szBuffer = new char [81];
        sprintf (szBuffer, "Unable to find %s.", FileName);
        MessageBox (NULL, szBuffer, "LoadFile error", MB_OK);
        delete szBuffer;
        return;
    }
    fclose (fp);
    hMF = GetMetaFile (FileName);
```

continues

LISTING 9.6. continued

```
    bDisk = TRUE;
}



// Load a metafile from the resource file
void WMetafile::LoadFile (char *ResourceName, HINSTANCE hInstance)
{
    HGLOBAL hResource;

    ResetAll ();
    hResource = LoadResource (hInstance,
                    FindResource (hInstance, ResourceName,
                    "METAFILE"));
    LockResource (hResource);
    hMF = SetMetaFileBits (hResource);
    UnlockResource (hResource);
}



// Set the bitmap default drawing background brush
void WMetafile::SetBackground (HBRUSH hBrush)
{
    Background = hBrush;
}



// Initialize the internal bitmap with size
// XSize and YSize and background hBackground
void WMetafile::InitBitmap (int XSize, int YSize,
            HBRUSH hBackground)
{
    HBITMAP hOldBitmap;
    HBRUSH hOldBrush;
    HDC hDC;
    HDC hMemDC;

    if (hMF == 0)
    {
        MessageBox (NULL, "Metafile not initialized!",
            "InitBitmap Error", MB_OK);
    }

    if (hBitmap != 0) DeleteObject (hBitmap);

    hDC = GetDC (NULL);  // Display
```

```
    hMemDC = CreateCompatibleDC (hDC);

    hBitmap = CreateCompatibleBitmap (hDC, XSize, YSize);
    ReleaseDC (NULL, hDC);

    hOldBitmap = (HBITMAP) SelectObject (hMemDC, hBitmap);

    // Clear the background
    if (hBackground == 0)
    {
        hBackground = (HBRUSH) GetStockObject (WHITE_BRUSH);
    }
    hOldBrush = (HBRUSH) SelectObject (hMemDC, hBackground);
    PatBlt (hMemDC, 0, 0, XSize, YSize, PATCOPY);
    SelectObject (hMemDC, hOldBrush);

    // Fill bitmap
    SetMapMode (hMemDC, MM_ANISOTROPIC);
    SetViewportExt (hMemDC, XSize, YSize);
    PlayMetaFile (hMemDC, hMF);
    SelectObject (hMemDC, hOldBitmap);
    DeleteDC (hMemDC);
}


// Draw the metafile directly (no bitmap)
void WMetafile::DrawMetafile (HDC hDC, RECT DrawRect)
{
    int OldDC;
    int nX, nY;

    OldDC = SaveDC (hDC);
    SetMapMode (hDC, MM_ANISOTROPIC);
    nX = DrawRect.right - DrawRect.left;
    if (nX < 0) nX = -nX;
    if (nX == 0) nX = 1;
    nY = DrawRect.bottom - DrawRect.top;
    if (nY < 0) nY = -nY;
    if (nY == 0) nY = 1;
    SetViewportExt (hDC, nX, nY);
    SetViewportOrg (hDC, DrawRect.left, DrawRect.top);
    PlayMetaFile (hDC, hMF);
    RestoreDC (hDC, OldDC);
}


void WMetafile::EnableTransition (Transition T)
```

continues

335

LISTING 9.6. continued

```
{
    if ((T < TOTAL_TRANSITIONS) && (T >= 0))
    {
        ValidTransitions [T] = TRUE;
    }
}


void WMetafile::DisableTransition (Transition T)
{
    if ((T < TOTAL_TRANSITIONS) && (T >= 0))
    {
        ValidTransitions [T] = FALSE;
    }

    // Ensure that at least one transition is valid
    for (int i = 0; i < TOTAL_TRANSITIONS; i++)
    {
        if (ValidTransitions [T] == TRUE) return;
    }
    // If you got to here, no transitions are valid!
    MessageBox (NULL,
        "No valid transitions.  Setting REPLACE true.",
        "DisableTransition error", MB_OK);
    ValidTransitions [REPLACE] = TRUE;
}




// Displays the metafile as a bitmap on the
// specified DC and with the specified transition

void WMetafile::DisplayBitmap (HDC hDC, int XOrg, int YOrg,
                    Transition Tran)
{
    switch (Tran)
    {
        case RANDOM:
            // Initialize random number generator
            // loop until a valid transition is found
          int i;
            while (TRUE)
          {
```

```
            i = random (TOTAL_TRANSITIONS);
            if (ValidTransitions [i] == TRUE) break;
        }
        // First value is "random", so add 1
        DisplayBitmap (hDC, XOrg, YOrg, (Transition)
                                        (REPLACE + i));
        break;

case REPLACE:
        ReplaceBitmap (hDC, XOrg, YOrg);
    break;

case FADE:
        FadeBitmap (hDC, XOrg, YOrg);
        break;

case TILE:
        TileBitmap (hDC, XOrg, YOrg);
        break;

case SPIRAL:
        SpiralBitmap (hDC, XOrg, YOrg);
        break;

case WIPE_LEFT:
        WipeLeftBitmap (hDC, XOrg, YOrg);
        break;

case WIPE_RIGHT:
        WipeRightBitmap (hDC, XOrg, YOrg);
        break;

case WIPE_TOP:
        WipeTopBitmap (hDC, XOrg, YOrg);
        break;

case WIPE_BOTTOM:
        WipeBottomBitmap (hDC, XOrg, YOrg);
        break;

case TUNNEL:
        TunnelBitmap (hDC, XOrg, YOrg);
        break;

case FROM_LEFT:
        FromLeftBitmap (hDC, XOrg, YOrg);
        break;
```

continues

337

LISTING 9.6. continued

```
            case FROM_RIGHT:
                FromRightBitmap (hDC, XOrg, YOrg);
                break;

            case FROM_TOP:
                FromTopBitmap (hDC, XOrg, YOrg);
                break;

            case FROM_BOTTOM:
                FromBottomBitmap (hDC, XOrg, YOrg);
                break;

            default:
                ReplaceBitmap (hDC, XOrg, YOrg);
              break;
    }
}


// Private functions

// Initialize a memory DC on which to draw the bitmap

void WMetafile::InitMemoryDC (HDC hDC, int &Width,
                         int &Height, HDC &hMemDC)
{
    BITMAP Bitmap;
    POINT pt;

    if (hBitmap == NULL)
    {
        MessageBox (NULL,
        "Must call InitBitmap prior to DrawBitmap.",
        "InitMemoryDC Error", MB_OK);
    }
    hMemDC = CreateCompatibleDC (hDC);
    SelectObject (hMemDC, hBitmap);
    SetMapMode (hMemDC, GetMapMode (hDC));
    GetObject (hBitmap, sizeof (BITMAP), (LPSTR) &Bitmap);
    pt.x = Bitmap.bmWidth;
    pt.y = Bitmap.bmHeight;
    DPtoLP (hDC, &pt, 1);
    Width = pt.x;
    Height = pt.y;
}
```

```
void WMetafile::ReplaceBitmap (HDC hDC, int XOrg, int YOrg)
{
    HDC hMemDC;
    int BitmapWidth, BitmapHeight;

    InitMemoryDC (hDC, BitmapWidth, BitmapHeight, hMemDC);
    BitBlt (hDC, XOrg, YOrg, BitmapWidth,
            BitmapHeight, hMemDC, 0, 0, ROPCode);

    SelectObject (hMemDC, (HBITMAP) NULL);
    DeleteDC (hMemDC);
}


void WMetafile::FadeBitmap (HDC hDC, int XOrg, int YOrg)
{
    const int Size = 25;
    HDC hMemDC;
    int BitmapWidth, BitmapHeight;
    int XPos, YPos;
    time_t Time;

    InitMemoryDC (hDC, BitmapWidth, BitmapHeight, hMemDC);


    // Fade in for three seconds
    Time = time (NULL);
    while (time (NULL) < Time + 3)
    {
        XPos = random (BitmapWidth - Size);
        YPos = random (BitmapHeight - Size);
        BitBlt (hDC, XOrg + XPos, YOrg + YPos, Size,
            Size, hMemDC, XPos, YPos, ROPCode);
    }
    BitBlt (hDC, XOrg, YOrg, BitmapWidth,
            BitmapHeight, hMemDC, 0, 0, ROPCode);

    SelectObject (hMemDC, (HBITMAP) NULL);
    DeleteDC (hMemDC);
}


void WMetafile::TileBitmap (HDC hDC, int XOrg, int YOrg)
{
```

continues

339

LISTING 9.6. continued

```
    const int Size = 100;
    HDC hMemDC;
    int BitmapWidth, BitmapHeight;
    int Row, Col;
    time_t Time;

    InitMemoryDC (hDC, BitmapWidth, BitmapHeight, hMemDC);

int OddEven;
 for (int Pass = 0; Pass < 2; Pass++)
 {
      for (Row = 0; Row <= (BitmapHeight / Size); Row++)
      {
          for (Col = 0; Col <= (BitmapWidth / Size); Col++)
          {
              OddEven = Pass + Row + Col;
              if (OddEven % 2 == 0)
            {
                  BitBlt (hDC, XOrg + (Col * Size), YOrg +
                          (Row * Size), Size,
                          Size, hMemDC, (Col * Size),
                          (Row * Size), ROPCode);
              }
          }
      }
      Time = time (NULL);
      while (time (NULL) != Time);
 }

    SelectObject (hMemDC, (HBITMAP) NULL);
    DeleteDC (hMemDC);
}


void WMetafile::SpiralBitmap (HDC hDC, int XOrg, int YOrg)
{
    const int Size = 100;
    HDC hMemDC;
    int BitmapWidth, BitmapHeight;
    int Row, Col;
    int Longest;
```

```
long BiosTime;

 InitMemoryDC (hDC, BitmapWidth, BitmapHeight, hMemDC);


 if (BitmapWidth > BitmapHeight) Longest = BitmapWidth;
 else Longest = BitmapHeight;

 int RowStart = -1;
 int ColStart = -1;
int X, Y;

 for (int i = 0; i < (Longest / Size) -1; i++) // 1 per spiral
 {
      RowStart++;
      ColStart++;
      Row = RowStart;
    Col = ColStart;
      // Right edge
      for (Row = RowStart; Row >= -RowStart; Row--)
      {
          BiosTime = biostime (0, 0);
          while (biostime (0, 0) == BiosTime);
          X = XOrg + (Col * Size) + (BitmapWidth / 2);
        Y = YOrg + (Row * Size) + (BitmapHeight / 2);
          BitBlt (hDC, X, Y, Size, Size, hMemDC, X, Y, ROPCode);


      }
      // Top edge
      for (Col = ColStart; Col >= -ColStart; Col--)
 {
          BiosTime = biostime (0, 0);
          while (biostime (0, 0) == BiosTime);
          X = XOrg + (Col * Size) + (BitmapWidth / 2);
        Y = YOrg + (Row * Size) + (BitmapHeight / 2);
          BitBlt (hDC, X, Y, Size, Size, hMemDC, X, Y,
                    ROPCode);
      }

    // Left edge
      for (Row = Row; Row <= RowStart; Row++)
      {
```

continues

LISTING 9.6. continued

```
                BiosTime = biostime (0, 0);
                while (biostime (0, 0) == BiosTime);
                X = XOrg + (Col * Size) + (BitmapWidth / 2);
            Y = YOrg + (Row * Size) + (BitmapHeight / 2);
                BitBlt (hDC, X, Y, Size, Size, hMemDC,
                        X, Y, ROPCode);
            }

            // Bottom edge
            for (Col = Col; Col <= ColStart; Col++)
            {
                BiosTime = biostime (0, 0);
                while (biostime (0, 0) == BiosTime);
                X = XOrg + (Col * Size) + (BitmapWidth / 2);
            Y = YOrg + (Row * Size) + (BitmapHeight / 2);
                BitBlt (hDC, X, Y, Size, Size, hMemDC,
                        X, Y, ROPCode);
            }
        }
    SelectObject (hMemDC, (HBITMAP) NULL);
    DeleteDC (hMemDC);
}


void WMetafile::WipeLeftBitmap (HDC hDC, int XOrg, int YOrg)
{
    const int Size = 25;
    HDC hMemDC;
    int BitmapWidth, BitmapHeight;

    InitMemoryDC (hDC, BitmapWidth, BitmapHeight, hMemDC);

    for (int i = 0; i <= BitmapWidth; i+= Size)
    {
        BitBlt (hDC, XOrg + i, YOrg, Size, BitmapHeight,
            hMemDC, i, 0, ROPCode);
    }
    SelectObject (hMemDC, (HBITMAP) NULL);
    DeleteDC (hMemDC);
}


void WMetafile::WipeRightBitmap (HDC hDC, int XOrg, int YOrg)
{
    const int Size = 25;
    HDC hMemDC;
```

```
        int BitmapWidth, BitmapHeight;

        InitMemoryDC (hDC, BitmapWidth, BitmapHeight, hMemDC);

        for (int i = BitmapWidth; i >= 0 - Size; i-= Size)
        {
            BitBlt (hDC, XOrg + i, YOrg, Size, BitmapHeight,
                hMemDC, i, 0, ROPCode);
        }
        SelectObject (hMemDC, (HBITMAP) NULL);
        DeleteDC (hMemDC);
    }


void WMetafile::WipeTopBitmap (HDC hDC, int XOrg, int YOrg)
    {
        const int Size = 2;
        HDC hMemDC;
        int BitmapWidth, BitmapHeight;

        InitMemoryDC (hDC, BitmapWidth, BitmapHeight, hMemDC);

        for (int i = 0; i <= BitmapHeight; i+= Size)
        {
            BitBlt (hDC, XOrg, YOrg + i, BitmapWidth, Size,
                hMemDC, 0, i, ROPCode);
        }
        SelectObject (hMemDC, (HBITMAP) NULL);
        DeleteDC (hMemDC);
    }


void WMetafile::WipeBottomBitmap (HDC hDC, int XOrg, int YOrg)
    {
        const int Size = 2;
        HDC hMemDC;
        int BitmapWidth, BitmapHeight;

        InitMemoryDC (hDC, BitmapWidth, BitmapHeight, hMemDC);

        for (int i = BitmapHeight; i >= 0 - Size; i-= Size)
        {
            BitBlt (hDC, XOrg, YOrg + i, BitmapWidth, Size,
                hMemDC, 0, i, ROPCode);
        }
        SelectObject (hMemDC, (HBITMAP) NULL);
        DeleteDC (hMemDC);
    }
```

continues

LISTING 9.6. continued

```
void WMetafile::TunnelBitmap (HDC hDC, int XOrg, int YOrg)
{
    const int Size = 30;
    HDC hMemDC;
    int BitmapWidth, BitmapHeight;
    int Largest;
    int X, Y;

    InitMemoryDC (hDC, BitmapWidth, BitmapHeight, hMemDC);


    if (BitmapWidth > BitmapHeight) Largest = BitmapWidth;
    else Largest = BitmapHeight;

    for (int i = 0; i <= (Largest /2); i+= Size)
    {
        X = (BitmapWidth / 2) - i;
        Y = (BitmapHeight / 2) - i;

        BitBlt (hDC, X + XOrg, Y + YOrg, i * 2, i * 2,
            hMemDC, X, Y, ROPCode);
    }
    BitBlt (hDC, XOrg, YOrg, BitmapWidth,
            BitmapHeight, hMemDC, 0, 0, ROPCode);
    SelectObject (hMemDC, (HBITMAP) NULL);
    DeleteDC (hMemDC);
}


void WMetafile::FromLeftBitmap (HDC hDC, int XOrg, int YOrg)
{
    const int Size = 100;
    HDC hMemDC;
    int BitmapWidth, BitmapHeight;

    InitMemoryDC (hDC, BitmapWidth, BitmapHeight, hMemDC);

    for (int i = 0; i <= BitmapWidth; i+= Size)
    {
        BitBlt (hDC, XOrg, YOrg, i, BitmapHeight,
            hMemDC, BitmapWidth - i, 0, ROPCode);
    }
    BitBlt (hDC, XOrg, YOrg, BitmapWidth,
            BitmapHeight, hMemDC, 0, 0, ROPCode);
```

```
        SelectObject (hMemDC, (HBITMAP) NULL);
        DeleteDC (hMemDC);
}


void WMetafile::FromRightBitmap (HDC hDC, int XOrg, int YOrg)
{
        const int Size = 100;
        HDC hMemDC;
        int BitmapWidth, BitmapHeight;

        InitMemoryDC (hDC, BitmapWidth, BitmapHeight, hMemDC);

        for (int i = BitmapWidth - Size; i >= 0; i -= Size)
        {
            BitBlt (hDC, i, YOrg, BitmapWidth - i, BitmapHeight,
                hMemDC, 0, 0, ROPCode);
        }
        BitBlt (hDC, XOrg, YOrg, BitmapWidth,
                BitmapHeight, hMemDC, 0, 0, ROPCode);
        SelectObject (hMemDC, (HBITMAP) NULL);
        DeleteDC (hMemDC);
}


void WMetafile::FromTopBitmap (HDC hDC, int XOrg, int YOrg)
{
        const int Size = 50;
        HDC hMemDC;
        int BitmapWidth, BitmapHeight;

        InitMemoryDC (hDC, BitmapWidth, BitmapHeight, hMemDC);

        for (int i = 0; i <= BitmapHeight; i += Size)
        {
            BitBlt (hDC, XOrg, YOrg, BitmapWidth, i,
                hMemDC, 0, BitmapHeight - i, ROPCode);
        }
        BitBlt (hDC, XOrg, YOrg, BitmapWidth,
                BitmapHeight, hMemDC, 0, 0, ROPCode);
        SelectObject (hMemDC, (HBITMAP) NULL);
        DeleteDC (hMemDC);
}


void WMetafile::FromBottomBitmap (HDC hDC, int XOrg, int YOrg)
```

continues

345

LISTING 9.6. continued

```
{
    const int Size = 50;
    HDC hMemDC;
    int BitmapWidth, BitmapHeight;

    InitMemoryDC (hDC, BitmapWidth, BitmapHeight, hMemDC);

    for (int i = BitmapHeight - Size; i >= 0; i-= Size)
    {
        BitBlt (hDC, XOrg, i, BitmapWidth, BitmapHeight - i,
            hMemDC, 0, 0, ROPCode);
    }
    BitBlt (hDC, XOrg, YOrg, BitmapWidth,
            BitmapHeight, hMemDC, 0, 0, ROPCode);
    SelectObject (hMemDC, (HBITMAP) NULL);
    DeleteDC (hMemDC);
}
```

Incorporating Sound

Sound BLASTER

Problem

You need to prepare an attention-getting presentation for use at a trade show. The presentation will describe your company and its products. It will consist of a series of slides displayed on a computer screen, perhaps using the WSlideShow class, described in Chapter 9, "Implementing a Screen Saver." You want to impress your boss by incorporating music and a voice narrative into the slide show, but how?

Solution

Sophisticated sound cards are available for the PC at a reasonable cost—less than $200. A wide variety of application software and drivers also is available. In addition, Microsoft Windows 3.1 includes DLLs that support all aspects of sound and video. This chapter presents a technical overview of the basics of adding sound to your application. The sample application adds a voice narrative to a short slide show.

To execute the code in this chapter, you need a third-party sound card for your PC. Although Microsoft Windows 3.1 sound drivers support your PC's internal speaker, the speaker's extremely limited capabilities preclude its use for anything more complex than simple beeps, arcade noises, and very simple music. For the examples in this chapter, I use Sound Blaster Pro, made by Creative Labs of Milpitas, CA. It is the most popular sound board for the PC. Sound Blaster Pro offers stereo recording and playback, *MIDI* (*Musical Instrument Digital Interface*) support, CD-ROM input, and a 20-voice sound synthesizer. All the examples in this chapter should also work with sound cards from other companies if they are supported by a Microsoft Windows 3.1 driver (from either Microsoft or the sound card company). If you haven't purchased a sound card yet, you might consider one of the newer 16-bit sound cards—for example, Sound Blaster Pro 16 or Pro Audio Spectrum 16. These offer noticeably better sound quality, and they are rapidly dropping in price.

Before I describe sound processing, I want to make sure that you understand what is meant by *multimedia* and how sound fits into the multimedia picture.

Sound as a Component of Multimedia

Multimedia is in. It's hot. It's rad. But what exactly does it mean?

The *media* in multimedia refers to a method of communicating information. Figure 10.1 shows the primary media that a computer can use to communicate with the user. Multimedia applications use multiple types of media to communicate. Current usage requires that at least one of the communication media be from either the sound or video categories. You are familiar with text as a method of communication. The two general forms of graphic communication, bitmaps and stored drawing commands, are discussed in Chapter 9, "Implementing a Screen Saver," and are incorporated in the WMetaFile class. I discuss sound in this chapter and video in Chapter 11, "Incorporating Video."

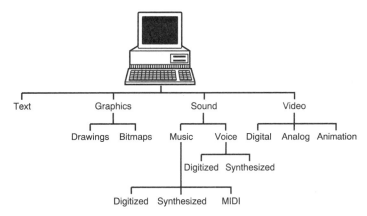

Figure 10.1. The components of multimedia.

Music

As a method of communication, sound generally can be classified as music—which includes special effects and unusual noises—and voice. Computers can produce music in a wide variety of ways. For example, one artist hooked up a computer to electronic clackers used to ring bells. The typical approach, however, is to use a combination of digitized sound, synthesized sound, and MIDI.

Digitized Sound

Digitized sound involves recording sound and storing it in digital format. As Figure 10.2 shows, you start with a source of analog sound—for example, a microphone or the output from a cassette player. Analog sound consists of small electric voltages that vary with time. (In other words, at any given instance, the voltage is slightly different from what it was at a previous instance.) For example, if the voltage varies sinusoidally (varies in the shape of a sine wave) with a frequency of 5,000 *hertz* (cycles per second), and this signal is connected to a speaker, a pure tone at 5,000 Hz is produced. The analog signal is fed into an *analog-to-digital* (*A/D*) converter. This device, normally a computer chip, samples the analog voltage at a regular rate (dictated by a very accurate clock) and outputs the voltage as a digital number. An 8-bit A/D converter can express the voltage over a range of 0 to 255, a 10-bit converter over a range of 0 to 1,023, a 12-bit converter over a range of 0 to 4,095, a 14-bit converter over a range of 0 to 16,383, and a full 16-bit A/D converter over a range of 0 to 65,535. Typically, for A/D chips, as the number of bits increases, the maximum sample rate decreases and the cost increases.

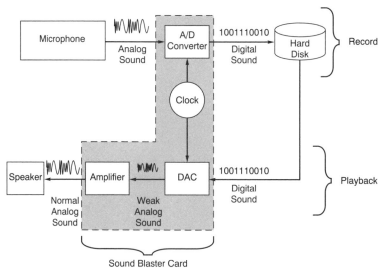

Figure 10.2. Digitized sound.

HINT: Although the number of bits supported by your A/D converter is fixed, you have much control over the sampling rate. For example, with Sound Blaster Pro, you can select sampling rates from 4 kHz (kilohertz) to 44.1 kHz. For maximum sound quality, you should select a sampling rate that is two times the maximum frequency being sampled. (Don't ask me why. It's based on something called the Nyquist sampling theorem, which is taught in electrical engineering.)

The frequencies that make up a typical spoken voice are all less than 4 kHz, so selecting an 8-kHz sampling rate captures full voice fidelity. (Higher sampling rates aren't necessary.) Human hearing covers a range up to about 22 kHz, so a 44-kHz sampling rate is necessary for full fidelity coverage over the entire spectrum of human hearing—for example, when you record high-fidelity music. CD players use 16-bit converters and a 44-kHz sampling rate.

Because Sound Blaster Pro—as well as most other sound cards— uses an 8-bit A/D converter, the amount of memory required to store uncompressed digitized sound is the sample rate times the number of seconds stored. For example, storing 10 seconds of speech sampled at 8 kHz requires 80,000 bytes of storage. Storing 10 seconds of high-fidelity music sampled at 44 kHz requires 440,000 bytes of storage. These storage requirements should be doubled for the newer 16-bit cards.

Sound Blaster Pro supports software compression and hardware decompression with *Adaptive Digital Pulse Code Modulation* (*ADPCM*). By default, each sample consists of the absolute voltage detected stored across the full range that the A/D converter supports—in this case, 0 to 255. This format is called 8-bit *Pulse Code Modulation* (*PCM*). ADPCM involves storing only the difference (variance up or down) from one sample to the next. Table 10.1 shows the three levels of ADPCM compression supported by Sound Blaster Pro.

TABLE 10.1. Levels of compression supported by Sound Blaster Pro.

Compression Scheme	Compression Ratio
4-bit ADPCM	2 to 1
3-bit ADPCM	3 to 1 (roughly)
2-bit ADPCM	4 to 1

When digitized sound is played back, the bits are read from the disk and fed to the *digital-to-analog converter* (*DAC*). The DAC reads a series of bits (8 in the case of Sound Blaster Pro) and then outputs the voltage corresponding to that value. If sound is to be played back without change, the output frequency must match the frequency used during recording. (Do you see what would happen if the frequencies didn't match?) Because the signal that the DAC puts out is weak, it is fed through an amplifier; then, it is ready to drive a speaker.

Synthesized Sound

Sound can be represented by analog voltages changing with various frequencies. If you generate the right frequency, you can produce the sound of a specific note. If you change the characteristics of the sine wave itself (the waveform), you can make the note sound like various musical instruments. If you use a *frequency modulation* (*FM*) synthesizer to produce the proper frequency and waveform, you can tell the FM synthesizer to play a series of notes that make up a melody. This is called one *voice*.

One voice plays a simple melody, but it can't play a chord. If a chord consists of three notes, you need one voice for each note, or three altogether. In addition, to properly emulate some musical instruments, you need more than one voice for each note. Extra voices enable you to reproduce the rich texture of an instrument. The PC speaker supports one voice. Sound Blaster Pro supports 20 voices.

MIDI

Virtually all digital musical instruments have adopted the MIDI protocol for communication among instruments, digital mixers, amplifiers, and

computers. The MIDI protocol defines a standard data packet that succinctly represents the sound being played. (I won't discuss MIDI further other than to mention that Sound Blaster Pro fully supports MIDI input and output.)

Voice

As with music, a human voice can be digitized and played back. The computer also can synthesize a voice. Digitized voice is identical to digitized music, except that the required sampling rates are lower. Speech synthesis relies on the fact that words in a language are made up of reoccurring sounds called *phonemes*. Table 10.2 shows a common set of phonemes for the English language. By combining phonemes, you can produce complete words of any length. Timing and inflection—that is, volume changes—can be used to make the voice sound more natural.

TABLE 10.2. Common English phonemes.

Phoneme	Sound
AA	Short **o** as in p**o**t
AE	Short **a** as in p**a**st
AH	Short **u** as in p**u**p
AO	Intermediate **o** as in c**au**ght
AW	Diphthong in cl**ou**d
AX	Schwa sound as **a** in **a**gainst
AY	Diphthong in **i**ce
b	Plosive in **b**it
CH	**ch** as in **ch**imney
d	Plosive in **d**ie
DH	**th** as in **th**en
DX	Intervocalic **t** as in bu**tt**er

continues

TABLE 10.2. continued

Phoneme	Sound
EH	Short **e** as in p**e**st
ER	**ur** as in f**ur**ther
EY	Diphthong in p**a**ce
f	Fricative in **f**it
g	Plosive in **g**one
h	**h** as in **h**elp
IH	Short **i** as in p**i**t
IX	Short duration sound between IH and AX, as in **D**avid
IY	Long **e** as in p**e**at
j	**j** as in **j**ug
k	Plosive in **k**it
KX	Unaspirated **k** as in ice **c**old
l	**l** as in **l**oose
m	Nasal in **m**ight
n	Nasal in **n**ight
NG	Nasal in pi**ng**
OW	Long **o** as in p**o**se
OY	Diphthong in n**oi**se
p	Plosive in **p**it
PX	Unaspirated **t** as in white **s**pot
r	**r** as in **r**ise
s	Sibilant in **s**it
SH	Sibilant in **sh**ower
t	Plosive in **t**in

Phoneme	Sound
TH	Fricative in **th**ing
TX	Unaspirated **t** as in miss**t**ate
UH	**u** sound as in h**oo**k
UW	Long **u** as in fl**u**te
v	**v** as in **v**igor
w	**w** as in **w**ater
WH	The sound in **wh**en
y	**y** as in **y**es
z	**z** as in **z**oo
ZH	**z** sound in plea**s**ure

Although some researchers still synthesize speech by typing the appropriate phonemes, most speech synthesis is accomplished by using a program that scans an ASCII input and uses a series of rules to determine the proper phonemes to output. Sound Blaster Pro includes such a program that reads ASCII input and outputs relatively accurate pronunciation to the speakers. Unfortunately, the program is only partially compatible with Windows. The speech driver loads itself into EMS (Expanded Memory Specification) and must be installed before you run Windows. Then you can execute the READ.EXE program supplied with Sound Blaster Pro in a DOS window to output speech.

Installing Sound Blaster Pro

The Sound Blaster Pro card is simple to install, and the several procedures apply to most other sound cards. It requires a full-size, 16-bit slot. You need to supply your own speakers and audio input devices—for example, a microphone. Although the factory configuration works fine on my computer, the card is equipped with jumpers that enable me to change the I/O address, the interrupt, and the DMA (Direct Memory Access) channel

used (see Figure 10.3). The Sound Blaster Pro card has jacks for line in, microphone in, volume control, stereo output, and a joystick (see Figure 10.4).

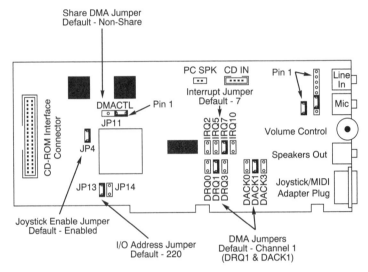

Figure 10.3. The Sound Blaster Pro card layout.

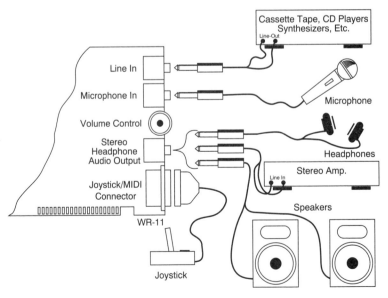

Figure 10.4. Sound Blaster Pro input/output capabilities.

With the hardware part of the installation complete, you need to install the drivers provided with the card. From Control Panel, select the Drivers icon. From the list of drivers, select Unlisted or Updated Driver, then enter the path to the disk or directory with the new drivers. Install the Creative Sound Blaster Pro 2 MIDI Synthesizer driver, the Creative Sound Blaster Pro Auxiliary driver, the Creative Sound Blaster Pro Wave driver, and the MIDI Audio driver. After you have installed all four drivers, restart Windows.

A Layered Approach to Multimedia Programming

As Figure 10.5 shows, you can incorporate multimedia capabilities into your application by using any combination of four approaches. Each approach is progressively closer to the hardware and therefore offers greater flexibility at the expense of simplicity and portability. Support for the multimedia API and multimedia string interface is included with Borland C++. Microsoft provides support in the form of a multimedia DLL with Windows 3.1 and later. The Microsoft sound recorder and player are two applications provided with Windows 3.1 and later. Typically you must purchase third-party applications, although Creative Labs currently is bundling multimedia-compatible presentation software with its Video Blaster board.

Sound Programming Using Third-Party Application Software

If your primary interest in multimedia is to produce presentations that incorporate sound or video, the best solution probably is a third-party presentation package that supports multimedia. For example, Tempra, PowerPoint, and Action! enable you to build presentations that include sound and music. In general, to incorporate sound into a presentation, you first record the sound by using the Microsoft Sound Recorder. This results in a .WAV sound file you can add to the presentation and play when a specified slide is displayed. The Microsoft Windows Multimedia Programmer's Reference contains the format for the .WAV file.

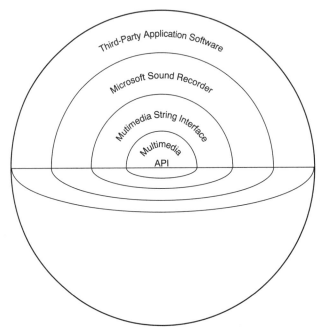

Figure 10.5. Approaches to multimedia programming.

Sound Programming Using the Microsoft Sound Recorder

The Sound Recorder is a simple application that enables you to record sound in a .WAV file and play stored .WAV files. Because the Sound Recorder supports Object Linking and Embedding (OLE), it can be embedded into other Windows applications. For example, suppose you want to add a voice comment to a Microsoft Word document. You would select Insert/Object/Sound, and the Sound Recorder would be executed (see Figure 10.6). To record your comment, select the record pushbutton on the Sound Recorder (it has a small microphone) and speak into the microphone attached to your sound card. When you are done, press the stop pushbutton (the square). When you close the Sound Recorder, a small microphone icon is left in your document (see Figure 10.7). Double-clicking on this icon causes the comment to be played. The SOUND.DOC file, included on the source disk, demonstrates this. (You need a sound card to play the sound back.)

Figure 10.6. The Sound Recorder launched within Word for Windows.

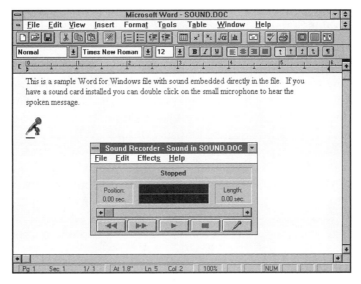

Figure 10.7. Embedded sound in a Word for Windows document.

Sound Programming Using the Multimedia String Interface

If you need to add pizazz to a presentation or to embed voice in an OLE-compatible application, by all means use the Sound Recorder. But what if you want to build capability for sound recording or playback into your own application? The first step is to decide whether you really need to include both capabilities, or whether one will suffice. For example, can you build in sophisticated sound recording capabilities, then let a presentation package or the Sound Recorder be responsible for playing back the files you generate? Likewise, can you use the Sound Recorder to record the music and voice files you need, then simply play them back in your application?

359

After you decide how much custom programming is required, you must decide whether you should use the string interface or program at the API level (discussed later in this chapter). Luckily, you can do almost all the typical multimedia programming functions by using the string interface; this greatly simplifies the programming task. The MCI string interface enables you to execute almost all MCI functions by passing a command string as a parameter in a call to the MCI `SendString()` multimedia API function. Return values are returned as a `NULL`-terminated string. All the MCI classes in this chapter use the MCI string interface. You will get a chance to see the real value of the `WStr` class in simplifying all of these string-handling chores. The string interface is fully documented in the *Microsoft Multimedia Programmer's Reference Guide.*

Generally, I try to use the string interface unless I absolutely must work at a lower level. Although using the API is no more difficult than using any other Windows API, the string interface is simpler to learn and easier to remember. If you purchase the Microsoft Multimedia Development Kit on CD-ROM (which I recommend if you get heavily into Multimedia), a program called MCI_Test is included that enables you to interactively type in strings for execution. All the multimedia classes implemented in this chapter and the next use the string interface. An example of when the lower-level API would be appropriate is an application to record a video segment, something that is supported by the API but not yet supported by the string interface.

Table 10.3 summarizes the MCI (Media Control Interface) string commands available. As the table indicates, some commands apply to a subset of the available multimedia devices. Monospace italic type in the command description represents a placeholder for a user-specified value.

INT: MCI string commands must have at least one space between each word in the command string. This is a common source of problems when concatenating strings to form a command. Remember that extra spaces are acceptable; include a space when you are in doubt.

TABLE 10.3. MCI string commands.

Command	Animation and Movie Player	CD Audio	MIDI Sequencer Player	Video Disk	Video Overlay	Waveform Audio
capability *device* can eject	*	*	*	*	*	*
capability *device* can freeze					*	
capability *device* can play	*	*	*	*	*	*
capability *device* can record	*	*	*	*	*	*
capability *device* can reverse	*			*		
capability *device* can save	*	*	*	*	*	*
capability *device* can stretch	*				*	
capability *device* compound device	*	*	*	*	*	*
capability *device* device type	*	*	*	*	*	*
capability *device* fast play rate	*			*		
capability *device* freeze [at *left top right bottom*]					*	
capability *device* has audio	*	*	*	*	*	*
capability *device* has video	*	*	*	*	*	*
capability *device* inputs						*
capability *device* normal play rate	*			*		
capability *device* outputs						*
capability *device* slow play rate	*			*		
capability *device* uses files	*	*	*	*	*	*
capability *device* uses palettes	*					

continues

TABLE 10.3. continued

Command	Animation and Movie Player	CD Audio	MIDI Sequencer Player	Video Disk	Video Overlay	Waveform Audio
capability *device* windows	*				*	
close *device*	*	*	*	*	*	*
cue *device* input						*
cue *device* output						*
delete [from *position*] [to *position*]						*
escape *device* *string*				*		
info *device* file	*				*	*
info *device* input						*
info *device* output						*
info *device* product	*	*	*	*	*	
info *device* window text	*				*	
load *device* *filename* [at *left top right bottom*]					*	
open [alias *alias*] [buffer *BufferSize*] [shareable] [type *type*]						*
open *device* [alias *alias*] [shareable] [type *device_type*]	*	*	*	*	*	*
open *device* [alias *alias*] [shareable] [type *device_type*] [nostatic] [parent *hwnd*] [shareable] [style *WindowStyle*]	*				*	

Command	Animation and Movie Player	CD Audio	MIDI Sequencer Player	Video Disk	Video Overlay	Waveform Audio
[style child] [style overlapped]						
[style popup]						
pause *device*	*	*	*	*		*
play *device*	*	*	*	*		*
play *device* fast	*			*		
play *device* from *position* to *position*	*	*	*	*		*
play *device* reverse	*					
play *device* scan	*			*		
play *device* slow	*			*		
play *device* speed *FPS*	*			*		
put *device* destination	*				*	
put *device* destination at *left top right bottom*	*				*	
put *device* frame [at *left top right bottom*]					*	
put *device* source	*				*	
put *device* source at *left top right bottom*	*				*	
put *device* video [at *left top right bottom*]					*	
realize *device* background	*					
realize *device* normal	*					
record *device* [insert]			*			*
[from *position* to *position*]						
[overwrite]						
resume *device*	*	*	*	*	*	*

continues

TABLE 10.3. continued

Command	Animation and Movie Player	CD Audio	MIDI Sequencer Player	Video Disk	Video Overlay	Waveform Audio
save *device* *filename*			*		*	*
save *device* *filename* [at *left top right bottom*]					*	
seek *device* to end	*	*	*	*		*
seek *device* to *position*	*	*	*	*		*
seek *device* to start	*	*	*	*		*
set *device* any input						*
set *device* any output						*
set *device* bitspersample *bits*						*
set *device* bytespersec *rate*						*
set *device* channels *number*						*
set *device* format tag pcm						*
set *device* format tag *tag*						*
set *device* input *channel*						*
set *device* output *channel*						*
set *device* samplespersec *rate*						*
set *device* time format bytes						*
set *device* time format samples						*
set *device* alignment *integer*						*
set *device* audio all off	*	*	*	*	*	*
set *device* audio all on	*	*	*	*	*	*
set *device* audio left off	*	*	*	*	*	*

Command	Animation and Movie Player	CD Audio	MIDI Sequencer Player	Video Disk	Video Overlay	Waveform Audio
set *device* audio left on	*	*	*	*	*	*
set *device* audio right off	*	*	*	*	*	*
set *device* audio right on	*	*	*	*	*	*
set *device* door closed		*		*		
set *device* door open		*		*		
set *device* master MIDI			*			
set *device* master none			*			
set *device* master SMPTE			*			
set *device* offset *time*			*			
set *device* port mapper			*			
set *device* port none			*			
set *device* port *PortNumber*			*			
set *device* slave file			*			
set *device* slave MIDI			*			
set *device* slave none			*			
set *device* slave SMPTE			*			
set *device* tempo *tempo*			*			
set *device* time format frames	*			*		
set *device* time format milliseconds	*	*	*	*	*	*
set *device* time format msf		*				
set *device* time format SMPTE 24				*		
set *device* time format SMPTE 25				*		

continues

365

TABLE 10.3. continued

Command	Animation and Movie Player	CD Audio	MIDI Sequencer Player	Video Disk	Video Overlay	Waveform Audio
set *device* time format SMPTE 30			*			
set *device* time format SMPTE 30 drop			*			
set *device* time format tmsf		*				
set *device* time format track				*		
set *device* video off	*			*	*	
set *device* video on	*			*	*	
status *device* alignment						*
status *device* bitspersample						*
status *device* bytespersec						*
status *device* channels						*
status *device* format tag						*
status *device* input						*
status *device* level						*
status *device* output						*
status *device* samplespersec						*
status *device* current track	*	*	*	*		*
status *device* disc size				*		
status *device* division type			*			
status *device* forward	*			*		
status *device* length	*	*	*	*		*
status *device* length track *TrackNumber*	*	*		*		*

Command	Animation and Movie Player	CD Audio	MIDI Sequencer Player	Video Disk	Video Overlay	Waveform Audio
status *device* master			*			
status *device* media present	*	*	*	*	*	*
status *device* media type				*		
status *device* mode	*	*	*	*	*	*
status *device* number of tracks	*	*	*	*		*
status *device* offset				*		
status *device* palette handle	*					
status *device* port			*			
status *device* position	*	*	*	*		*
status *device* position track *number*	*	*	*	*		*
status *device* ready	*	*	*	*	*	*
status *device* side				*		
status *device* slave			*			
status *device* speed	*			*		
status *device* start position	*	*	*	*		*
status *device* tempo			*			
status *device* time format	*	*	*	*		*
status *device* time format hms				*		
status *device* window handle	*				*	
step *device* [by *frames*] [reverse]	*			*		
stop *device*	*	*	*	*		*
unfreeze *device* [at *left top right bottom*]					*	

continues

TABLE 10.3. continued

Command	Animation and Movie Player	CD Audio	MIDI Sequencer Player	Video Disk	Video Overlay	Waveform Audio
update *device* [hdc *hDC*] [at *ClipLeft ClipTop*	*					
ClipRight ClipBottom]						
where *device* destination	*				*	
where *device* frame					*	
where *device* source	*				*	
window *device* [handle *hWnd*] [handle default]	*				*	
[state hide] [state iconic] [state maximized]						
[state minimized] [state no action]						
[state normal] [text *caption*]						

INT: A table like Table 10.3 is useful when you are designing class inheritance hierarchies. The objects are found across the top, and the functions are down the left side.

To design the MCI class hierarchy, I began by highlighting all functions that pertained to all objects. This described the required capabilities of a generic class that all MCI objects would inherit. Because the resultant WMCI class wasn't useful by itself, I made it an abstract class by specifying—but not defining—one of its functions. Then I looked for and highlighted functions that were applicable to waveform devices and that were present for most other devices. This produced a set of functions that were applicable to all MCI devices except video overlays. I called this

intermediate class WMCIDevice, and I put the indicated functionality in the class.

WMCIDevice is a child of WMCI, and it is the parent of all classes except the VideoOverlay class. It is an abstract class because it does not provide a definition for the abstract function defined in WMCI. Finally, I took the functions that were present for MCI sound devices but that were not already highlighted. This defined the required functionality for the WSound class. Because WSound defines the WMCI abstract function, it is not an abstract class.

The chpt10 sample application displays two slides by using the slide viewer class defined when I built my screen saver, and it adds sound to each slide. Table 10.4 describes the files that make up the sample application. This list is somewhat longer than the lists in other chapters, because I tried to make the MCI multimedia classes general-purpose, reusable classes. Remember that to run the sample application, you need a sound card for your computer. Figure 10.8 shows the inheritance relationships among the classes that make up this application. Figure 10.9 shows the creation relationships among the classes.

TABLE 10.4. Files required for the chpt10 application.

File	Description
WMETAFILE.CPP and WMETAFILE.H	WMetafile class defined in Chapter 9, "Implementing a Screen Saver"
WSLIDESHOW.CPP and WSLIDESHOW.H	WSlideShow class defined in Chapter 9
CHPT10.CPP	Main application class and main window for the chpt10 program
CHPT10.PRJ	chpt10 project file

continues

TABLE 10.4. continued

File	Description
SOUND1.MF and SOUND2.MF	Windows metafiles used for the `chpt10` demonstration
SOUND1.WAV and SOUND2.WAV	Files containing sound that go with SOUND1.MF and SOUND2.MF
WMCI.H and WMCI.CPP	`WMCI` class header and source files. This is the abstract class from which all MCI classes are derived.
WMCIDEVICE.H and WMCIDEVICE.CPP	`WMCIDevice` class header and source files. This is an abstract class from which all MCI devices (everything but video overlays) are derived.
WSOUND.H and WSOUND.CPP	`WSound` class header and source files. This class encapsulates a waveform audio MCI device—for example, Sound Blaster Pro.
WSOUNDSLIDE.H and WSOUNDSLIDE.CPP	`WSoundSlide` class header and source files. This class adds sound capability to the `WSlideShow` class.

File	Description
WSTR.H and WSTR.CPP	WStr class header and source files. The string-handling capabilities of this class are particularly useful for this application.

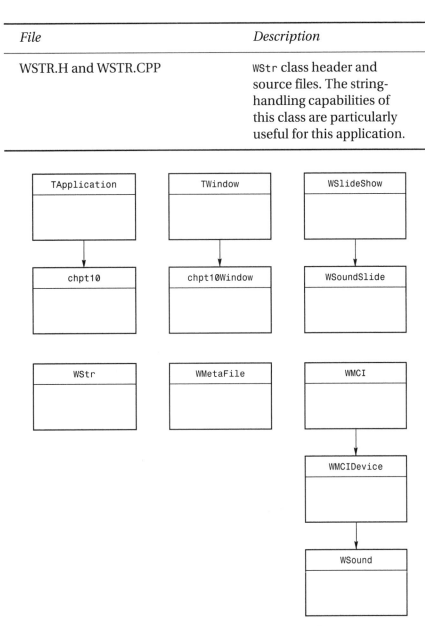

Figure 10.8. Inheritance relationships among chpt10 *classes.*

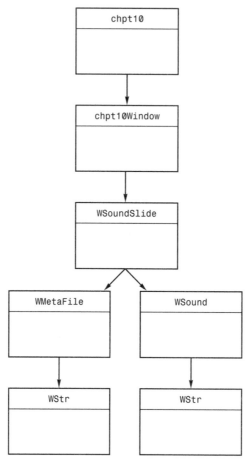

Figure 10.9. Creation relationships among chpt10 *classes.*

The *chpt10* Sample Application

Listing 10.1 shows the main application code for the chpt10 sample application. The only significant difference between this code and the code in Chapter 9, "Implementing a Screen Saver," is the use of the WSoundSlide class rather than the WSlideShow class.

LISTING 10.1. chpt10 sample application.

```
#define WIN31
#define STRICT
#define _CLASSDLL

// #include files for both PC and SUN
#include  "WSoundSlide.h"

#ifdef __BORLANDC__
     // PC-specific #includes
#    include   <owl.h>

#endif

#ifdef Unix
     // UNIX-specific #includes

#endif


//****************************************************
// chpt10Window - chpt10 main window
//
//     Purpose:
//         This class is the main window for the
//         chpt10 application.
//
//     Notes:
//
//     Copyright:
//             Copyright (c) 1993, William H. Roetzheim
//             All Rights Reserved
//
//****************************************************
_CLASSDEF (chpt10Window)
class chpt10Window : public TWindow
{
    private:
        PWSoundSlide SlideShow;

    public:
        chpt10Window (PTWindowsObject Parent, LPSTR Title,
                            PTModule Module = NULL);
        ~chpt10Window ();
       void Start ();
};
```

continues

LISTING 10.1. continued

```
//******************************************************
// chpt10 - chpt10 application class
//
//      Purpose:
//          This class is the overall application
//          executive for chpt10.
//
//      Notes:
//
//      Copyright:
//              Copyright (c) 1993, William H. Roetzheim
//              All Rights Reserved
//
//******************************************************

_CLASSDEF (chpt10)
class chpt10 : public TApplication
{
    private:
        // Private data members ********************
        //    None


        // Private member functions ***************
        //    None

    public:
        // Public data members ********************

        // Public member functions ****************
        // Constructors and destructors
        chpt10 (char *szName, HINSTANCE hInstance,
                HINSTANCE hPrevInstance, LPSTR lpCmdLine,
                int nCmdShow);

        // Member functions
        virtual void InitMainWindow ();
        virtual void IdleAction ();
};


//******************************************************
// Constructors and destructors for chpt10Window
//
```

```
//    Copyright:
//            Copyright (c) 1993, William H. Roetzheim
//            All Rights Reserved
//
//****************************************************

chpt10Window::chpt10Window (PTWindowsObject Parent,
     LPSTR Title, PTModule Module)
     : TWindow (Parent, Title, Module)
{
     ShowCursor (FALSE);
     Attr.Style = WS_POPUP;
     SlideShow = new WSoundSlide ("Sound*.mf");
}


void chpt10Window::Start ()
{

     SlideShow->Start (TRUE);
}

chpt10Window::~chpt10Window ()
{
     ShowCursor (TRUE);
     delete SlideShow;

    // Refresh the entire display
     InvalidateRect (NULL, NULL, TRUE);
     UpdateWindow (NULL);
}




//****************************************************
// Constructors and destructors for chpt10
//
//    Copyright:
//            Copyright (c) 1993, William H. Roetzheim
//            All Rights Reserved
//
//****************************************************

#pragma argsused  // Turn off arguments not used warning
chpt10::chpt10(char *szName, HINSTANCE hInstance,
              HINSTANCE hPrevInstance, LPSTR lpCmdLine,
               int nCmdShow)
```

continues

375

LISTING 10.1. continued

```
                : TApplication (szName, hInstance,
                hPrevInstance, lpCmdLine, nCmdShow)
{
    return;
}




//****************************************************
// Member functions for class
//
//    Copyright:
//            Copyright (c) 1993, William H. Roetzheim
//            All Rights Reserved
//
//****************************************************


//****************************************************
// chpt10::IdleAction - Perform background processing
//
//    Purpose:
//        This function enables you to perform a small amount
//        of processing when Windows has nothing else to
//        do. In this case, a slide is displayed. It would
//        be even better to break the slide display into
//        smaller pieces (a single slide can take up to a
//        couple seconds to display).
//
//    General Notes:
//
//     Testing Notes:
//
//    Copyright:
//            Copyright (c) 1993, William H. Roetzheim
//            All Rights Reserved
//
//****************************************************

void chpt10::IdleAction ()
{
    ((Pchpt10Window) MainWindow)->Start ();
    PostQuitMessage (0);
}


void chpt10::InitMainWindow ()
```

```
{
    MainWindow = new chpt10Window (NULL, NULL, NULL);
}



// Here is the main () for the program
int PASCAL WinMain (HINSTANCE hInstance,
    HINSTANCE hPrevInstance, LPSTR lpCmdLine,
    int)
{

    // Create chpt10 application from class
    chpt10 ochpt10 ("chpt10", hInstance,
                    hPrevInstance, lpCmdLine, SW_NORMAL);

    // Start created application running
    ochpt10.Run ();  // Runs till window closed

    // Return termination status when window closed
    return ochpt10.Status;
}
```

The *WSoundSlide* Class

Listings 10.2 and 10.3 show the listings for the header and source code for the WSoundSlide class. It is a child of the WSlideShow class, from which it inherits almost all its functionality. WSoundSlide overrides NextSlide in WSlideShow, attempting to play a sound file after each slide is displayed. The sound files are assumed to be in the same directory as the slide show metafiles.

This version of WSoundSlide assumes that the metafiles and sound files are ordered in the directory appropriately. For example, the version assumes that the first sound file matches the first metafile, and so on. To make this class useful as a general-purpose class, you need to replace it with an equivalent one that stores the metafile and sound filenames internally, reads them from a disk, or uses the filename rather than the file position in the directory.

The code that plays the waveform audio file is very simple:

```
WSound Sound ((WStr) ffBlock.ff_name);
Sound.Play (1);
```

An instance of the WSound class is created, and at that time it is passed a waveform audio filename. The Play function is then used. It is passed a starting position of 1 (the beginning of the file).

LISTING 10.2. WSOUNDSLIDE.H header file listing.

```
// WSLIDESHOW.H - Header file for WSlideShow class

#ifndef WSlideShow_H
#    define WSlideShow_H

// Note that the following code is executed only
// if this file has not been previously included


// #include files for both PC and SUN
#include <dir.h>
#include "WStr.h"
#include "WMetaFile.h"


#ifdef __BORLANDC__
    // PC-specific #includes
#    include    <owl.h>

#endif

#ifdef Unix
    // UNIX-specific #includes

#endif

//****************************************************
// WSlideShow - Slide show class
//
//    Purpose:
//        Display a series of metafiles with
//        special effects.
//
```

```
//      Notes:
//
//      Copyright:
//              Copyright (c) 1993, William H. Roetzheim
//              All Rights Reserved
//
//****************************************************

_CLASSDEF (WSlideShow)
class WSlideShow
{
    protected:
            // Private data members *******************
            WStr FileName;  // Allows wildcards
            // ValidTransitions is used when drawing random
            // transitions
            BOOL ValidTransitions [TOTAL_TRANSITIONS];

            BOOL EscapePressed;  // Has user pressed the Esc key?
            int  SlideNumber;    // Next slide number to be drawn



            // Private member functions ****************
            BOOL Go ();  // Was Esc pressed?

    public:
            // Public data members ********************


            // Public member functions ****************
            // Constructors and destructors
            WSlideShow (WStr FileName);

            // Standard functions
            virtual void ResetAll(void);

            // Member functions
            virtual void Start(BOOL LoopBack = FALSE);
        virtual int NextSlide ();
            virtual void EnableTransition (Transition);
            virtual void DisableTransition (Transition);
};

#endif WSlideShow_H
```

LISTING 10.3. WSOUNDSLIDE.CPP source code listing.

```
//  WSOUNDSLIDE.CPP - Source file for WSoundSlide class

#include "WSoundSlide.h"  // ALL other #include statements
                          // are in this file

//****************************************************
// Constructors and destructors for WSoundSlide
//
//     Copyright:
//             Copyright (c) 1993, William H. Roetzheim
//             All Rights Reserved
//
//****************************************************

WSoundSlide::WSoundSlide (WStr File)
              : WSlideShow (File)
{
    return;
}




//****************************************************
// Member functions for class
//
//     Copyright:
//             Copyright (c) 1993, William H. Roetzheim
//             All Rights Reserved
//
//****************************************************

//****************************************************
// WSoundSlide::Start - Start a complete slide show
//
//     Purpose:
//         Displays all slides matching FileName (including
//         wildcards). If LoopBack is TRUE, the slide show
//         continues until Esc is pressed.
//
//     General Notes:
//         For real-world slide shows, you will want to
//         modify this class (or derive a class from it)
//         so that the delay between slides and the
//         transition from one slide to the next can be
//         set on a slide-by-slide basis. (For example, you
//         might want a slide with lots of text displayed
```

```
//         longer than a simple slide.)
//
//      Testing Notes:
//
//      Copyright:
//              Copyright (c) 1993, William H. Roetzheim
//              All Rights Reserved
//
//****************************************************


//****************************************************
// WSoundSlide::NextSlide - Display the current slide
//
//      Purpose:
//          Displays the current slide, then returns
//          the number of the next slide to be displayed.
//          Also displays any sound stored in a file
//          that has the same name as the slide but a
//          .WAV extension.
//
//      General Notes:
//
//      Testing Notes:
//
//      Copyright:
//              Copyright (c) 1993, William H. Roetzheim
//              All Rights Reserved
//
//****************************************************

int WSoundSlide::NextSlide ()
{
    struct ffblk ffBlock;
    int Flag;
    int SoundNumber = SlideNumber;
    char Buffer [MAXPATH + 40];

    WSlideShow::NextSlide ();


    // Modify the end of the FileName
    strcpy (Buffer, FileName);
    char * End = strrchr (Buffer, '.');
    if (End != NULL) End[0] = 0;
    strcat (Buffer, ".WAV");

    // Play the sound at SlideNumber
```

continues

LISTING 10.3. continued

```
Flag = findfirst (Buffer, &ffBlock, 0);
for (int i = 0; i < SoundNumber; i++)
    Flag = findnext (&ffBlock);

if (Flag == 0)
{
    // Play the file ffBlock.ff_name
    WSound Sound ((WStr) ffBlock.ff_name);
    Sound.Play (1);
}
return SlideNumber;
}
```

The *WMCI* Class

Listings 10.4 and 10.5 show the code for the WMCI class. The WMCI class is an abstract class used by all other MCI classes through inheritance. As it is written, this is a useful, general-purpose class. If you prefer the MCI API (discussed later), simply replace the function bodies with appropriate API calls. The class is abstract because the Open function, also known as a pure virtual function, is specified but not defined (note the = 0):

```
virtual void Open (RWStr FileName) = 0;
```

The class maintains a variable, Status, that provides the error code (or 0 for no error) returned by the last function. In addition, a message box is displayed with any MCI errors that are encountered. You can use the GetError function to return a string representation of the Status variable error. For example, you might use it for an error log file. All other functions are self-explanatory; they are derived from the information in Table 10.3.

LISTING 10.4. WMCI.H header file listing.

```
// WMCI.H - Header file for WMCI class

#ifndef WMCI_H
#    define WMCI_H

// Note that the following code is executed only
```

```
// if this file has not been previously included


// #include files for both PC and SUN
#include   "WStr.h"
#include   <mmsystem.h>

#ifdef __BORLANDC__
    // PC-specific #includes
#    include   <owl.h>

#endif

#ifdef Unix
    // UNIX-specific #includes

#endif

//*******************************************************
// WMCI - Abstract class representing generic device
//
//     Purpose:
//         MCI commands that are present for all MCI
//         devices are found here.
//
//     Notes:
//
//     Copyright:
//             Copyright (c) 1993, William H. Roetzheim
//             All Rights Reserved
//
//*******************************************************

_CLASSDEF (WMCI)
class WMCI
{
    protected:
        // Protected data members ******************
        WStr DeviceName;


        // Protected member functions **************
        virtual WStr SendCommand (RWStr Command);
        virtual void Open (RWStr FileName) = 0;


    public:
        // Public data members *********************
```

continues

LISTING 10.4. continued

```
            DWORD Status;


            // Public member functions ******************
            // Constructors and destructors
            ~WMCI ();

            // Member functions
            virtual BOOL    CanEject ();
            virtual BOOL    CanPlay ();
            virtual BOOL    CanRecord ();
            virtual BOOL    CanSave ();
            virtual BOOL    CompoundDevice ();
            virtual BOOL    HasAudio ();
            virtual BOOL    HasVideo ();
            virtual BOOL    UsesFiles ();
            virtual BOOL    Ready ();
            virtual BOOL    MediaPresent ();

            virtual void    AudioAllOff ();
            virtual void    AudioAllOn ();
            virtual void    AudioLeftOff ();
            virtual void    AudioLeftOn ();
            virtual void    AudioRightOff ();
            virtual void    AudioRightOn ();

            virtual void    SetTimeMilliseconds ();

            virtual WStr    GetType ();
            virtual WStr    GetMode ();
            virtual WStr    GetProduct ();
            virtual WStr    GetName ();
            virtual WStr    GetError ();
};

#endif WMCI_H
```

LISTING 10.5. WMCI.CPP source code listing.

```
// WMCI.CPP - Source file for WMCI class

#include "WMCI.h"   // ALL other #include statements
                     // are in this file
```

```
//****************************************************
// Constructors and destructors for WMCI
//
//    Copyright:
//            Copyright (c) 1993, William H. Roetzheim
//            All Rights Reserved
//
//****************************************************


// Uses default constructor


WMCI::~WMCI ()
{
    WStr Command = "close " + DeviceName;
    SendCommand (Command);
}




//****************************************************
// Member functions for class
//
//    Copyright:
//            Copyright (c) 1993, William H. Roetzheim
//            All Rights Reserved
//
//****************************************************


// Returns TRUE if device can eject the media
BOOL WMCI::CanEject ()
{
    WStr Return;
    WStr Command = "capability " + DeviceName + " can eject";
    Return = SendCommand (Command);
    if (Return == "true") return TRUE;
    else return FALSE;
}


// Returns TRUE if the device can play
BOOL WMCI::CanPlay ()
{
    WStr Return;
    WStr Command = "capability " + DeviceName + " can play";
    Return = SendCommand (Command);
    if (Return == "true") return TRUE;
```

continues

LISTING 10.5. continued

```
        else return FALSE;
}


// Returns TRUE if the device supports recording
BOOL WMCI::CanRecord ()
{
    WStr Return;
    WStr Command = "capability " + DeviceName + " can record";
    Return = SendCommand (Command);
    if (Return == "true") return TRUE;
    else return FALSE;
}

// Returns TRUE if the device can save data
BOOL      WMCI::CanSave ()
{
    WStr Return;
    WStr Command = "capability " + DeviceName + " can save";
    Return = SendCommand (Command);
    if (Return == "true") return TRUE;
    else return FALSE;
}


// Returns TRUE if the device requires an element name
BOOL WMCI::CompoundDevice ()
{
    WStr Return;
    WStr Command = "capability " + DeviceName +
                   " compound device";
    Return = SendCommand (Command);
    if (Return == "true") return TRUE;
    else return FALSE;
}


// Returns TRUE if the device supports audio playback
BOOL WMCI::HasAudio ()
{
    WStr Return;
    WStr Command = "capability " + DeviceName + " has audio";
    Return = SendCommand (Command);
    if (Return == "true") return TRUE;
    else return FALSE;
}
```

```
// Returns TRUE if the device supports video
BOOL WMCI::HasVideo ()
{
    WStr Return;
    WStr Command = "capability " + DeviceName + " has video";
    Return = SendCommand (Command);
    if (Return == "true") return TRUE;
    else return FALSE;
}


// Returns TRUE if the element of a compound device is
// a file path name

BOOL WMCI::UsesFiles ()
{
    WStr Return;
    WStr Command = "capability " + DeviceName + " uses files";
    Return = SendCommand (Command);
    if (Return == "true") return TRUE;
    else return FALSE;
}


BOOL WMCI::Ready ()
{
    WStr Return;
    WStr Command = "status " + DeviceName + " ready";
    Return = SendCommand (Command);
    if (Return == "true") return TRUE;
    else return FALSE;
}


BOOL WMCI::MediaPresent ()
{
    WStr Return;
    WStr Command = "status " + DeviceName + " media present";
    Return = SendCommand (Command);
    if (Return == "true") return TRUE;
    else return FALSE;
}



void WMCI::AudioAllOff ()
{
    WStr Command = "set " + DeviceName + " audio all off";
    SendCommand (Command);
}

void WMCI::AudioAllOn ()
```

continues

LISTING 10.5. continued

```
{
     WStr Command = "set " + DeviceName + " audio all on";
     SendCommand (Command);
}

void WMCI::AudioLeftOff ()
{
     WStr Command = "set " + DeviceName + " audio left off";
     SendCommand (Command);
}

void WMCI::AudioLeftOn ()
{
     WStr Command = "set " + DeviceName + " audio left on";
     SendCommand (Command);
}

void WMCI::AudioRightOff ()
{
     WStr Command = "set " + DeviceName + " audio right off";
     SendCommand (Command);
}

void WMCI::AudioRightOn ()
{
     WStr Command = "set " + DeviceName + " audio right on";
     SendCommand (Command);
}

void WMCI::SetTimeMilliseconds ()
{
     WStr Command = "set " + DeviceName +
                    " time format milliseconds";
     SendCommand (Command);
}

WStr WMCI::GetType ()
{
     WStr Command = "capability " + DeviceName + " device type";
     return SendCommand (Command);
}

WStr WMCI::GetMode ()
{
     WStr Command = "status " + DeviceName + " mode";
     return SendCommand (Command);
```

```
}


WStr WMCI::GetProduct ()
{
    WStr Command = "info " + DeviceName + " product";
    return SendCommand (Command);
}



WStr WMCI::GetName ()
{
    return DeviceName;
}


WStr WMCI::GetError ()
{
    char Buffer [81];
    mciGetErrorString (Status, Buffer, 81);
    return (WStr) Buffer;
}



// Private member functions

WStr WMCI::SendCommand (RWStr Command)
{
    char Buffer [81];

    Status = mciSendString (Command, Buffer, 81, NULL);

    if (Status != 0)
    {
        if (mciGetErrorString (Status, Buffer, 81))
        {
            MessageBox (NULL, Buffer, "WMCI", MB_OK);
        }
        else MessageBox (NULL, "Unknown MCI error.",
                "WMCI", MB_OK);
        return (WStr) "";
    }
    else return (WStr) Buffer;
}
```

The *WMCIDevice* Class

Listings 10.6 and 10.7 show the code for the WMCIDevice class. This class is a child of WMCI. It adds functions that apply to all MCI devices but not to video overlays. The functions Play, Seek, SeekEnd, and SeekStart are particularly useful. The Play function plays the file or buffer—whether video, audio, animation, or whatever. You can optionally specify a starting position and an ending position using From and To. If they are not specified, the starting position is the current location, and the ending position is the end of the file or buffer. Seek is used to advance to a specified position in the file or buffer. SeekEnd and SeekStart perform the positioning functions. The default for all four functions is for the command to block until completion (Wait = TRUE). You can specify nonblocking by setting Wait = FALSE. Because the WMCIDevice class does not define an Open function and is a child of WMCI, it is an abstract class.

HINT: By default, MCI string commands return control to your program immediately. If you want to block until the command is complete, you must add the wait option to the command. Because I have encapsulated an MCI device in a C++ class, the default behavior (nonblocking) presents a potential problem. I open the device in the class constructor and close the device in the class destructor.

Suppose that you create an instance of the class, then call the Play function in the default nonblocking mode. If the class instance goes out of scope before the Play function completes the play, the Close command is executed, and play stops when the class destructor is called. I handle this problem by modifying the MCI default behavior to ensure command blocking by default. The nonblocking version of the commands can be used if the class remains in scope until the command is completed.

LISTING 10.6. WMCIDEVICE.H header file listing.

```
// WMCIDEVICE.H - Header file for WMCIDevice class

#ifndef WMCIDevice_H
```

```
#      define WMCIDevice_H

// Note that the following code is executed only
// if this file has not been previously included


// #include files for both PC and SUN
#include   "WStr.h"
#include   "WMCI.h"

#ifdef __BORLANDC__
      // PC-specific #includes
#      include    <owl.h>

#endif

#ifdef Unix
      // UNIX-specific #includes

#endif

//*****************************************************
// WMCIDevice - Commands common to MCI devices
//
//     Purpose:
//          Abstract class to handle MCI device commands.
//          This class handles commands that are common
//          to all MCI devices except Video Overlay.
//
//     Notes:
//
//     Copyright:
//          Copyright (c) 1993, William H. Roetzheim
//          All Rights Reserved
//
//*****************************************************

_CLASSDEF (WMCIDevice)
class WMCIDevice : public WMCI
{
     private:
          // Private data members ********************


          // Private member functions ***************

     public:
          // Public data members *********************
```

continues

LISTING 10.6. continued

```
// Public member functions *****************

// Member functions
virtual int        GetCurrentTrack ();
virtual long   GetLength ();
virtual int        GetTotalTracks ();
virtual int    GetPosition ();
virtual int        GetPosition (int TrackNumber);
virtual int        GetStart ();
virtual WStr   GetTimeFormat ();
virtual void   Stop ();
virtual void   Pause ();
virtual void   Play (int From = -1, int To = -1,
                     int Wait = TRUE);
virtual void   Resume ();
virtual void   Seek (int Position, int Wait = TRUE);
virtual void   SeekEnd (int Wait = TRUE);
virtual void   SeekStart (int Wait = TRUE);
};

#endif WMCIDevice_H
```

LISTING 10.7. WMCIDEVICE.CPP source code listing.

```
// WMCIDEVICE.CPP - Source file for WMCIDevice class

#include "WMCIDevice.h"  // ALL other #include statements
                         // are in this file


//*****************************************************
// Member functions for class
//
//     Copyright:
//          Copyright (c) 1993, William H. Roetzheim
//          All Rights Reserved
//
//*****************************************************

int      WMCIDevice::GetCurrentTrack ()
```

```
{
    WStr Return;
    WStr Command = "status " + DeviceName + " current track";
    Return = SendCommand (Command);
    return Return.ToInt ();
}


long WMCIDevice::GetLength ()
{
    WStr Return;
    WStr Command = "status " + DeviceName + " current track";
    Return = SendCommand (Command);
    return Return.ToInt ();
}


int     WMCIDevice::GetTotalTracks ()
{
    WStr Return;
    WStr Command = "status " + DeviceName + " number of tracks";
    Return = SendCommand (Command);
    return Return.ToInt ();
}


int  WMCIDevice::GetPosition ()
{
    WStr Return;
    WStr Command = "status " + DeviceName + " position";
    Return = SendCommand (Command);
    return Return.ToInt ();
}

int     WMCIDevice::GetPosition (int TrackNumber)
{
    WStr Return;
    WStr Command = "status " + DeviceName + " position track" +
        + " " + ToString (TrackNumber);
    Return = SendCommand (Command);
    return Return.ToInt ();
}

int     WMCIDevice::GetStart ()
{
    WStr Return;
    WStr Command = "status " + DeviceName + " start position";
    Return = SendCommand (Command);
```

continues

LISTING 10.7. continued

```
    return Return.ToInt ();
}

WStr      WMCIDevice::GetTimeFormat ()
{
    WStr Command = "status " + DeviceName + " time format";
    return SendCommand (Command);
}

void WMCIDevice::Stop ()
{
    WStr Command = "stop " + DeviceName;
    SendCommand (Command);
}


void WMCIDevice::Pause ()
{
    WStr Command = "pause " + DeviceName;
    SendCommand (Command);
}


void WMCIDevice::Play (int From, int To, int Wait)
{
    WStr sFrom = "";
    WStr sTo = "";

    if (From != -1)
    {
        sFrom = "from " + ToString(From);
    }

    if (To != -1)
    {
        sTo = "to " + ToString (To);
    }

    WStr Command = "play " + DeviceName + sFrom + sTo;

    if (Wait == TRUE) Command += " wait";
    SendCommand (Command);
}


void WMCIDevice::Resume ()
```

```
{
    WStr Command = "resume " + DeviceName;
    SendCommand (Command);
}


void      WMCIDevice::Seek (int Position, int Wait)
{
    WStr Command = "seek " + DeviceName + " to " +
                    ToString (Position);
    if (Wait == TRUE) Command += " wait";
    SendCommand (Command);
}


void WMCIDevice::SeekEnd (int Wait)
{
    WStr Command = "seek " + DeviceName + " to end";
    if (Wait == TRUE) Command += " wait";
    SendCommand (Command);
}


void      WMCIDevice::SeekStart (int Wait)
{
    WStr Command = "seek " + DeviceName + " to start";
    if (Wait == TRUE) Command += " wait";
    SendCommand (Command);
}
```

The *WSound* Class

Listings 10.8 and 10.9 contain the code for the WSound class. This class encapsulates an MCI waveform audio device. It provides a large number of member functions specific to waveform audio. Its constructor takes either a filename (the file must already exist and either be empty or contain waveform audio data) or a buffer size in seconds. Three functions that are particularly useful for this class are Record, Delete, and Save.

Record is used to record audio information into the file or buffer. This information overwrites any information already in the file or buffer. (Use RecordInsert to insert rather than to overwrite.) Again, you can optionally specify a From position or a To position (or both) in the file or buffer. The

Delete function deletes either all or a portion of the file or buffer. The Save function writes the internal buffer to the file. Note that if you record to the internal buffer, then delete the object without saving to a file, the recording is lost. You can test for this condition. You can prompt the user in the class destructor if you want to add this test.

LISTING 10.8. WSOUND.H header file listing.

```
// WSOUND.H - Header file for WSound class

#ifndef WSound_H
#    define WSound_H

// Note that the following code is executed only
// if this file has not been previously included


// #include files for both PC and SUN
#include  "WStr.h"
#include  "WMCIDevice.h"


#ifdef __BORLANDC__
     // PC-specific #includes
#    include   <owl.h>
#    include <mmSystem.h>

#endif

#ifdef Unix
     // UNIX-specific #includes

#endif

//******************************************************
// WSound - Sound recorder and player
//
//     Purpose:
//          Encapsulates multimedia sound playing
//          and recording capabilities.
//
//     Notes:
//
//     Copyright:
//             Copyright (c) 1993, William H. Roetzheim
```

```
//          All Rights Reserved
//
//****************************************************

_CLASSDEF (WSound)
class WSound : public WMCIDevice
{
    private:
        // Private data members ********************


        // Private member functions ****************
        virtual void Open (RWStr FileName);
      virtual void Open (int BufferSize);

    public:
        // Public data members *********************


        // Public member functions *****************
        // Constructors and destructors
        WSound (RWStr FileName);
        WSound (int BufferSize);

        // Member functions
        virtual void    CueInput ();
        virtual void    CueOutput ();

        virtual long    GetTrackLength (int Track);
        virtual int         GetInputs ();
        virtual int         GetOutputs ();
        virtual WStr    GetFile ();
        virtual WStr    GetInputDevice ();
        virtual WStr    GetOutputDevice ();
        virtual int         GetAlignment ();
        virtual int         GetBitsPerSample ();
        virtual long    GetBytesPerSecond ();
        virtual int         GetChannels ();
        virtual WStr    GetFormatTag ();
        virtual int         GetInput ();
        virtual int         GetLevel ();
        virtual int         GetOutput ();
        virtual long    GetSamplesPerSecond ();

        virtual void    SetAlignment (int Alignment);
        virtual void    SetBitsPerSample (int Bits);
        virtual void    SetBytesPerSecond (long Bytes);
        virtual void    SetChannels (int Channels);
```

continues

LISTING 10.8. continued

```
        virtual void    SetFormatTag (RWStr Tag);
        virtual void    SetFormatPCM ();
        virtual void    SelectInput (int Input);
        virtual void    SelectOutput (int Output);
        virtual void    SetSamplesPerSecond (long Samples);
        virtual void    SelectTimeFormatBytes ();
        virtual void    SelectTimeFormatSamples ();
        virtual void    RecordInsert (int From = -1, int To = -1,
                                      int Wait = TRUE);
        virtual void    Record (int From = -1, int To = -1,
                                int Wait = TRUE);
        virtual void    Delete (int From = -1, int To = -1,
                                int Wait = TRUE);
        virtual void    Save (RWStr FileName, int Wait = TRUE);
};


#endif WSound_H
```

LISTING 10.9. WSOUND.CPP source code listing.

```cpp
// WSOUND.CPP - Source file for WSound class

#include "WSound.h"  // ALL other #include statements
                     // are in this file

//****************************************************
// Constructors and destructors for WSound
//
//      Copyright:
//              Copyright (c) 1993, William H. Roetzheim
//              All Rights Reserved
//
//****************************************************

WSound::WSound (RWStr FileName)
{
    Open (FileName);
}


WSound::WSound (int BufferSize)
{
    Open (BufferSize);
```

```
}



//****************************************************
// Member functions for class
//
//     Copyright:
//                Copyright (c) 1993, William H. Roetzheim
//                All Rights Reserved
//
//****************************************************

// Prepares device for input. An optional command, but
// it speeds up record command for some devices.

void WSound::CueInput ()
{
    WStr Command = "cue " + DeviceName + " input";
    SendCommand (Command);
}



// Prepares device for output. An optional command, but
// it speeds up play command for some devices.

void WSound::CueOutput ()
{
    WStr Command = "cue " + DeviceName + " output";
    SendCommand (Command);
}



// Returns the length of the specified track

long WSound::GetTrackLength (int Track)
{
    WStr Return;
    WStr Command = "status " + DeviceName + " length track "
                        + ToString(Track);
    Return = SendCommand (Command);
    return Return.ToLong ();
}



// Returns the total number of input devices (audio channels)
int      WSound::GetInputs ()
{
```

continues

LISTING 10.9. continued

```
    WStr Return;
    WStr Command = "capability " + DeviceName + " input";
    Return = SendCommand (Command);
   return Return.ToInt ();
}


// Returns the total number of output devices (e.g., speakers)

int      WSound::GetOutputs ()
{
    WStr Return;
    WStr Command = "capability " + DeviceName + " output";
    Return = SendCommand (Command);
   return Return.ToInt ();
}


// Returns current filename

WStr WSound::GetFile ()
{
    WStr Return;
    WStr Command = "info " + DeviceName + " file";
    Return = SendCommand (Command);
   return Return;
}


// Returns current input device name

WStr WSound::GetInputDevice ()
{
    WStr Return;
    WStr Command = "info " + DeviceName + " input";
    Return = SendCommand (Command);
   return Return;
}


// Returns current output device name
WStr WSound::GetOutputDevice ()
{
    WStr Return;
    WStr Command = "info " + DeviceName + " output";
    Return = SendCommand (Command);
   return Return;
```

```
}


// Returns record alignment for data file in bytes
int       WSound::GetAlignment ()
{
    WStr Return;
    WStr Command = "status " + DeviceName + " alignment";
    Return = SendCommand (Command);
   return Return.ToInt ();
}


// Returns the current bits per sample

int       WSound::GetBitsPerSample ()
{
    WStr Return;
    WStr Command = "status " + DeviceName + " bitspersample";
    Return = SendCommand (Command);
   return Return.ToInt ();
}


// Returns the current bytes per second
long WSound::GetBytesPerSecond ()
{
    WStr Return;
    WStr Command = "status " + DeviceName + " bytespersec";
    Return = SendCommand (Command);
   return Return.ToLong ();
}


// Returns the number of available channels
int WSound::GetChannels ()
{
    WStr Return;
    WStr Command = "status " + DeviceName + " channels";
    Return = SendCommand (Command);
   return Return.ToInt ();
}


// Returns the format tag
WStr WSound::GetFormatTag ()
{
    WStr Return;
```

continues

LISTING 10.9. continued

```
        WStr Command = "status " + DeviceName + " format tag";
        Return = SendCommand (Command);
     return Return;
}


// Returns the current input that is set
int        WSound::GetInput ()
{
     WStr Return;
     WStr Command = "status " + DeviceName + " input";
     Return = SendCommand (Command);
    return Return.ToInt ();
}


// Returns the current audio sample value
int        WSound::GetLevel ()
{
     WStr Return;
     WStr Command = "status " + DeviceName + " level";
     Return = SendCommand (Command);
    return Return.ToInt ();
}

// Returns the current output that is set
int        WSound::GetOutput ()
{
     WStr Return;
     WStr Command = "status " + DeviceName + " output";
     Return = SendCommand (Command);
    return Return.ToInt ();
}

// Returns the number of samples per second
long WSound::GetSamplesPerSecond ()
{
     WStr Return;
     WStr Command = "status " + DeviceName + " bitspersample";
     Return = SendCommand (Command);
    return Return.ToLong ();
}


// Sets the record byte alignment for storage
void WSound::SetAlignment (int Alignment)
```

```
{
    WStr Command = "set " + DeviceName + " alignment " +
                        ToString (Alignment);
    SendCommand (Command);
}


// Sets the bits per sample
void WSound::SetBitsPerSample (int Bits)
{
    WStr Command = "set " + DeviceName + " bitspersample " +
                        ToString (Bits);
    SendCommand (Command);
}

// Sets the bytes per second
void WSound::SetBytesPerSecond (long Bytes)
{
    WStr Command = "set " + DeviceName + " bytespersecond " +
                        ToString (Bytes);
    SendCommand (Command);
}


// Sets the channels used for playing and recording
void WSound::SetChannels (int Channels)
{
    WStr Command = "set " + DeviceName + " channels " +
                        ToString (Channels);
    SendCommand (Command);
}


// Sets the format type for playing and recording
void WSound::SetFormatTag (RWStr Tag)
{
    WStr Command = "set " + DeviceName + " format tag " + Tag;
    SendCommand (Command);
}


// Sets the format to PCM
void WSound::SetFormatPCM ()
{
    WStr Command = "set " + DeviceName + " format tag pcm";
    SendCommand (Command);
}
```

continues

LISTING 10.9. continued

```cpp
// Selects an input device
void WSound::SelectInput (int Input)
{
    WStr Command = "set " + DeviceName + " input " +
                        ToString (Input);
    SendCommand (Command);
}


// Selects an output device
void WSound::SelectOutput (int Output)
{
    WStr Command = "set " + DeviceName + " output " +
                        ToString (Output);
    SendCommand (Command);
}


// Specifies the samples per second
void WSound::SetSamplesPerSecond (long Samples)
{
    WStr Command = "set " + DeviceName + " samplespersec " +
                        ToString (Samples);
    SendCommand (Command);
}


// Specifies that bytes should be used for position information
void WSound::SelectTimeFormatBytes ()
{
    WStr Command = "set " + DeviceName + " time format bytes";
    SendCommand (Command);
}


// Specifies that samples should be used for position information
void WSound::SelectTimeFormatSamples ()
{
    WStr Command = "set " + DeviceName + " time format samples";
    SendCommand (Command);
}


// Inserts recording
void WSound::RecordInsert (int From, int To, int Wait)
{
```

```
    WStr sFrom = "";
    WStr sTo = "";

    if (From != -1) sFrom = " from " + ToString(From);
    if (To != -1) sTo = " to " + ToString(To);
    WStr Command = "record " + DeviceName + " insert " +
                        sFrom + sTo;
    if (Wait == TRUE) Command += " wait";
    SendCommand (Command);
}



// Overwrites recording
void WSound::Record (int From, int To, int Wait)
{
    WStr sFrom = "";
    WStr sTo = "";

    if (From != -1) sFrom = " from " + ToString(From);
    if (To != -1) sTo = " to " + ToString (To);
    WStr Command = "record " + DeviceName +
                        sFrom + sTo;
    if (Wait == TRUE) Command += " wait";
    SendCommand (Command);
}

// Deletes part of recording
void WSound::Delete (int From, int To, int Wait)
{
    WStr sFrom = "";
    WStr sTo = "";

    if (From != -1) sFrom = " from " + ToString(From);
    if (To != -1) sTo = " to " + ToString(To);
    WStr Command = "delete " + DeviceName +
                        sFrom + sTo;
    if (Wait == TRUE) Command += " wait";
    SendCommand (Command);
}


// Saves the current buffer to the file
void WSound::Save (RWStr FileName, int Wait)
{
    WStr Command = "save " + DeviceName + FileName;
    if (Wait == TRUE) Command += " wait";
```

continues

LISTING 10.9. continued

```
    SendCommand (Command);
}



void        WSound::Open (RWStr FileName)
{
    DeviceName = " Audio ";
    WStr Command = (WStr) "open " +
                FileName + " alias Audio type waveaudio";
    SendCommand (Command);
}
void        WSound::Open (int BufferSize)
{
    DeviceName = " Audio " ;
    WStr Command = (WStr) "open alias type waveaudio " +
                        "buffer " + ToString(BufferSize);
    SendCommand (Command);
}
```

Sound Programming Using the Multimedia API

Although the MCI string interface meets all my multimedia programming requirements, you might have occasion to use the multimedia API functions directly. These are standard C functions that can be called just like other Windows API functions. Table 10.5 summarizes the functions available. These functions are documented in the *Microsoft Windows Multimedia Programmer's Reference,* which is available in bookstores. They also are supplied as part of SDK documentation.

INT: Even if you don't intend to do multimedia programming, you might want to look at the timer services available through the multimedia API. These timer functions provide periodic and one-time events at a higher resolution than what is available through standard Windows timers.

In Chapter 11, "Incorporating Video," I extend the multimedia classes in this chapter (by using inheritance) to support video and video overlays.

TABLE 10.5. Windows multimedia API functions.

Category	Function	Description
MIDI queries	midiInGetNumDevs	Returns the number of MIDI input devices in the system
	midiInGetDevCaps	Returns the capabilities of a specified MIDI input device
	midiOutGetNumDevs	Returns the number of MIDI output devices in the system
	midiOutGetDevCaps	Returns the capabilities of a specified MIDI output device
MIDI opening and closing	midiInOpen	Opens a MIDI device for recording
	midiInClose	Closes an input MIDI device
	midiOutOpen	Opens a MIDI device for playback
	midiOutClose	Closes an output MIDI device
MIDI device IDs	midiInGetID	Gets the MIDI input device ID
	midiOutGetID	Gets the MIDI output device ID

continues

TABLE 10.5. continued

Category	Function	Description
MIDI send messages	midiOutLongMsg	Sends a buffer to a MIDI device
	midiOutShortMsg	Sends a nonsystem exclusive message to a MIDI device
	midiOutPrepareHeader	Prepares a MIDI data buffer for playback
	midiOutReset	Turns off all notes on all channels for a MIDI device
	midiOutUnprepareHeader	Removes header information from an output buffer
MIDI receive messages	midiInAddBuffer	Provides a buffer for use by incoming messages
	midiInPrepareHeader	Prepares an input buffer for use
	midiInUnprepareHeader	Removes header infor-mation from an input buffer
MIDI input control	midiInStart	Starts input
	midiInStop	Stops input
	midiInReset	Stops input and marks pending data buffers as done
MIDI volume caching	midiOutCacheDrumPatches	Preloads a specified set of key-based percussion patches

Category	Function	Description
	`midiOutCachePatches`	Preloads a specified set of patches
	`midiOutGetVolume`	Gets the current volume
	`midiOutSetVolume`	Sets the current volume
MIDI errors	`midiInGetErrorText`	Gets a text description of the current input error
	`midiOutGetErrorText`	Gets a text description of the current output error
Auxiliary audio services	`auxGetDevCaps`	Gets capabilities
	`auxGetNumDevs`	Gets the number of devices present
	`auxGetVolume`	Gets the current volume
	`auxSetVolume`	Sets the current volume
Multimedia Movie Player (MMP) loading	`mmpClose`	Closes a movie player
	`mmpOpen`	Opens a movie player
MMP file handling	`mmpFileLoaded`	Checks to see whether a file is loaded
	`mmpFreeFile`	Frees a movie file
	`mmpLoadFile`	Loads a movie file
MMP information	`mmpError`	Returns error information
	`mmpGetFileInfo`	Returns movie file information

continues

TABLE 10.5. continued

Category	Function	Description
	mmpGetInfo	Accesses a label list and a script channel in a movie file
	mmpGetMovieInfo	Returns information about the current movie file
	mmpGetPaletteHandle	Returns a palette handle for the current movie file
	mmpSetInfo	Changes a label list and a script channel for a movie file
MMP animation	mmpAnimate	Displays the next frame
	mmpAnimStatus	Returns animation status
	mmpAnimStopped	Determines whether a movie is stopped
	mmpStartAnimating	Starts animating a movie
	mmpStopAnimating	Stops animating a movie
MMP playback window	mmpGetStage	Returns stage window information
	mmpSetDC	Sets a device context for MMP
	mmpSetStage	Assigns a playback window for MMP
	mmpUpdate	Updates an invalid rectangle in the stage window

Category	Function	Description
MMP playback	`mmpGetCurFrame`	Returns the current frame number
	`mmpGetFrameHook`	Returns the frame callback function hook
	`mmpGetMute`	Checks to see whether a sound track is muted
	`mmpGetRepeat`	Checks to see whether a movie will repeat
	`mmpGoToFrame`	Jumps to a specified frame number
	`mmpIsLastFrame`	Is this the last frame?
	`mmpSetMute`	Disables or enables audio mute
	`mmpSetFrameHook`	Sets the frame callback function
	`mmpSetRepeat`	Determines whether a movie should repeat
Basic multimedia I/O (MMIO)	`mmioClose`	Closes a file
	`mmioOpen`	Opens a file
	`mmioRead`	Reads from a file
	`mmioSeek`	Seeks within a file
	`mmioWrite`	Writes to a file
Buffered MMIO	`mmioAdvance`	Fills or flushes a buffer
	`mmioFlush`	Flushes a buffer to disk
	`mmioGetInfo`	Gets buffer information
	`mmioSetBuffer`	Changes the size of a buffer

continues

TABLE 10.5. continued

Category	Function	Description
	mmioSetInfo	Sets I/O buffer information
MMIO-RIFF files	mmioAscend	Advances to the next chunk
	mmioCreateChunk	Creates a new chunk
	mmioDescend	Descends into a chunk
	mmioFOURCC	Converts four characters to FOURCC code
	mmioStringToFOURCC	Converts a NULL-terminated string to FOURCC code
MMIO custom	mmioInstallIOProc	Installs, removes, or relocates a custom I/O procedure
	mmioSendMessage	Sends a message to an I/O procedure
Media Control Interface (MCI) services	mciSendCommand	Sends a command message to MCI
	mciSendString	Sends a command string to MCI
	mciExecute	A simple version of mciSendString
	mciGetDeviceID	Returns the device ID
	mciGetErrorString	Returns an error string
MCI time and date	MCI_HMS_HOUR	Returns the hours field of a packed time
	MCI_HMS_MINUTE	Returns the minutes field of a packed time

Category	Function	Description
	MCI_HMS_SECOND	Returns the seconds field of a packed time
	MCI_MSF_FRAME	Returns the frame field of a minutes/seconds/ frames field
	MCI_MSF_MINUTE	Returns the minutes field of a minutes/ seconds/frames field
	MCI_MSF_SECOND	Returns the seconds field of a minutes/ seconds/frames field
	MCI_TMSF_FRAME	Returns the frame from a tracks/minutes/ seconds/frames field
	MCI_TMSF_SECOND	Returns the seconds from a tracks/minutes/ seconds/frames field
	MCI_TMSF_TRACK	Returns the track from a track/minutes/ seconds/frames field
	MCI_MAKE_HMS	Creates DWORD from hours, minutes, and seconds
	MCI_MAKE_MSF	Creates DWORD from minutes, seconds, and frames
	MCI_MAKE_TMSF	Creates DWORD from tracks, minutes, seconds, and frames
Joystick services	joyGetDevCaps	Returns joystick capabilities

continues

TABLE 10.5. continued

Category	Function	Description
	joyGetNumDevs	Returns the number of joysticks supported by the driver
	joyGetPos	Gets the position and button state of a joystick
	joyGetThreshold	Returns the joystick movement threshold
	joyReleaseCapture	Releases joystick capture
	joySetCapture	Captures joystick messages
	joySetThreshold	Sets the movement threshold of a joystick
Timer services	timeBeginPeriod	Sets timer resolution
	timeEndPeriod	Clears timer resolution
	timeGetDevCaps	Returns the capabilities of the timer driver
	timeGetSystemTime	Returns the system time as an MMTIME structure in milli-seconds
	timeGetTime	Returns system time in milliseconds
	timeKillEvent	Cancels a time event
	timeSetEvent	Sets a timer event
Screen Saver	DefScreenSaverProc	A default Windows procedure for screen savers

Category	Function	Description
Bitmaps	DisplayDIB	Displays a 256-color bitmap on a standard VGA
Debugging	mmsystemGetVersion	Gets the version number
	OutputDebugStr	Sends a debug string to COM1 or to a monochrome display adapter

CHAPTER 11

Incorporating
Video

Problem

In Chapter 10, "Incorporating Sound," I discussed the various components of multimedia, including still and moving video. If you're like me, a million ideas came to mind. Can I create applications incorporating images for identification? Real-estate applications where the prospective buyer can actually see a picture of the house on the computer? A myriad of training applications? What's involved? What equipment do you need and how do you write the necessary software?

Solution

With the advent of low-cost video display and capture software, and Microsoft's introduction of Video for Windows, incorporating video into your application is not as far-fetched as you might think. Low-cost video capture and display can be accomplished with products costing about $200 (for example, Video Blaster, used in this chapter). High-quality video display using Microsoft's Audio Video Interleave (AVI) standard can be accomplished using a standard PC with a VGA card capable of displaying 256 colors and no additional hardware.

The Video Blaster board accepts input from as many as three composite video sources (both the U.S. NTSC standard and the European PAL standard) and displays live video in a fully resizable and movable window. It also supports frame capture and import in a wide variety of formats (PCX, TIFF, BMP, MMP, GIF, and Targa) and supports audio mixing from stereo line-in, CD audio, stereo FM, and microphone input sources. Using the Microsoft Video for Windows software (included with Video Blaster), you can capture live video and audio segments using the Microsoft Audio Video Interleave (AVI) format. AVI is discussed in more detail later. In addition to Microsoft Video for Windows, my copy of Video Blaster includes presentation software (MMPlay, Tempra Show, and Macromind Action) and image editing software (Tempra GIF and BitEdit).

Understanding Animation, Analog Video, and Digital Video

In Chapter 10's discussion of multimedia, I broke video down into animation, analog video, and digital video. Animation consists of a series of computer-generated images that normally are produced and stored ahead of time, then displayed when desired. Most really impressive computer-generated graphics (for example, the mirrored bouncing balls that are popular in computer showrooms) take an incredible amount of computer time to generate (hours or days) but support snappy animation when simply played back from disk or memory. In order to focus on analog and digital video in more detail, I don't discuss computer animation further.

A Bit of Background

Recall from Chapter 10 that analog signals consist of continuously variable electrical voltages, and analog signals consist of discretely varying voltages that represent a 1 or a 0. For all modern computer monitors, the signal at the monitor is analog. (The exceptions are EGA monitors and the IBM monochrome monitors.) You can feed a composite video signal, such as the output from your VCR or camcorder, directly into your VGA monitor and have it displayed. The signal must simply be input into the appropriate pins on the DB-15 connector. At the computer end, however, all modern display cards work using a digital buffer. (Vector graphic displays on some early computers such as the Tektronix were an exception.)

The display is stored as a series of pixels, each of which is represented with 1 to 24 bits. The standard VGA display with 640-by-480 resolution and 16 colors represents the display as 640 pixels by 480 pixels by 4 bits and requires a total of 153,600 bytes of video storage on the card. The same display in 256-color mode requires $640 \times 480 \times 8$ bits of video storage, or 307,200 total bytes. An expensive graphics display supporting 1280-by-1024 resolution with 16,777,216 available colors requires $1280 \times 1024 \times 24$ bits of video storage, or 3,932,160 total bytes.

A standard television set has a resolution of approximately 400 horizontal by 483 vertical. "Wait a minute," you might be thinking. "The picture on my TV looks a heck of a lot better than the computer graphics on my computer screen." You're right, and you've just discovered an important principle of human perception. The perceived quality of photographic-type images is much more dependent on the number of colors displayed (or shades of gray for black-and-white) than on the resolution of the pictures. Your home television uses an analog input whose bandwidth gives it a color palette of more than 4 million colors. Even with the relatively poor resolution of a television, your eye easily fills in the details and perceives a pleasing, realistic picture. In fact, the higher resolution for computer monitors is really driven by text font legibility more than anything else. In general, multimedia work requires a display with 256 colors (black-and-white or pictures where the color palette is optimized for the specific pictures displayed), with more than 256 available colors being desired when possible. The 16,777,216 colors provided by 24 bits of color information approach the color resolution of the human eye, so it is unlikely that future standards will need to go beyond this level.

Analog Video: A Television in a Window

The computer stores bits representing pixels, but the monitor expects analog voltages. What happens in between? The answer is obvious if you consider how digital sound is output to a speaker (an analog device). The display adapter uses a specialized digital-to-analog (DAC) converter to convert the digital information to its analog equivalent. You might be starting to grasp how a board such as Video Blaster can overlay an incoming analog signal (for example, output from a VCR) onto your VGA computer. When you install Video Blaster, you unplug your monitor from the VGA card and plug it into Video Blaster, which is responsible for producing the output to the monitor. In normal operation, Video Blaster uses the feature connector socket on your VGA adapter to intercept the VGA card output and send it to the monitor. When you want to overlay an external video signal onto the display, Video Blaster simply combines the VGA output with the external signal and outputs the result to your monitor. The result is video in a window. Frame capture using Video Blaster is the inverse. Video Blaster uses an analog-to-digital (A/D) converter to sample the incoming

external video analog signal and converts the signal to a stream of bytes that can be saved as a bitmap.

The easiest way to display video in a window is to use the Video Kit program provided with Video Blaster (see Figure 11.1). This program displays a resizable window with a live video image in the client area. Menu selections enable you to freeze and capture a frame in various bit-oriented formats and to adjust visual aspects of the picture (brightness, contrast, and so on).

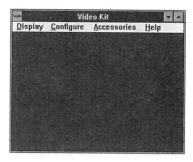

Figure 11.1. The Video Kit program in operation.

I have defined three classes, all derived from `WMCIDevice` as shown in Figure 11.2, to support video overlays and AVI. Because video overlays and AVI playback are both forms of video, they have much in common. These common features are found in the abstract class `WVideo`. `WAVI` contains member functions for capabilities unique to AVI, and `WOverlay` contains member functions for capabilities unique to video overlays. These classes are included in the listings at the end of this chapter.

As shown in Listing 11.1, creating a video overlay window from within your application is simple. The key code consists of three lines:

```
PWOverlay Overlay;
Overlay = new WOverlay (" overlapped ", HWindow);
Overlay->WindowShow ();
```

The static string " `overlapped` " creates an overlapped video overlay window. Other options are " `child` " and " `popup` ". The `HWindow` parameter sets the parent window value of the video overlay window. Leaving this value out (or setting it to –1) creates a video overlay window with no parent.

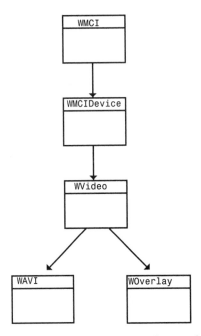

Figure 11.2. WAVI *and* WOverlay *inheritance relationships.*

LISTING 11.1. chpt11 header and source files.

```
#define DIALOG_VERSION
#define SET_TEXT

#define         _CLASSDLL
#define   WIN31
#define   STRICT
#include   <owl.h>
#include   <edit.h>
#include   "WOverlay.h"
#include   "WAVI.h"



//*******************************************************
// chpt11 - chpt11 application class
//
//      Purpose:
```

```
//          This class is the overall application
//          executive for chpt11.
//
//      Notes:
//          None
//
//      Copyright:
//              Copyright (c) 1993, William H. Roetzheim
//              All Rights Reserved
//
//****************************************************

_CLASSDEF (chpt11)
class chpt11 : public TApplication
{
    public:
          // Public member functions *****************
          // Constructors and destructors
          chpt11 (LPSTR szName, HINSTANCE hInstance,
                    HINSTANCE hPrevInstance, LPSTR lpCmdLine,
                    int nCmdShow);

          // Member functions
          virtual void InitMainWindow ();
};



_CLASSDEF (chpt11Window)
class chpt11Window : public TWindow
{
    private:
          PWOverlay Overlay;
        PWAVI   AVI;

    public:
          chpt11Window ();
        ~chpt11Window ();

          virtual void SetupWindow ();
};

//****************************************************
// Constructors and destructors for chpt11
//
//      Copyright:
//              Copyright (c) 1993, William H. Roetzheim
//              All Rights Reserved
```

continues

LISTING 11.1. continued

```
//
//****************************************************

#pragma argsused  // Turn off arguments not used warning
chpt11::chpt11(LPSTR szName, HINSTANCE hInstance,
          HINSTANCE hPrevInstance, LPSTR lpCmdLine,
          int nCmdShow)
          : TApplication (szName, hInstance,
          hPrevInstance, lpCmdLine, nCmdShow)
{
    return;
}



//****************************************************
// Member functions for class chpt11
//
//     Copyright:
//             Copyright (c) 1993, William H. Roetzheim
//             All Rights Reserved
//
//****************************************************

void chpt11::InitMainWindow ()
{
    MainWindow = new chpt11Window ();
}



chpt11Window::chpt11Window ()
    : TWindow (NULL, "Video Test")
{
    return;
}

chpt11Window::~chpt11Window ()
{
    delete Overlay;
    delete AVI;
}


void chpt11Window::SetupWindow ()
{
```

```
    TWindow::SetupWindow ();
    Overlay = new WOverlay (" overlapped ", HWindow);
    Overlay->WindowShow ();

    AVI = new WAVI ((WStr) "wndsurf1.avi");
    AVI->Play ();
}


// Here is the main () for the program
int PASCAL WinMain (HINSTANCE hInstance,
    HINSTANCE hPrevInstance, LPSTR lpCmdLine,
    int)
{
    // Create chpt11 application from class
    chpt11 ochpt11 ("chpt11", hInstance,
                    hPrevInstance, lpCmdLine, SW_NORMAL);

    // Start created application running
    ochpt11.Run ();  // Runs till window closed

    // Return termination status when window closed
    return ochpt11.Status;
}
```

Audio Video Interleave

Audio Video Interleave, or AVI, is a new Microsoft file format that intersperses audio and video information in the same file (see Figure 11.3). The file consists of one or more frames. Each frame includes digitized audio information and a single digital picture. For example, a 10-second video clip captured at the rate of 15 frames per second would consist of 150 frames. The digital picture may be compressed or not compressed. Microsoft's Video for Windows supports a variety of compression schemes, including Microsoft Video 1, Intel Indeo Video, and a fuzzy version of run-length encoding (RLE) in which close matches are considered "good enough." Compression is accomplished off-line in nonreal time. Decompression is accomplished during playback in real time with or without special hardware installed. During playback, you can specify a frame rate at which you would like the bitmaps displayed. Video for Windows

attempts to achieve this frame rate, but it skips over frames if the CPU cannot display the frames fast enough. Even when Video for Windows skips over frames, however, it is smart enough to pick out the interleaved audio and play the complete audio segment without any gaps.

```
                  Frame 1            Frame 2            Frame 3
          ┌─────┬─────────┬───────┬─────────┬───────┬─────────┬───────┬──────┐
          │     │         │       │         │       │         │       │      │
          │Header│ Digital │Digital│ Digital │Digital│ Digital │Digital│      ⌇
          │     │ Audio   │Video  │ Audio   │Video  │ Audio   │Video  │      ⌇
          │     │         │       │         │       │         │       │      │
          └─────┴─────────┴───────┴─────────┴───────┴─────────┴───────┴──────┘
```

Figure 11.3. The AVI file format.

To play back an AVI clip using the WAVI class (shown at the end of this chapter), you need only three lines of significant code:

```
PWAVI     AVI;
AVI = new WAVI ((WStr) "wndsurf1.avi");
AVI->Play ();
```

These lines read the file WNDSURF1.AVI, a sample AVI file included with Video for Windows, then play the file. Although the file plays on any Windows 3.1-compatible display, the quality is degraded significantly unless you are in a display mode that supports 256 colors. Remember that playing the file doesn't require Video Blaster or any other specialized video hardware. Unfortunately, even this short video clip is more than 1MB in size—well beyond anything I could include on the source disk.

HINT: The MCI string interface currently doesn't support any commands to capture AVI video. This currently is best accomplished using the VidCap utility provided with Microsoft Video for Windows. Although you can do video capture from within your application using the low-level MCI API, Microsoft warns that these functions are likely to change over the next year. For most applications, it's probably best to either capture the video outside of your application or use WinExec() to execute VidCap directly from within your application.

Video Classes and the Sample Application

Listings 11.2–11.7 show the WVideo, WAVI, and WOverlay header and source code listings.

LISTING 11.2. WVIDEO.H header file listing.

```
// WVIDEO.H - Header file for WVideo class

#ifndef WVideo_H
#    define WVideo_H

// Note that the following code is executed only
// if this file has not been previously included


// #include files for both PC and SUN
#include   "WStr.h"
#include   "WMCIDevice.h"


#ifdef __BORLANDC__
     // PC-specific #includes
#    include    <owl.h>
#    include <mmSystem.h>

#endif

#ifdef Unix
     // UNIX-specific #includes

#endif

//******************************************************
// WWide - Video overlay and animation abstract class
//
//     Purpose:
//         Encapsulates multimedia video animation and
//         overlay capability. Items specific to either
//         animation OR overlays are found in WAnimation
//         or WOverlay.
//
//     Notes:
//
//     Copyright:
```

continues

LISTING 11.2. continued

```
//          Copyright (c) 1993, William H. Roetzheim
//          All Rights Reserved
//
//****************************************************

_CLASSDEF (WVideo)
class WVideo : public WMCIDevice
{
    protected:
        // Protected data members ******************


        // Protected member functions **************
        RECT ParseRectString (WStr);

    public:
        // Public data members ********************


        // Public member functions ***************
        // Member functions
        virtual    BOOL CanStretch ();
        virtual HWND    GetWindowHandle ();
        virtual RECT    GetDestination ();
        virtual RECT    GetSource ();
        virtual int     GetMaxWindows ();
        virtual WStr    GetWindowText ();

       virtual void     SetVideoOff ();
        virtual    void SetVideoOn ();
        virtual void    SetWindowHandle (HWND);
        virtual void    SetDefaultWindow ();
        virtual void    WindowHide ();
        virtual void    WindowIconic ();
        virtual void    WindowMaximized ();
        virtual void    WindowMinimized ();
        virtual void    WindowNormal ();
        virtual void    WindowShow ();
        virtual void    SetWindowText (WStr);
        virtual void    SetDestinationRectangle (RECT* = NULL);
        virtual void    SetSourceRectangle (RECT* = NULL);
};

#endif WVideo_H
```

428

LISTING 11.3. WVIDEO.CPP source code listing.

```cpp
// WVIDEO.CPP - Source file for WVideo class

#include "WVideo.h"  // ALL other #include statements
                      // are in this file


//*****************************************************
// Member functions for class
//
//    Copyright:
//            Copyright (c) 1993, William H. Roetzheim
//            All Rights Reserved
//
//*****************************************************

// Returns TRUE if the device can stretch frames to fill
// a specified Rectangle

BOOL WVideo::CanStretch ()
{
    WStr Return;
    WStr Command = "capability " + DeviceName + " can stretch";
    Return = SendCommand (Command);
    if (Return == "true") return TRUE;
    else return FALSE;
}

HWND WVideo::GetWindowHandle ()
{
    WStr Return;
    WStr Command = "status " + DeviceName + " window handle";
    Return = SendCommand (Command);
   return (HWND) (* (char *) Return);
}


RECT WVideo::GetDestination ()
{
    WStr Return;
    WStr Command = "where " + DeviceName + " destination";
    Return = SendCommand (Command);
    return ParseRectString (Return);
}

RECT WVideo::GetSource ()
```

continues

LISTING 11.3. continued

```
{
    WStr Return;
    WStr Command = "where " + DeviceName + " destination";
    Return = SendCommand (Command);
    return ParseRectString (Return);
}

int     WVideo::GetMaxWindows ()
{
    WStr Return;
    WStr Command = "capability " + DeviceName + " windows";
    Return = SendCommand (Command);
    return Return.ToInt ();
}

WStr WVideo::GetWindowText ()
{
    WStr Command = "info " + DeviceName + " window text";
    return SendCommand (Command);
}


void WVideo::SetVideoOff ()
{
    WStr Command = "set " + DeviceName + " video off";
    SendCommand (Command);
}

void WVideo::SetVideoOn ()
{
    WStr Command = "set " + DeviceName + " video on";
    SendCommand (Command);
}

void WVideo::SetWindowHandle (HWND Handle)
{
    WStr Command = "window " + DeviceName + " handle " +
        ToString ((int) Handle);
    SendCommand (Command);
}

void     WVideo::SetDefaultWindow ()
{
    WStr Command = "set " + DeviceName + " handle default";
    SendCommand (Command);
}

void     WVideo::WindowHide ()
```

```
{
    WStr Command = "set " + DeviceName + " state hide";
    SendCommand (Command);
}

void      WVideo::WindowIconic ()
{
    WStr Command = "window " + DeviceName + " state iconic";
    SendCommand (Command);
}

void      WVideo::WindowMaximized ()
{
    WStr Command = "window " + DeviceName + " state maximized";
    SendCommand (Command);
}

void      WVideo::WindowMinimized ()
{
    WStr Command = "window " + DeviceName + " state minimized";
    SendCommand (Command);
}

void WVideo::WindowNormal ()
{
    WStr Command = "window " + DeviceName + " state normal";
    SendCommand (Command);
}

void WVideo::WindowShow ()
{
    WStr Command = "window " + DeviceName + " state show";
    SendCommand (Command);
}

void WVideo::SetWindowText (WStr NewText)
{
    WStr Command = "window " + DeviceName + " text " +
        NewText;
    SendCommand (Command);
}

void WVideo::SetDestinationRectangle (RECT * Rect)
{
    WStr Command = "put " + DeviceName + " destination ";
    if (Rect != NULL)
    {
        Command += "at " + ToString (Rect->left) + " ";
```

continues

431

LISTING 11.3. continued

```
        Command += ToString (Rect->top) + " ";
        Command += ToString (Rect->right) + " ";
        Command += ToString (Rect->bottom);
    }
    SendCommand (Command);
}

void WVideo::SetSourceRectangle (RECT * Rect)
{
    WStr Command = "put " + DeviceName + " source ";
    if (Rect != NULL)
    {
        Command += "at " + ToString (Rect->left) + " ";
        Command += ToString (Rect->top) + " ";
        Command += ToString (Rect->right) + " ";
        Command += ToString (Rect->bottom);
    }
    SendCommand (Command);
}



// Private member functions

// Parse a Rectangle from a WStr
RECT WVideo::ParseRectString (WStr String)
{
    RECT Rect;
    Rect.left = String.ToInt();
    String = String.Slice (String.Find (" "), String.Length());
    Rect.top = String.ToInt ();
    String = String.Slice (String.Find (" "), String.Length());
    Rect.right = String.ToInt ();
    String = String.Slice (String.Find (" "), String.Length());
    Rect.bottom = String.ToInt ();
    return Rect;
}
```

LISTING 11.4. WAVI.H header file listing.

```
// WOVERLAY.H - Header file for WOverlay class

#ifndef WOverlay_H
```

```
#     define WOverlay_H

// Note that the following code is executed only
// if this file has not been previously included


// #include files for both PC and SUN
#include  "WVideo.h"


#ifdef __BORLANDC__
     // PC-specific #includes

#endif

#ifdef Unix
     // UNIX-specific #includes

#endif

//****************************************************
// WOverlay - Video overlay
//
//     Purpose:
//         Encapsulates multimedia Overlay capabilities.
//
//     Notes:
//
//     Copyright:
//             Copyright (c) 1993, William H. Roetzheim
//             All Rights Reserved
//
//****************************************************

_CLASSDEF (WOverlay)
class WOverlay : public WVideo
{
    private:
        // Private data members *******************

        // Private member functions ***************
        virtual void Open (WStr Style, HWND = (HWND) -1);
        virtual void Open (RWStr);

    public:
        // Public data members ********************
```

continues

LISTING 11.4. continued

```
           // Public member functions *****************
           // Member functions
           WOverlay (WStr Style = "overlapped",
                    HWND hWnd = (HWND) -1);

     virtual BOOL    CanFreeze ();

      virtual void    Freeze (RECT * Rect = NULL);
      virtual void    UnFreeze (RECT * Rect = NULL);
      virtual void    Save (WStr Filename);
    virtual void     Load (WStr Filename, RECT * Rect = NULL);
      virtual void    SetFrameRectangle (RECT* = NULL);
      virtual void    SetVideoRectangle (RECT* = NULL);
    virtual RECT     GetFrame ();
};

#endif WOverlay_H
```

LISTING 11.5. WAVI.CPP source code listing.

```
// WOVERLAY.CPP - Source file for WOverlay class

#include "WOverlay.h"  // ALL other #include statements
                       // are in this file

//****************************************************
// Constructors and destructors for WOverlay
//
//     Copyright:
//          Copyright (c) 1993, William H. Roetzheim
//          All Rights Reserved
//
//****************************************************

WOverlay::WOverlay (WStr Style, HWND hWnd)
{
    Open (Style, hWnd);
}

//****************************************************
// Member functions for class
//
//     Copyright:
```

```
//          Copyright (c) 1993, William H. Roetzheim
//          All Rights Reserved
//
//******************************************************
BOOL WOverlay::CanFreeze ()
{
    WStr Return;
    WStr Command = "capability " + DeviceName + " can reverse";
    Return = SendCommand (Command);
    if (Return == "true") return TRUE;
    else return FALSE;
}

void WOverlay::Freeze (RECT * Rect)
{
    WStr Command = "freeze " + DeviceName;
    if (Rect != NULL)
    {
        Command += "at " + ToString (Rect->left) +
                   " " + ToString (Rect->top) +
                   " " + ToString (Rect->right) +
                   " " + ToString (Rect->bottom);
    }
    SendCommand (Command);
}

void WOverlay::UnFreeze (RECT * Rect)
{
    WStr Command = "unfreeze " + DeviceName;
    if (Rect != NULL)
    {
        Command += "at " + ToString (Rect->left) +
                   " " + ToString (Rect->top) +
                   " " + ToString (Rect->right) +
                   " " + ToString (Rect->bottom);
    }
    SendCommand (Command);
}

void WOverlay::Save (WStr Filename)
{
    WStr Command = "save " + DeviceName + Filename;
    SendCommand (Command);
}

void WOverlay::Load (WStr Filename, RECT * Rect)
{
    WStr Command = "load " + DeviceName + Filename;
```

continues

435

LISTING 11.5. continued

```
    if (Rect != NULL)
    {
        Command += "at " + ToString (Rect->left) +
                   " " + ToString (Rect->top) +
                   " " + ToString (Rect->right) +
                   " " + ToString (Rect->bottom);
    }
    SendCommand (Command);
}

void WOverlay::SetFrameRectangle (RECT* Rect)
{
    WStr Command = "put " + DeviceName + " frame ";
    if (Rect != NULL)
    {
        Command += "at " + ToString (Rect->left) +
                   " " + ToString (Rect->top) +
                   " " + ToString (Rect->right) +
                   " " + ToString (Rect->bottom);
    }
    SendCommand (Command);
}

void WOverlay::SetVideoRectangle (RECT* Rect)
{
    WStr Command = "put " + DeviceName + " video ";
    if (Rect != NULL)
    {
        Command += "at " + ToString (Rect->left) +
                   " " + ToString (Rect->top) +
                   " " + ToString (Rect->right) +
                   " " + ToString (Rect->bottom);
    }
    SendCommand (Command);
}

RECT WOverlay::GetFrame ()
{
    WStr Return;
    WStr Command = "where " + DeviceName + " frame ";
    Return = SendCommand (Command);
    return ParseRectString (Return);
}
```

```
// Private member functions
void WOverlay::Open (WStr Style, HWND hWnd)
{
    DeviceName = " Video ";
    WStr Command = (WStr) "open overlay" +
                " alias Video ";
    Command += " style " + Style;
    if (hWnd != (HWND) -1)
    {
        Command +=  " parent " + ToString ((int) hWnd);
    }
    SendCommand (Command);
}



void WOverlay::Open (RWStr)
{
    Open ("overlapped");
}
```

LISTING 11.6. WOVERLAY.H header file listing.

```
// WAVI.H - Header file for WAVI class

#ifndef WAVI_H
#     define WAVI_H

// Note that the following code is executed only
// if this file has not been previously included


// #include files for both PC and SUN
#include  "WVideo.h"


#ifdef __BORLANDC__
    // PC-specific #includes

#endif

#ifdef Unix
```

continues

LISTING 11.6. continued

```
     // UNIX-specific #includes

#endif

//****************************************************
// WAVI - Video AVI
//
//     Purpose:
//         Encapsulates multimedia AVI capabilities.
//
//     Notes:
//
//     Copyright:
//             Copyright (c) 1993, William H. Roetzheim
//             All Rights Reserved
//
//****************************************************

_CLASSDEF (WAVI)
class WAVI : public WVideo
{
    private:
        // Private data members ********************

        // Private member functions ****************
        virtual void Open (RWStr FileName, RWStr Style,
                           HWND hWnd = (HWND) -1);
        virtual void Open (RWStr FileName);

    public:
        // Public data members *********************

        // Public member functions *****************
        // Member functions
                           WAVI (RWStr, RWStr, HWND);
                           WAVI (RWStr);
        virtual BOOL    CanReverse ();
       virtual BOOL     UsesPalettes ();
        virtual int       GetFastPlayRate ();
        virtual int       GetNormalPlayRate ();
        virtual int       GetSlowPlayRate ();
        virtual   int     GetSpeed ();
        virtual void    RealizeBackgroundPalette ();
        virtual void    RealizeForegroundPalette ();
```

```
            virtual   void SetTimeFrames ();
            virtual   void PlayReverse ();
            virtual void   Scan ();
            virtual void   Slow ();
            virtual void   PlaySpeed (int Speed);
            virtual void   StepForward (int Frames = 1);
            virtual void   StepReverse (int Frames = 1);
            virtual void   Update (HDC = (HDC) -1, RECT * = NULL);
};


#endif WAVI_H
```

LISTING 11.7. WOVERLAY.CPP source code listing.

```
// WAVI.CPP - Source file for WAVI class

#include "WAVI.h"  // ALL other #include statements
                   // are in this file

//****************************************************
// Constructors and destructors for WAVI
//
//     Copyright:
//            Copyright (c) 1993, William H. Roetzheim
//            All Rights Reserved
//
//****************************************************

WAVI::WAVI (RWStr FileName, RWStr Style, HWND hWnd = (HWND) -1)
{
    Open (FileName, Style, hWnd);
}

WAVI::WAVI (RWStr FileName)
{
    Open (FileName);
}

//****************************************************
// Member functions for class
//
//     Copyright:
//            Copyright (c) 1993, William H. Roetzheim
```

continues

LISTING 11.7. continued

```
//          All Rights Reserved
//
//********************************************************

BOOL WAVI::CanReverse ()
{
    WStr Return;
    WStr Command = "capability " + DeviceName + " can reverse";
    Return = SendCommand (Command);
    if (Return == "true") return TRUE;
    else return FALSE;
}


BOOL WAVI::UsesPalettes ()
{
    WStr Return;
    WStr Command = "capability " + DeviceName + " uses palettes";
    Return = SendCommand (Command);
    if (Return == "true") return TRUE;
    else return FALSE;
}

int     WAVI::GetFastPlayRate ()
{
    WStr Return;
    WStr Command = "capability " + DeviceName + " fast play rate";
    Return = SendCommand (Command);
    return Return.ToInt ();
}

int     WAVI::GetNormalPlayRate ()
{
    WStr Return;
    WStr Command = "capability " + DeviceName +
                   " normal play rate";
    Return = SendCommand (Command);
    return Return.ToInt ();
}

int     WAVI::GetSlowPlayRate ()
{
    WStr Return;
    WStr Command = "capability " + DeviceName + " slow play rate";
    Return = SendCommand (Command);
    return Return.ToInt ();
}
```

```
int      WAVI::GetSpeed ()
{
    WStr Return;
    WStr Command = "status " + DeviceName + " speed";
    Return = SendCommand (Command);
    return Return.ToInt ();
}

void WAVI::RealizeBackgroundPalette ()
{
    WStr Command = "realize " + DeviceName + " background";
    SendCommand (Command);
}

void WAVI::RealizeForegroundPalette ()
{
    WStr Command = "realize " + DeviceName + " normal";
    SendCommand (Command);
}

void WAVI::SetTimeFrames ()
{
    WStr Command = "set " + DeviceName + " time format frames";
    SendCommand (Command);
}

void WAVI::PlayReverse ()
{
    WStr Command = "play " + DeviceName + " reverse";
    SendCommand (Command);
}

void WAVI::Scan ()
{
    WStr Command = "play " + DeviceName + " scan";
    SendCommand (Command);
}

void     WAVI::Slow ()
{
    WStr Command = "play " + DeviceName + " slow";
    SendCommand (Command);
}

void WAVI::PlaySpeed (int Speed)
{
    WStr Command = "play " + DeviceName + " speed"
                    + ToString (Speed);
```

continues

LISTING 11.7. continued

```
    SendCommand (Command);
}

void WAVI::StepForward (int Frames)
{
    WStr Command = "step " + DeviceName + " by"
                    + ToString (Frames);
    SendCommand (Command);
}

void WAVI::StepReverse (int Frames)
{
    WStr Command = "step " + DeviceName + " reverse by" +
                    ToString (Frames);
    SendCommand (Command);
}

void     WAVI::Update (HDC hDC, RECT * Rect)
{
    WStr Command = "update " + DeviceName;
    if (hDC != (HDC) -1)
    {
        Command += " hdc " + ToString ((int) hDC);
    }

    if (Rect != NULL)
    {
        Command += " at " + ToString (Rect->left) + " " +
                            ToString (Rect->top) + " " +
                            ToString (Rect->right) + " " +
                            ToString (Rect->bottom);
    }
    SendCommand (Command);
}


// Private member functions
void WAVI::Open (RWStr FileName, RWStr Style, HWND hWnd)
{
    DeviceName = " AVI ";
    WStr Command = (WStr) "open " +
                FileName + " alias AVI type AVIVideo";
    Command += " style " + Style;
    if (hWnd != (HWND) -1)
    {
```

```
            Command += " parent " + ToString ((int) hWnd);
    }
     SendCommand (Command);
}


void WAVI::Open (RWStr FileName)
{
    Open (FileName, (WStr) " overlapped ");
}
```

CHAPTER 12

Miscellaneous Tricks and Techniques

User-Defined Resources

The Resource Workshop enables you to add user-defined resources to your application's resource area. This option is often used to include things such as static data files, text files, graphic metafiles, and help or tutorial files. This offers at least two advantages over keeping these items as separate files. First, loading data from a resource is significantly faster than loading the same data from a disk file. This is true even if you eliminate the file opening overhead for a disk file. Second, installation is simplified when all your application files are contained in a single executable file rather than in multiple files, which could be installed improperly or erased later by mistake.

Don't be concerned that your application will get too large. (I recently wrote a program whose application file was over 1.5MB!) Only the executable code is loaded from the executable file at runtime. All resources are loaded into RAM only when they are specifically required, and the memory is freed when the resource is no longer needed. The only caution with this approach is *never* to modify a resource after you have loaded it into RAM (for example, to load a text file resource and then to modify the text). If you do, the result is a UAE.

More DLL Hints

When writing a DLL, you must not explicitly export your WEP function in the .DEF file. Borland exports WEP for you automatically. Exporting it yourself can cause a UAE or a Windows crash when your application is loaded.

When you analyze the output of WinSpector in a postmortem of a UAE that occurred during program execution, check whether the DS register equals the SS register. If it doesn't, this is the probable cause of the crash. For a Windows .EXE file, this typically indicates that you haven't properly exported a function. If the UAE occurs within a DLL, however, the DS and SS registers normally should *not* be the same.

Use of Memory Models

I strongly recommend that you use the large memory model for all your programming when you work with Borland C++. Borland's large model differs from Microsoft's in that it has one data segment and multiple code segments, and all pointers default to far. This is roughly equivalent to Microsoft's medium model. Borland's large model simplifies much of your coding when you work with Windows. Because Windows doesn't support multiple segments of class DATA, you shouldn't use Borland's huge model or Microsoft's large model. An application that is compiled with the huge model and that contains multiple segments of class DATA will cause a UAE or a Windows crash when it is loaded.

Borland C++ and High-Resolution Screens

If you are fortunate enough to have a 1024 by 768 (or higher) resolution screen, you might have run into problems reading some fonts in Borland C++. The cause of the problem is two statements that Borland C++ adds to the WIN.INI file. These statements, found in the [FontSubstitutes] section, read

```
Helv=MS Sans Serif
Tms Rmn=MS Serif
```

To use the appropriate Windows 3.1 True Type character sets instead, change these statements to read

```
Helv=Arial
Tms Rmn=Times New Roman
```

Working with Dynamic List Boxes

It is relatively common for an application to have list boxes whose contents are changed at runtime. For example, you might have a database application that fills a list box based on the information in a database. It is not uncommon to want to associate information with every entry in the list box. Suppose, for example, you have an application that enables you to select an entry from an address book. Then the application automatically prints a mailing label. Further assume that the application stores the names in the database sorted by zip code, but that the list box should be sorted by name. The application reads the database, and for each record, it adds an entry to the list box. The complete address is stored in the database and is not part of the list box. When the user clicks on a name, how do you get the address information from the database?

One possibility is to reread the database while looking for a match on the selected string. Adding an index based on name to the database is another approach. A more elegant method is to store the database record number in the list box entry itself. This can be accomplished easily by appending the record number to the string before you add it to the list box. To avoid confusing the user, you should ensure that the entry is not in the visible portion of the list box. The best way to do this is to set a tab stop in the list box that is off the screen. For example, to set a single list box tab at 200—guaranteed to be off the screen—you would type

```
SendMessage (hListBoxWindow, LB_SETTABSTOPS, 1, 200);
```

Then you would include a tab character between the text to be displayed and the text to be hidden. For example, to insert a string with my name and 5 as the record number, you would type

```
WStr Buffer = "Roetzheim, William" + "\t" + WStr (5);
```

The string Roetzheim, William is displayed in the list box, but the 5 is tabbed to the invisible area. When the selected string is returned, however, the 5 is included. It can be parsed out and used to access the appropriate record in the database directly.

Distributing Your Code

Both Borland and Microsoft include all the code you need to distribute your code in a compressed format without having to pay any royalties. The Compress program is a DOS-based program with this syntax:

```
COMPRESS [-r] source destination
```

The -r switch tells Compress to rename the files automatically by adding an underscore to the end of the file's extension, or by replacing the last character with an underscore if the extension is already three characters long. Compress stores the original filename in the file itself, so you don't need to worry about losing it. I recommend that you always use the -r switch to prevent users from trying to read or execute compressed files.

The DOS counterpart of Compress is EXPAND. The syntax is identical. The -r switch tells the EXPAND program to rename the file with its original filename. The Windows DLL equivalent of EXPAND is LZexpand. The prototypes for all functions in the library are found in LZEXPAND.H. The LZexpand DLL is often used by the installation programs shipped with your application. The following code fragment uses LZexpand to copy the TEST.EX_ file from the floppy drive to the hard drive and simultaneously expand it:

```
OFSTRUCT Source, Destination;
HFILE SourceFile, DestinationFile;
char szBuffer [MAXPATH];

// Open the source file
SourceFile = LZOpenFile ("A:\\Test.ex_", &Source, OF_READ);

// Get the original filename
GetExpandedName ("A:\\Test.ex_", szBuffer);

// Create the destination file
DestinationFile = LZOpenFile (szBuffer, &Destination, OF_CREATE);

// Copy and decompress
LZCopy (Source, Destination);

// Close the files
LZClose (Source);
LZClose (Destination);
```

449

Network Problems with the Resource Compiler

If you are running Borland C++ on a network, and you get I/O errors from the resource compiler, it is probably because the resource compiler is trying to create a temporary file on a network drive. For reasons unknown, this causes problems on some networks. The solution is to force the resource compiler to use a specific directory for its temporary files by setting the environment variable TMP (for example, set TMP=c:\TEMP).

Scroll Bar Hints

Most programmers know that they must initialize a scroll bar's range to match the desired scroll range. Many programmers do this properly but then forget that the range often varies when the window changes size. You should respond to a WM_SIZE message by overriding the WMSize member function and adjusting the scroll bar range whenever the window size changes.

If you're not careful, you can introduce a bug when you adjust the scroll bar range in response to a WM_SIZE message. This bug is very common, even in commercial software. To see it in action, make a window small and drag the thumb box to somewhere in the center of the scroll bar. Next, maximize the window and attempt to drag the thumb box again. When you try to click on the thumb box, it jumps away! The problem is caused by code that adjusts the scroll bar range (in response to the WM_SIZE message) but doesn't change the thumb box to match. To avoid this problem, remember that whenever you change the scroll bar range, you must also call SetScrollPos() to reposition the thumb box.

Problem-Solving Techniques

I've given you many interesting and, I hope, fun solutions to problems I've encountered in my own programming endeavors. I thought that it would be worthwhile to share with you the approaches I use to solve many Windows programming problems. These problems typically can be summarized as follows:

> *I want my application to do* X, *but I'm not sure how to accomplish this.*

Given this scenario, I begin by studying the OWL classes involved. I look at all the member functions and data elements, for the classes I am using and for all the parent classes up the inheritance chain. I check whether any member functions or data elements seem appropriate. If so, I experiment with the function or data element involved and try to make it do what I want. When experimenting with a new member function, I use the following sources of information:

> ➤ The description of the function in the *ObjectWindows for C++ User's Guide*

> ➤ The descriptions of the function and of related functions available in the online help

> ➤ Samples of function usage in Borland's sample code delivered with the compiler

> ➤ Studying the actual OWL source code

To find sample code that demonstrates well the use of an unusual function, I search all online code files for the function. This can be accomplished either by using a word processor that can search for a keyword in text files (Word for Windows, for example) or by using Borland's grep utility from a DOS shell. Then I study how Borland uses the function to see whether it is appropriate for my application.

If I strike out, I pull out my Microsoft Windows Software Development Kit reference volume and study the available Windows API functions. Again I look for a function or set of functions that will enable me to accomplish my objective.

If I still don't have any luck, I flip to Chapter 6 of the same volume and study the available messages. Can I send (or receive and process) a message that does what I want?

The next place to look is CompuServe. Both the Borland and the Microsoft forums have extensive code libraries that provide source code to do many interesting things. Unfortunately, it might be difficult to find exactly the right source code. Generally, I find that the best route is to download the latest index of files in a library, study the descriptions of the code provided, then download the individual files that seem to be likely candidates. Even if the code doesn't solve my problem, it often gives me enough of a lead to solve it on my own.

If I find nothing helpful, I post a message on CompuServe and hope that someone else—perhaps one of Borland's or Microsoft's technical support people—has an answer. If even this doesn't work, I play my final card: I go to a trade show where Borland and Microsoft have large booths, and I bug the people there. Eventually, they put me in touch with a technical individual, normally at the show anyway, who can answer my question.

The Final Word

I sincerely hope that you have enjoyed reading this book and perhaps have even learned a trick or two. If you find mistakes in this book or on the source disk, please help me correct them. Forward any mistakes to me on CompuServe at address 71542,1717. Feel free to incorporate the code from this book into your own programs, but be sure to review the class designs for robustness. I've left out quite a bit of error- and exception-handling code to keep the classes simple and short, but your production code should include this important processing.

Appendix A

Code for a
Support Class

This appendix contains the code for WStr, a class that encapsulates a considerable amount of string-handling capability. Several classes in this book use the WStr class. I use it frequently in my own development efforts.

LISTING A.1. WSTR.H header file listing.

```
//   STR.H - String-handling class

#ifndef STR_H
     #define   STR_H

#include  <string.h>
#include  <stdlib.h>
#include  <stdio.h>
#include   <owl.h>
#include  <Windows.h>

#define        INVALID        -1


//******************************************************
// class WStr - Generic string class
//
//    Description:
//         Provides basic string-manipulation capabilities,
//         such as those found in BASIC or Ada.
//
//    Creation Parameters and Notes:
//         WStr (char *szText)      // Create from C string
//         WStr (int nSize = 40)    // Create setting buffer size
//         WStr (WStr& sOldString)  // Create from existing WStr
//
//    Destructor Behavior:
//         The space is deallocated.
//
//    Parent Classes:
//         None
//
//    Child Classes:
//         TBD
//
//    Notes:
//         1.   New space for the string is allocated as required.
//
```

```
//          2.    Friend functions are used in several locations
//                as operators. This is done so that the first
//                parameter, which normally would be the pointer,
//                is explicitly stated as a Wstr object. In this
//                way, the compiler can automatically cast a
//                char * (for example, "Test") to a WStr object
//                during execution of the method/operator.
//
//    Copyright:
//          Copyright (c) 1991, William H. Roetzheim
//          All Rights Reserved
//
//*****************************************************

_CLASSDEF (WStr)
class WStr : public TStreamable
{
    private:
        // Functions required for streamable classes
        virtual const Pchar streamableName () const;
        WStr (StreamableInit);

    protected:
        int       nBufSize;    // Buffer size
        char      *szBuffer;   // Pointer to buffer

    public:
        // Constructors
        WStr ();               // Default constructor
        WStr (char *szText);   // Create from C string
        WStr (int nSize);      // Create setting buffer size
        WStr (WStr& sString);  // Create from existing String

        // Destructor
        ~WStr();

        // Member functions
        int Length ();  // Get length
        int Find (WStr& sString, int nStart = 0);
        int Find (char *szString, int nStart = 0);
        char Slice (int nCharacter);   // Get character
        WStr Slice (int nStart, int nStop);   // Get slice

        // Functions required because streamable
        virtual void write (Ropstream);
        virtual Pvoid read (Ripstream);
```

continues

455

LISTING A.1. continued

```
void DeleteAll ();  // Helper function
  static PTStreamable build ();
  // Type conversion
  int  ToInt ();       // Convert string to int
  long ToLong ();      // Convert string to long
  double ToDouble ();  // Convert string to double

  // Operators
  // Type conversion operators
  operator char *();  // Convert string to C style

  // Additive operators
  WStr operator + (WStr& sString);
  WStr operator + (char *szString);
  friend WStr operator +
          (char *szString1, WStr& sString2);
  WStr operator - (WStr& sString);
  WStr operator - (char *szString);
  friend WStr operator -
          (char *szString1, WStr& sString2);

  // Bitwise operators
  WStr operator ^ (WStr& sString2);
  WStr operator ^ (char *szString2);
  friend WStr operator ^
          (char *szString1, WStr& sString2);

  // Assignment operators
  WStr& operator = (WStr& sString);     // Assignment
  WStr& operator = (char *szString);    // Assignment
  WStr& operator += (WStr& sString);    // Concatenate
  WStr& operator += (char *szString);   // Concatenate
  WStr& operator -= (WStr& sString);    // Find and remove
  WStr& operator -= (char *szString);   // Find and remove
  WStr& operator ^= (WStr& sString);    // EOR
  WStr& operator ^= (char *szString);   // EOR

  // Relational operators
  BOOL operator < (WStr& sString);
  BOOL operator < (char *szString);
  friend BOOL operator <
          (char *szString1, WStr& sString2);
  BOOL operator > (WStr& sString);
  BOOL operator > (char *szString);
  friend BOOL operator >
          (char *szString1, WStr& sString2);
  BOOL operator <= (WStr& sString);
```

```
            BOOL operator <= (char *szString);
            friend BOOL operator <=
                    (char *szString1, WStr& sString2);
            BOOL operator >= (WStr& sString);
            BOOL operator >= (char *szString);
            friend BOOL operator >=
                    (char *szString1, WStr& sString2);

            // Equality operators
            BOOL operator == (WStr& sString);
            BOOL operator == (char *szString);
            friend BOOL operator ==
                    (char *szString1, WStr& sString2);
            BOOL operator != (WStr& sString);
            BOOL operator != (char *szString);
            friend BOOL operator !=
                    (char *szString1, WStr& sString2);
};

//    ToString converts numbers to WStr objects
// Convert int to string
    WStr ToString (int nValue, WStr sFormat = "%d");
    WStr ToString (int nValue, char *szString);
// Convert long to string
    WStr ToString (long lValue, WStr sFormat = "%ld");
    WStr ToString (long lValue, char *szString);
// Convert float to string
    WStr ToString (double dValue, WStr sFormat = "%f");
    WStr ToString (double dValue, char *szString);

#endif
```

LISTING A.2. WSTR.CPP source file listing.

```
//    STR.CPP - String-handling methods

#include   "WStr.h"


/********************************************************
*     ToString - Family of functions to convert number to Str
*
*     Parameters:
*          First parameter is int, long, or double.
```

continues

LISTING A.2. continued

```
*          Second optional parameter is format string in
*          printf() format.
*
*     Returns:
*          Str object representing formatted number.
*
*     Notes:
*          The formatted strings cannot exceed MAX_STR_LEN
*          length.
*
*     Copyright:
*          Original code by William H. Roetzheim
*          (619) 669-6970
*          Copyright (c) 1991 by William H. Roetzheim
*          All Rights Reserved
******************************************************* /

// This #define specifies the maximum length of a string
// used to receive an ASCII representation of a numeric
// value. This class supports strings of arbitrary length
// and is not limited by this #define at all.

#define    MAX_STR_LEN 41

WStr ToString (int nValue, WStr sFormat)
{
     char szBuffer [MAX_STR_LEN];

     sprintf (szBuffer, sFormat, nValue);
     WStr sReturnString = szBuffer;
     return sReturnString;
}

WStr ToString (int nValue, char *szFormat)
{
     return ToString (nValue, (WStr) szFormat);
}

WStr ToString (long lValue, WStr sFormat)
{
     char szBuffer [MAX_STR_LEN];

     sprintf (szBuffer, sFormat, lValue);
     WStr sReturnString = szBuffer;
     return sReturnString;
}
```

```
WStr ToString (long lValue, char *szFormat)
{
    return ToString (lValue, (WStr) szFormat);
}


WStr ToString (double dValue, WStr sFormat)
{
    char szBuffer [MAX_STR_LEN];

    sprintf (szBuffer, sFormat, dValue);
    WStr sReturnString = szBuffer;
    return sReturnString;
}

WStr ToString (double dValue, char *szFormat)
{
    return ToString (dValue, (WStr) szFormat);
}




/*********************************************************
 *    WStr::WStr - Default constructor for String object
 *
 *    Parameters:
 *         None
 *
 *    Class Variables Used:
 *         nBufSize
 *         szBuffer
 *
 *    Files:
 *         None
 *
 *    Returns:
 *         Nothing
 *
 *    Notes:
 *         None
 *
 *    Copyright:
 *         Original code by William H. Roetzheim
 *         (619) 669-6970
 *         Copyright (c) 1991 by William H. Roetzheim
 *         All Rights Reserved
 *********************************************************/
```

continues

LISTING A.2. continued

```cpp
WStr::WStr ()
{
    nBufSize = 1;
    szBuffer = new char [nBufSize];
    szBuffer[0] = 0;
}




/********************************************************
*    WStr::WStr - Constructor for String object
*
*    Parameters:
*         char *szText - NULL-terminated initial string
*
*    Class Variables Used:
*         nBufSize
*         szBuffer
*
*    Files:
*         None
*
*    Returns:
*         Nothing
*
*    Notes:
*         String will be initialized to the length of Text.
*
*    Copyright:
*         Original code by William H. Roetzheim
*         (619) 669-6970
*         Copyright (c) 1991 by William H. Roetzheim
*         All Rights Reserved
********************************************************/

WStr::WStr (char *szText)
{
    nBufSize = strlen (szText) + 1;
    szBuffer = new char [nBufSize];
    memcpy (szBuffer, szText, nBufSize);
}
```

```
/*********************************************************
*    WStr::WStr - Another constructor for String object
*
*     Parameters:
*          int nSize = 40   // Initial length
*
*     Class Variables Used:
*          nBufSize
*          szBuffer
*
*     Files:
*          None
*
*     Returns:
*          Nothing
*
*     Notes:
*          nSize is the maximum string that can be stored
*          without reallocation.
*
*     Copyright:
*          Original code by William H. Roetzheim
*          (619) 669-6970
*          Copyright (c) 1991 by William H. Roetzheim
*          All Rights Reserved
*********************************************************/

WStr::WStr (int nSize)
{
    if (nSize < 0) nSize = 0;
    nBufSize = nSize + 1;
    szBuffer = new char [nBufSize];
    szBuffer[0] = 0;
}




/*********************************************************
*    Str::WStr - Another creator for String object
*
*     Parameters:
*          WStr& sString
*
*     Class Variables Used:
*          nBufSize
*          szBuffer
*
```

continues

LISTING A.2. continued

```
*    Files:
*        None
*
*    Returns:
*        Nothing
*
*    Notes:
*        None
*
*    Copyright:
*        Original code by William H. Roetzheim
*        (619) 669-6970
*        Copyright (c) 1991 by William H. Roetzheim
*        All Rights Reserved
*******************************************************/

WStr::WStr (WStr& sString)
{
    nBufSize = sString.nBufSize;
    szBuffer = new char [nBufSize];
    memcpy (szBuffer, sString.szBuffer, nBufSize);
}


/*******************************************************
*    WStr::~WStr - Destructor for String class
*
*    Parameters:
*        None
*
*    Class Variables Used:
*        szBuffer
*
*    Files:
*        None
*
*    Returns:
*        Nothing
*
*    Notes:
*        None
*
*    Copyright:
*        Original code by William H. Roetzheim
*        (619) 669-6970
*        Copyright (c) 1991 by William H. Roetzheim
*        All Rights Reserved
*******************************************************/
```

```
WStr::~WStr()
{
    delete[] szBuffer;
}




/********************************************************
*    Member functions required for streamable classes
*
*    Parameters:
*        Various
*
*    Class Variables Used:
*        All
*
*    Copyright:
*        Original code by William H. Roetzheim
*        (619) 669-6970
*        Copyright (c) 1991 by William H. Roetzheim
*        All Rights Reserved
********************************************************/
WStr::WStr (StreamableInit)
{
    DeleteAll ();
}




const Pchar WStr::streamableName () const
{
    return "WStr";
}




void WStr::write (Ropstream)
{
    int i;
    for (i = 0; i <= strlen (szBuffer); i++)
    {
            // os << szBuffer[i];
     }
}




// This function reads only strings up to 1024
// bytes in length
```

continues

LISTING A.2. continued

```
Pvoid WStr::read (Ripstream is)
{
    char *szTemp = new char [1025];
    szTemp [1024] = 0;
    int i = 0;
    while ((!is.eof()) && (i < 1024))
    {
        // is >> szTemp [i];
        if (szTemp [i++] == 0) break;
    }
    *this = szTemp;
    delete[] szTemp;

    return this;
}


void WStr::DeleteAll ()
{
    delete[] szBuffer;
    szBuffer = new char [1];
    szBuffer [0] = 0;
    nBufSize = 1;
}



PTStreamable WStr::build ()
{
    return new WStr (streamableInit);
}



/********************************************************
*    WStr::Length - Returns the current length of a string
*
*    Parameters:
*         None
*
*    Files:
*         None
*
*    Returns:
*         int giving the current length
*
```

```
*     Notes:
*          None
*
*     Copyright:
*          Original code by William H. Roetzheim
*          (619) 669-6970
*          Copyright (c) 1991 by William H. Roetzheim
*          All Rights Reserved
******************************************************/

int WStr::Length ()
{
     return strlen (szBuffer);
}


/*********************************************************
*     WStr::Find - Find the first occurence of the string
*
*     Parameters:
*          WStr& sString - String object to look for
*          int nStart = 0 - Place to start looking
*
*     Class Variables Used:
*          szBuffer
*
*     Files:
*          None
*
*     Returns:
*          int with the starting character in this object's
*          string where the string being searched for was
*          found, or INVALID if not found.
*
*     Notes:
*          None
*
*     Copyright:
*          Original code by William H. Roetzheim
*          (619) 669-6970
*          Copyright (c) 1991 by William H. Roetzheim
*          All Rights Reserved
******************************************************/
int WStr::Find (WStr& sString, int nStart)
{
     int          i;
```

continues

465

LISTING A.2. continued

```
        // Is a match even possible?
        if ((sString.Length () > Length ()) ||
            (sString.Length () == 0))
            return INVALID;

        // Use a brute-force approach to looking for a match
        for (i = nStart; i <= Length () - sString.Length ();
            i++)
        {
            if (memcmp (&szBuffer[i],
                sString.szBuffer, sString.Length ()) == 0)
            {
                return i;
            }
        }
        return INVALID;
}

// Alternate Find()
int WStr::Find (char *szString, int nStart)
{
    WStr sTemp = szString;
    return Find (sTemp, nStart);
}




/******************************************************
*    Slice - Returns a character of a string
*
*    Parameters:
*        nCharacter
*
*    Class Variables Used:
*        szBuffer
*
*    Returns:
*        Character at specified position
*
*    Notes:
*        1.    Function is overloaded with Slice
*              (nStart, nStop);
*
```

```
*    Copyright:
*        Original code by William H. Roetzheim
*        (619) 669-6970
*        Copyright (c) 1991 by William H. Roetzheim
*        All Rights Reserved
******************************************************/
char WStr::Slice (int nCharacter)
{
    if ((nCharacter >= 0) && (nCharacter < Length ()))
        return szBuffer      [nCharacter];
    else return 0;
}



/******************************************************
*    Slice - Returns a slice (segment) of a string
*
*    Parameters:
*        nStart
*        nStop
*
*    Class Variables Used:
*        szBuffer
*
*    Returns:
*        String sliced from specified range
*
*    Notes:
*        1.    Function is overloaded with Slice (nCharacter);
*
*    Copyright:
*        Original code by William H. Roetzheim
*        (619) 669-6970
*        Copyright (c) 1991 by William H. Roetzheim
*        All Rights Reserved
******************************************************/
WStr WStr::Slice (int nStart, int nStop)
{
    if (nStart >= Length ()) nStart = Length () - 1;
    if (nStop < nStart) nStop = nStart;

    if (nStop >= Length ()) nStop = Length () - 1;

    WStr sTemp (nStop - nStart + 1);
    memcpy (sTemp.szBuffer, &szBuffer[nStart],
        nStop - nStart + 1);
```

continues

467

LISTING A.2. continued

```
        sTemp.szBuffer[nStop - nStart + 1] = 0;
        return sTemp;
}


/*******************************************************
 *      Type conversion methods for string class
 *
 *      Notes:
 *              None
 *
 *      Copyright:
 *              Original code by William H. Roetzheim
 *              (619) 669-6970
 *              Copyright (c) 1991 by William H. Roetzheim
 *              All Rights Reserved
 *******************************************************/
int WStr::ToInt ()
{
        return atoi (szBuffer);
}

long WStr::ToLong()
{
        return atol (szBuffer);
}

double WStr::ToDouble()
{
        return atof (szBuffer);
}

/*******************************************************
 *      Operators for String class
 *
 *      Notes:
 *              None
 *
 *      Copyright:
 *              Original code by William H. Roetzheim
 *              (619) 669-6970
 *              Copyright (c) 1991 by William H. Roetzheim
 *              All Rights Reserved
 *******************************************************/
```

```
WStr::operator char*()
{
    return szBuffer;
}

WStr WStr::operator + (WStr& sString)
{
  WStr sTemp (Length () + sString.Length ());
  strcpy (sTemp.szBuffer, szBuffer);
  strcat (sTemp.szBuffer, sString.szBuffer);
  return sTemp;
}

WStr WStr::operator + (char *szString)
{
    WStr sTemp = szString;
    return (*this + sTemp);
}


WStr operator + (char *szString1, WStr& sString2)
{
    WStr sTemp = szString1;
    return (sTemp + sString2);
}


WStr WStr::operator - (WStr& sString)
{
    int        nDeleteStart;

    nDeleteStart = Find (sString);

    if (nDeleteStart != INVALID)
    {
        WStr sTemp (Length () - sString.Length ());

        // Pick up first portion of base string
        memcpy (sTemp.szBuffer, szBuffer, nDeleteStart);

        // Pick up trailing portion of base string
        memcpy (&sTemp.szBuffer[nDeleteStart],
                &szBuffer [nDeleteStart +
                sString.Length ()], Length () + 1 -
                nDeleteStart - sString.Length ());
```

continues

LISTING A.2. continued

```
            return sTemp;
        }
        else return *this;
}

WStr WStr::operator - (char *szString)
{
        WStr sTemp = szString;
        return (*this - sTemp);
}


WStr operator - (char *szString1, WStr& sString2)
{
        WStr sTemp = szString1;
        return (sTemp - sString2);
}



WStr WStr::operator ^ (WStr& sString)
{
        int        i;
        int        nIndex;

        WStr sTemp (Length ());
        memcpy (sTemp.szBuffer, szBuffer, Length () + 1);

        if (sString.Length () > 0)
        {
            nIndex = 0;
            for (i = 0; i < Length (); i++)
            {
                sTemp.szBuffer[i] = szBuffer[i] ^
                sString.szBuffer[nIndex++];
                if (nIndex >= sString.Length ()) nIndex = 0;
            }
        }
        return sTemp;
}

WStr WStr::operator ^ (char *szString)
{
        WStr sTemp = szString;
        return (*this ^ sTemp);
}
```

```
WStr operator ^ (char *szString1, WStr& sString2)
{
    WStr sTemp = szString1;
    return (sTemp ^ sString2);
}


WStr& WStr::operator = (WStr& sString)
{
    nBufSize = sString.Length () + 1;
    delete[] szBuffer;
    szBuffer = new char [nBufSize];
    memcpy (szBuffer, sString.szBuffer, nBufSize);
    return *this;
}


WStr& WStr::operator = (char *szString)
{
    WStr sTemp = szString;
    return (*this = sTemp);
}


WStr& WStr::operator += (WStr& sString)
{
    return (*this = *this + sString);
}


WStr& WStr::operator += (char *szString)
{
    WStr sTemp = szString;
    return (*this = *this + sTemp);
}


WStr& WStr::operator -= (WStr& sString)
{
    return (*this = *this - sString);
}


WStr& WStr::operator -= (char *szString)
{
    WStr sTemp = szString;
    return (*this = *this - sTemp);
}
```

continues

LISTING A.2. continued

```cpp
WStr& WStr::operator ^= (WStr& sString)
{
    return (*this = *this ^ sString);
}


WStr& WStr::operator ^= (char *szString)
{
    WStr sTemp = szString;
    return (*this = *this ^ sTemp);
}



BOOL WStr::operator < (WStr& sString)
{
    return (strcmp (szBuffer, sString.szBuffer) < 0);
}

BOOL WStr::operator < (char *szString)
{
    WStr sTemp = szString;
    return (*this < sTemp);
}


BOOL operator < (char *szString1, WStr& sString2)
{
    WStr sTemp = szString1;
    return (sTemp < sString2);
}


BOOL WStr::operator > (WStr& sString)
{
    return (strcmp (szBuffer, sString.szBuffer) > 0);
}

BOOL WStr::operator > (char *szString)
{
    WStr sTemp = szString;
    return (*this > sTemp);
}
```

```
BOOL operator > (char *szString1, WStr& sString2)
{
    WStr sTemp = szString1;
    return (sTemp > sString2);
}


BOOL WStr::operator <= (WStr& sString)
{
    return (strcmp (szBuffer, sString.szBuffer) <= 0);
}

BOOL WStr::operator <= (char *szString)
{
    WStr sTemp = szString;
    return (*this <= sTemp);
}


BOOL operator <= (char *szString1, WStr& sString2)
{
    WStr sTemp = szString1;
    return (sTemp <= sString2);
}


BOOL WStr::operator >= (WStr& sString)
{
    return (strcmp (szBuffer, sString.szBuffer) >= 0);
}

BOOL WStr::operator >= (char *szString)
{
    WStr sTemp = szString;
    return (*this >= sTemp);
}


BOOL operator >= (char *szString1, WStr& sString2)
{
    WStr sTemp = szString1;
    return (sTemp >= sString2);
}
```

continues

LISTING A.2. continued

```
BOOL WStr::operator == (WStr& sString)
{
    return (strcmp (szBuffer, sString.szBuffer) == 0);
}

BOOL WStr::operator == (char *szString)
{
    WStr sTemp = szString;
    return (*this == sTemp);
}


BOOL operator == (char *szString1, WStr& sString2)
{
    WStr sTemp = szString1;
    return (sTemp == sString2);
}


BOOL WStr::operator != (WStr& sString)
{
    return !(*this == sString);
}

BOOL WStr::operator != (char *szString)
{
    WStr sTemp = szString;
    return (*this != sTemp);
}


BOOL operator != (char *szString1, WStr& sString2)
{
    WStr sTemp = szString1;
    return (sTemp != sString2);
}
```

INDEX

M

P

R

Y-Z

Add to Your Sams Library Today with the Best Books for Programming, Operating Systems, and New Technologies!

Yes, please send me the productivity-boosting material I have checked below. Make check payable to Sams Publishing.

☐ **Check enclosed**

Charge to my credit card:

☐ **VISA**   ☐ **MasterCard**   ☐ **American Express**

Acct: _____

Expiration date: _____

Signature: _____

Name: _____

Company: _____

Address: _____

City: _____

State: _____ ZIP: _____

Phone: _____

The easiest way to order is to pick up the phone and call 1-800-428-5331 between 9:00 a.m. and 5:00 p.m. EST. For faster service please have your credit card available.

ISBN #	Quantity	Description of Item	Unit Cost	Total Cost
0-672-30168-7		Advanced C (Book/Disk)	$39.95	
0-672-30158-X		Advanced C ++ (Book/Disk)	$39.95	
0-672-30287-X		Tom Swan's Code Secrets (Book/Disk)	$39.95	
0-672-30309-4		Programming Sound for DOS & Windows (Book/Disk)	$39.95	
0-672-30240-3		OS/2 2.1 Unleashed (Book/Disk)	$34.95	
0-672-30288-8		DOS Secrets Unleashed (Book/Disk)	$39.95	
0-672-30298-5		Windows NT: The Next Generation	$22.95	
0-672-30274-8		Mastering Borland C++ (Book/Disk)	$39.95	
0-672-30226-8		Windows Programmer's Guide to OLE/DDE (Book/Disk	$34.95	
0-672-30236-5		Windows Programmer's Guide to DLLs & Memory Management (Book/Disk)	$34.95	
0-672-30030-3		Windows Programmer's Guide to Serial Communications (Book/Disk)	$39.95	
0-672-30177-6		Windows Programmer's Guide to Borland C++ Tools (Book/Disk)	$39.95	
0-672-30097-4		Windows Programmer's Guide to Resources (Book/Disk)	$34.95	
0-672-30067-2		Windows Programmer's Guide to MS Foundation Class Library (Book/Disk)	$34.95	
0-672-30106-7		Windows Programmer's Guide to ObjectWindows Library (Book/Disk)	$34.95	
0-672-30137-7		Secrets of the Borland C++ Masters (Book/Disk)	$44.95	
0-672-30190-3		Windows Resource and Memory Management (Book/Disk)	$29.95	
0-672-30249-7		Multimedia Madness! (Book/Disk - CD-ROM)	$44.95	
☐ 3 1/2" Disk ☐ 5 1/4" Disk		Shipping and Handling: See information below.		
		TOTAL		

Shipping and Handling: $4.00 for the first book and $1.75 for each additional book. Floppy disk: add $1.75 for shipping and handling. If you need to have it NOW, we can ship product to you in 24 hours for an additional charge of approximately $18.00, and you will receive your item overnight or in two days. Overseas shipping and handling add $20.00 per book and $8.00 for up to three disks. Prices subject to change. Call for availability and pricing information on latest editions.

11711   N. College Avenue,   Suite 140,   Carmel, Indiana   46032

1-800-428-5331— Orders   1-800-835-3202—FAX   1-800-858-7674 — CustomersService

What's on the Disk

The *Uncharted Windows Programming* disk contains more than 2.4MB of software, including

> ➤ All sample code from the book

> ➤ Code for more than 30 Windows classes

> ➤ U/Win, a suite of more than 30 Windows utilities that provides support functions and file management for software development. It includes a utility for unloading DLLs from memory.

Installing the Disk

The software included with this book is stored in a compressed form. You can't use the software without first installing it to your hard drive. The installation program runs from within Windows.

1. From File Manager or Program Manager, select File/Run.

2. Type `<drive>INSTALL` and press Enter. `<drive>` is the letter of the drive that contains the installation disk. For example, if the disk is in drive B:, type `B:INSTALL` and press Enter.

Follow the on-screen instructions in the installation program. When the installation is complete, be sure to read the file README.TXT. It contains information about the files and programs that were installed.

 NOTE: To install the files on the disk, you need at least 2.5MB of free space on your hard drive.